T·A·R·O·T
CORRESPONDENCES

Ancient
SECRETS
for
EVERYDAY
Readers

Includes Over 100 Essential Tables & Charts

T. SUSAN CHANG

Llewellyn Publications
Woodbury, Minnesota

FIRST EDITION
Fifth Printing, 2021

The meditative approaches in this book are not a substitute for psychotherapy or counseling nor are they a substitute for medical treatment. They are intended to provide clients with information about their inner workings that can add another helpful dimension to treatment with a trained medical or mental health professional, as their circumstances may warrant.

Book design by Bob Gaul
Mystical Tarot Deck on cover © Lo Scarabeo
Cover design by Kevin R. Brown
Editing by Laura Kurtz
For interior art credits please see page 376
Tarot Decks Used:
   Animal Totem Tarot © 2016 by Leeza Robertson and Eugene Smith, Llewellyn Publications
   Dame Fortune's Wheel Tarot © 2009, Lo Scarabeo
   Mystical Tarot © 2017 by Luigi Costa, Lo Scarabeo
   Pictorial Key Tarot © 1910 by Arthur Edward Waite
   Steampunk Tarot © 2012 by Barbara Moore and Aly Fell, Llewellyn Publications
   Tabula Mundi © 2014 by M.M. Meleen
   Tarot de Marseille © 2016 by Camoin and Jodorowsky, Lo Scarabeo

Llewellyn Publications is a registered trademark of Llewellyn Worldwide Ltd.

Library of Congress Cataloging-in-Publication Data
The Library of Congress has already cataloged an earlier printing under LCCN: 2018289253

Llewellyn Worldwide Ltd. does not participate in, endorse, or have any authority or responsibility concerning private business transactions between our authors and the public.
  All mail addressed to the author is forwarded, but the publisher cannot, unless specifically instructed by the author, give out an address or phone number.
  Any Internet references contained in this work are current at publication time, but the publisher cannot guarantee that a specific location will continue to be maintained. Please refer to the publisher's website for links to authors' websites and other sources.

Llewellyn Publications
A Division of Llewellyn Worldwide Ltd.
2143 Wooddale Drive
Woodbury, MN 55125-2989
www.llewellyn.com

Printed in the United States of America

CONTENTS

Part Two: The Reader's Guide to Using Correspondences

Part Three: Individual Card Tables

ACKNOWLEDGMENTS

When I picked up my first Rider Waite deck in 1997, I was simply intrigued and curious like anyone else. I had no idea that over the next two decades, tarot would go from being a pastime to an obsession to a belief system to a way of life. For the most part I conducted my tarot life under the radar until 2015, when I stumbled into the global tarot community on Facebook. Since then, many readers across the world have shared their company, their conversation, and the joy of tarot with me.

First and foremost I would like to thank my friend, near-neighbor, and collaborator, Mel Meleen. *Tarot Correspondences* has an esoteric twin in the Fortune's Wheelhouse podcast, which Mel and I launched and hosted during the writing of this book. Fortune's Wheelhouse has helped to fuel and inspire this book, and works as a card-by-card audio companion to much of the material explored herein. I am indebted to Mel for her friendship and conversation, and the answers to many last-minute frantic questions on technical points in this book that no one else would comprehend. My thanks go also to our podcast listeners and the Fortune's Wheelhouse Academy Facebook group for their encouragement, patronage, and fellowship.

Peter ("Spiffo") Stuart, accomplice on the opposite side of the world, virtually held my hand as I found my way into the tarot community and a life hijacked by the cards. The Department of Akashic Records has your number, my friend.

Thanks to Marcus Katz's Tarot Professionals Facebook group and the Tarot Readers Development and Study Group (among others) I've enjoyed the fellowship and encouragement of many online tarot friends around the world, among them Jason Colmer, Djamila Zon, Michael Bridge-Dickson, and Sasha Bekier. Ted Myatt is an unflagging source of bright ideas and experimental practices.

Inspirit Crystals in Northampton, Massachusetts, where I read cards weekly, has offered a congenial environment for the practical application of my studies—as well as an enviably stocked bookshelf where I could conduct research when business was slow. Bud, Barry, Emily, Asherah,

Rosie, Don, Drew, et. al.—thank you for welcoming me into the Inspirit family. And Josh Berkowitz, thank you for lending a helping hand as I crashed, grasping for purchase and scratched by twigs, through the ineffable branches of the Tree of Life.

My thanks also go to the customers of Tarotista on Etsy, whose enthusiastic support for my Arcana Cases has helped to underwrite these esoteric adventures.

A number of tarot luminaries have lighted my way. Wald and Ruth Amberstone helped get me started in tarot way back in 1996, at the Tarot School in New York. Rachel Pollack, both in print and in delightful person, has been a source of inspiration and entertainment. In the final stages of this book's composition, Christine Payne-Towler defeated a host of email gremlins to share her astro-alpha-numeric *tour de force* with me.

The astrologer Chris Warnock shared his incisive observations with me over the course of several absorbing conversations on the subject of divination. And the astrologer Austin Coppock generously shared his insights on the relationship between tarot, decans, and much more.

At Llewellyn I would like to offer one million thank-yous to editor and tarot diva Barbara Moore, whose clarity and kindness have been a beacon in the construction of this book. I can't thank her enough for "getting" what I was trying to do with this book from the first tentative email pitch. Nanette Stearns and Bob Gaul have tackled the complex production challenges posed by this book with deftness and grace. Special thanks go to production editor Laura Kurtz, who deserves an alchemically transmuted gold medal for wrangling innumerable tables crawling with glyph text. And publicist Vanessa Wright helped walk this blinking and bespectacled book into the light of day.

Thank you to the many local friends who have put up with hours of tarot sermons and practice sessions—particularly Mark Nickels, Ivy Mabius, and the members of the on-again, off-again Tarot of the Valley group.

Above all, thank you to my family—Randy, Noah, and Zoe—for putting up with me and my eight jobs—and all the morning chanting. The house may not be clean, but it is certainly thoroughly banished!

INTRODUCTION

USING TAROT CORRESPONDENCES
IN EVERYDAY TAROT

If you're reading this book, chances are you're a tarot reader. Maybe you've been reading for decades, or maybe you just picked up your first deck. In either case, you are a traveler on a lifelong journey working with the cards. And for one reason or another you have a hunch that a strong, wonky dose of esoteric knowledge is going to help you become a better reader. Enter the correspondences—a paradise of neatly organized data points for your inner nerd/witch/wizard/systems fanatic.

WHAT ARE TAROT CORRESPONDENCES?

Correspondences are patterns and connections inherited from esoteric systems. In tarot, correspondences line up with specific cards. For example, if you are familiar with astrology, you know that there's a basic system that includes planets, elements, and the signs of the zodiac. Each of these corresponds to a tarot card. For example, the planet Jupiter *corresponds* to the Wheel of Fortune. The sign of Virgo *corresponds* to the Hermit.

Tarot correspondences date back to about the mid-eighteenth century (tarot itself dates back only to the mid-fifteenth century, despite any rumors about ancient Egypt you may have heard). Because of tarot's powerful symbolic imagery, you can find correspondences to innumerable mythologies, cosmogonies,

> What is esoteric? In standard dictionary terms, *esoteric* means "confined to an inner circle". In Greek, *eso-* means "within" and *esoteros* means "*more* within". So, esoteric matters are confined to the few, say, initiates of an esoteric order. Opposite to "esoteric" is "exoteric," or public.
>
> In practice, when we refer to esotericism in tarot, we're talking about occult systems of knowledge and mystical practices such as those shared by initiatory orders.

and belief systems in the cards. By connecting the cards to the age-old arts of magic and astrology, you can unearth many correspondences to the natural world. Some of these extended systems appear in the tables at the front and back of the book.

In terms of incorporating the esoterics into your tarot practice, we will be focusing on four main systems in this book: the elements, astrology, numbers, and Kabbalah. These correspondences lie hidden beneath the face of many decks, including even most contemporary ones. Often they are so well hidden that the deck creators themselves are unaware they are using them. They might draw a fierce warrior on the 7 of Wands, never realizing that card was once associated with the war god Mars. They might draw the Star pouring the traditional urns of water onto the ground, never realizing that she is associated with Aquarius, the water-bearer. Yet the iconography of tarot is so persistent that these correspondences travel forward in time, reproduced again and again in new decks, just waiting to be decoded by the right reader.

CORRESPONDENCES ARE A VITAL SYSTEM OF METAPHOR

How many times do we stretch for a metaphor to explain something we see in the cards as readers? "It's like when you're swimming in the ocean and the shore suddenly seems so, so far away." "It's like you're knitting together the fabric of your relationship." We reach for metaphors without even thinking; it comes as naturally to us as reaching for our favorite coffee mug on the desk. And many of these metaphors are unconsciously based in imagery, associations, language, and myths deeply embedded in the cards.

Every new reader, at one point or another, finds themselves stuck with a particular card, unable to get beyond its surface image. "I think the 2 of Pentacles means *change*," you think, "but what kind? and why?" But what if that change was caused by the forces of contraction and expansion, Jupiter and Saturn, endlessly cycling, like the pistons in an engine? What if you knew this card was astrologically associated with the end of one year and the beginning of the next—between December and January, when the days begin to lengthen? Wouldn't it make sense that there's an infinity sign on the card indicating all things are possible? And wouldn't it follow that's when people make New Year's resolutions—the simplest kind of magic spell for creating change?

All this insight is hidden inside the 2 of Pentacles, and once it is revealed, there's no limit to what may be extrapolated from that knowledge: Long trips, pen pals, exercise, relocation, and so on. But correspondences are a key that brings these shades to light, a linchpin that anchors you so you can travel to far-off interpretive lands.

WHY DOES TAROT NEED CORRESPONDENCES?

As every witch, ceremonial magician, and scholar of the magical arts knows, it always comes down to "this goes with that." This *doctrine of sympathy* is our inheritance from the Hermetic thinkers of seventeen centuries ago, and it still packs a punch. Correspondences aren't just the reference material or the data set behind the magic—they *are* the magic. They are embedded in the structure of every modern deck whether we recognize it or not.

Yet in the world of tarot reading, many of us have believed that studying the correspondences is a purely academic pursuit for the librarians and brainiacs among us who are content to pore over fine print in ivory towers for months at a stretch. Isn't it easier to simply open our heart chakras or channel a friendly angel? What I'm doing with this book is building a bridge between these worlds. To paraphrase the astrologer Bernadette Brady, you need both the eagle and the lark—the engineer and the poet. Each has a place at a tarot reader's table.

You don't need to know that the Empress is associated with the Hebrew letter ד or *daleth*, which means "door." You don't have to memorize it or study it or understand why that is. But if you've heard or read, even once, that the Empress is associated with "door," that becomes part of your inner tarot experience. And the next time you see the Empress when you're reading for someone you may find yourself saying "What creative forces do you wish to invite into your life? Open the door and let them in!" You may not even realize why you said what you did, and that's okay; it's good, even. Tarot is an art, and you don't have to prove you've mastered it by taking an exam and being able to regurgitate a complete set of seventy-eight correspondences. You only have to be able to help someone.

CORRESPONDENCES ARE A FRIEND TO THE IMAGINATION, NOT ITS ENEMY

I believe correspondences don't just reveal *why* we see the images we do in each card—they are also a fertile place to plant the seed of our own interpretations. They are a language which blossoms in the presence of a rich and flexible imagination.

As tarot readers, we are the caretakers of a living language of pictures, one we use every day to help ourselves and others in our passage through life. It's a language that evolves every day we use it, and its vocabulary is as deep and rich as we're willing to make it. The better we speak tarot, the better readers we become … and the less often we come up dry in a reading.

As readers, we're always looking for more in each card, digging for treasure to share with those we read for, hunting for wisdom for ourselves. This is true whether you've been reading for two months or forty years: by expanding the language, the imagery, the metaphors we associate with each card, we join them up with our own lived experience.

DIVINATION AND MAGIC:
THE ROLE OF THE CORRESPONDENCES IN EACH

Divination and magic are kissing cousins. It's as if we go to the same place to do different work. If it's a library, the diviner is the kind of reader who goes there to browse and read and hunt for information—knowledge for its own sake. The magician is the patron who takes out books to use as a tool—knowledge as a weapon and utensil for creating change. If it's a garden, the diviner tells you when and where to plant and what pests you must deter; the magician plants the seed and harvests the crop when it has grown to maturity.

If I had to choose a single metaphor to describe the place where both divination and magic occur, I'd call it the backstage of reality—its blueprint, map, or foundation. When you do a reading you look at the map, figure out where you're going, decide on the best route between point A and point B, determine whether point B is really where you want to go in the first place, and consider what obstacles you're likely to face getting there. When you do magic, you redraw the map so that point A is now a short hop from point B, rather than a three-day slog.

Each method can benefit from the other. What good does it do the magician to take a shortcut if the destination turns out to be a terrible place to be? What good does it do the diviner to have the perfect plan if action does not follow? Neither fate nor free will completely rules our lives.

So, if you think of yourself mainly as a reader, never forget that magic—essentially the power to change your path—is always available to you. And if you are a magician, never forget that divination—essentially, the power of navigation—is a vital part of every shortcut.

The correspondences are the keys to getting backstage, like the passcode that unlocks the GPS. Suppose you draw the Empress, complete with a retinue of correspondences that includes the goddess Venus, the color green, the day Friday, bees, doves, roses, and swans. As a reader, you fill your mind with these associations. And whatever the question—Will my business grow? Can I become pregnant? What do I need more of in my life?—you can be sure that somewhere in that garden of details is the answer.

As a magician, you don't stop at answers. You instead invite the Empress to take charge of your affairs (or one part of them). You call her on her day, at her hour, in her dignity and with her tokens, and you ask her for her help, please, in bringing love or peace or wealth into your life. Then you thank her, leave the room, close the door behind you ... and you don't look back.

ABOUT CORRESPONDENCES
AND THE GOLDEN DAWN

The correspondences I use in this book are primarily based on those used by the Golden Dawn, an esoteric organization that got its start in England in the last days of the nineteenth century. It was members of the Golden Dawn, Pamela Colman Smith and Arthur Edward Waite, who gave us the most commonly used tarot deck in the English-speaking world: the Rider Waite Smith deck (first published in 1909). Trailing far behind in popularity but still significant is Aleister Crowley and Lady Frieda Harris's Thoth deck (created in the 1940s but not published until 1969), which was also heavily influenced by the Golden Dawn correspondences. Sometimes tarot decks in this lineage are called "English school" decks.

Golden Dawn correspondences are also found at the heart of the Western ceremonial magical traditions. It's not that I use them because I'm an initiate of any of those traditions—I'm not. The correspondences worked out by the Golden Dawn and its followers are the most extensive set of correspondences available. They are applicable to the majority of modern tarot decks and, with a little latitude for which elements go with which suits, can be used by the majority of Western magicians (including those brought up in Wicca, Neopaganism, and Hermetic Qabalah).

There are other correspondence systems besides the Golden Dawn's. Probably the most widespread one is that used in the Continental tarot tradition, sometimes called the "French school." The big difference between the two lies in the way the correspondences are assigned to the major arcana—different astrological correspondences, different Hebrew letter correspondences. The minors don't have correspondences at all. You can find out more about some of these alternate systems in Table 4: Alternate Astro-Alpha-Numeric Correspondences (p. 33).

When you use a modern-day tarot deck, there's a very good chance that its meanings derive in some form or another from the Rider Waite Smith deck. And the pictorial language of the Rider Waite Smith deck is based in the correspondences. For the most part, the decks I've used in this book—M. M. Meleen's Tabula Mundi, Luigi Costa's Mystical Tarot, Leeza Robertson's Animal Totem tarot, and Barbara Moore's Steampunk Tarot—draw directly or indirectly on Golden Dawn-based decks; i.e., Thoth or Rider Waite Smith. The Dame Fortune's Wheel Tarot (derived from Etteilla) and the Lo Scarabeo Tarot de Marseille are exceptions. I tend to use these mostly when working with numbers, a language common to all decks rather than astrological or kabbalistic attributions.

Can one use Golden Dawn correspondences on a deck from a different system? Most readers would say no. My view is that you are the reader, and it's not easy to turn off the perspective, knowledge, and habits of interpretation you've developed. As a matter of respect, it's good to understand whatever you can about the deck you're using. You may not be able to switch systems as easily as going from manual to automatic transmission, or from a PC to a Mac.

That said, don't let a different correspondence system dissuade you from using a deck you're drawn to, whether it's the Dalí Universal Tarot or Christine Payne-Towler's Tarot of the Holy Light (both wonderful decks that are not based on English school correspondences). As powerful as correspondences are, they are only part of your toolbox. You'll still be bringing your ability to read visual clues, your intuition, and your common sense to readings.

USING THIS BOOK

The tables in part one are organized specifically for tarot, which means that the 78 cards of the tarot are split up into groups of 22, 40, and 16: major arcana, numeric minor arcana, and court cards respectively. I've also included a section dealing with correspondences to the number 4—suits, directions, elements, and so on, given how central the fourfold division is in esoteric systems.

If you'd like to look up an individual card, you can do that as well; there's a table listing correspondences for every card in part three at the back of the book.

You can use the charts to help you dive deeper into any individual card, to design magical workings and tarot spells, to memorize (if that's something you like to do). If you don't already have an idea of what you would do with a compendium of tarot correspondences, consider starting with part two.

Part two is devoted to different techniques you can use with the correspondences, divided into the four main categories: elements, astrology, numbers, and Kabbalah. Each chapter is a deep dive into using that single technique in a reading. The final chapters offer ways of combining all the correspondences into a glorious, powerful, synthetic system that helps you journey deep into the cards—and work magic, if you wish.

Use this book as a tool. You don't have to memorize the tables (unless that's fun for you) and you don't have to try every technique. Dive in anywhere, use what you like, disregard the rest. If a system doesn't work for you, adapt it until it does or even devise your own. Try not to get hung up on the inconsistencies and infelicities that inevitably have arisen over six centuries of tarot history. Life's too short … and far too magical.

PART ONE

CORRESPONDENCE
TABLES

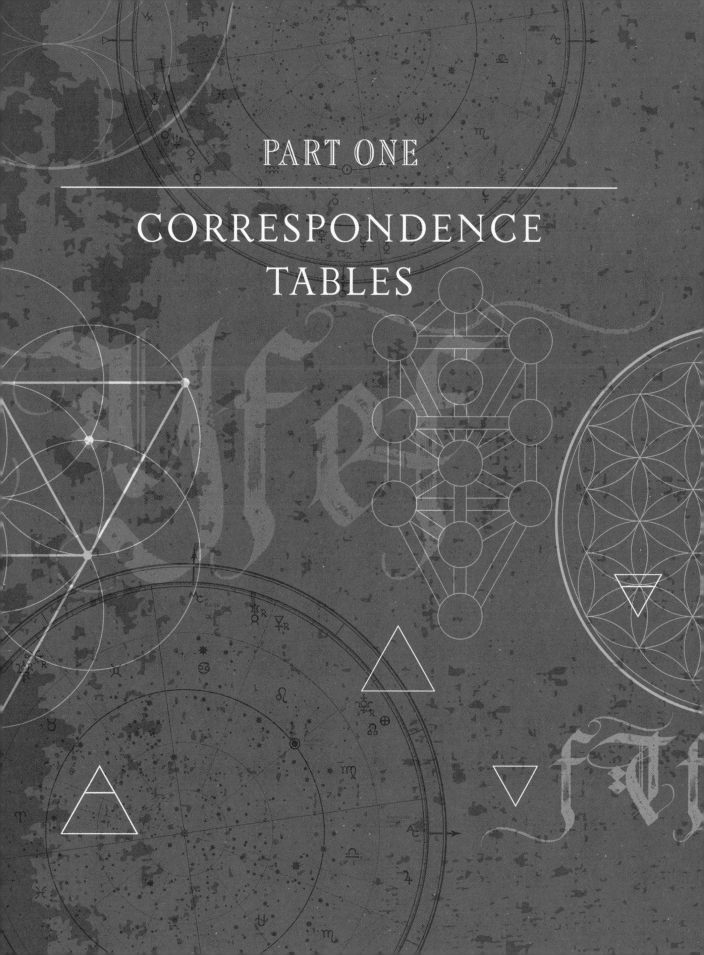

CORRESPONDENCES FOR THE 22 MAJOR ARCANA

TABLE 1—CONVENTIONAL, HISTORICAL, AND HERMETIC TITLES

Arabic number	Roman numeral	Conventional card title	Alternate English titles*	Romance language titles	Hermetic titles
0	0	The Fool	The Foolish Man, 'The Unnumbered Card', the Crocodile	Le Mat, Le Fou, Il Matto, Mattello, Il Pazzo, Le Fol	The spirit of Ether
01	I	The Magician	The Juggler, The Magus, the Mountebank, the Thimble-Rigger, the Quarter-penny	Le Jongleur, Il Bagat, Le Pagad, Le Bateleur, Il Bagatino, Il Bagatto, Il Bagattel, Il Ciabattino	The Magus of Power
02	II	The High Priestess (The Priestess)	The Popess, Pope Joan, the Door of the Occult Sanctuary	La Papesse, La Papessa, Junon, La Pances	The Priestess of the Silver Star
03	III	The Empress	The Queen, Isis-Urania	L'Imperatrice	Daughter of the Mighty Ones
04	IV	The Emperor	The King, the Cubic Stone	L'Empéreur, L'Imperatore, L'Imperadore	Son of the Morning, Chief Among the Mighty

TABLE 1—CONVENTIONAL, HISTORICAL, AND HERMETIC TITLES

Arabic number	Roman numeral	Conventional card title	Alternate English titles*	Romance language titles	Hermetic titles
05	V	The Hierophant	The Pope, The High Priest, Master of the Arcanum, Master of the Sacred Mysteries	Jupiter, Le Pape, Il Papa, Pontifex Pontificum	Magus of the Eternal Gods
06	VI	The Lovers	The Lover, Love, The Two Roads, the Ordeal	L'Amoureux, L'Amore, Gli Amanti, Gli Inamorati	Children of the Voice Divine, the Oracles of the Mighty Gods
07	VII	The Chariot	The Triumphal Car, The Chariot of War, Chariot of Osiris, the Cubic Chariot	Victoriae Premium, Il Carro, Le Chariot, La Carrozza	Child of the Power of the Waters, Lord of the Triumph of Light
08	VIII	Strength (Lust)	Fortitude, Force, The Tamed Lion	La Force, La Fortezza, La Forza	Daughter of the Flaming Sword, Leader of the Lion
09	IX	The Hermit	The Old Man, the Veiled Lamp	Rerum Edax (Devourer of Things), L'Eremite, Le Vieillard, Capuchin, Le Prêtre, L'Eremita, Il Gobbo, L'Ermita, Il Vecchio	The Magus of the Voice of Light, The Prophet of the Gods

TABLE 1—CONVENTIONAL, HISTORICAL, AND HERMETIC TITLES

Arabic number	Roman numeral	Conventional card title	Alternate English titles*	Romance language titles	Hermetic titles
10	X	The Wheel of Fortune	The Wheel, The Sphinx	Omnium Dominatrix (Mistress of Everything), La Roue de Fortune, La Ruota, Rota di Fortuna, Ruota della Fortuna, Fortuna	The Lord of the Forces of Life
11	XI	Justice (Adjustment)	Themis	La Justice, La Giustizia	Daughter of the Lord of Truth, The Holder of the Balances
12	XII	The Hanged Man	The Hanging Man, The Traitor, Prudence, The Sacrifice	Le Pendu, Il Penduto, L'Appeso, Il Traditore, L'Impiccato	The Spirit of the Mighty Waters
13	XIII	Death	The Scythe, "the Unnamed Card"	La Mort, Il Morte, La Morte	The Child of the Great Transformers, Lord of the Gates of Death
14	XIV	Temperance (Art)	Time, The Solar Spirit	Atrempance, La Temperance, La Temperanza	Daughter of the Reconcilers, The Bringer Forth of Life

TABLE 1—CONVENTIONAL, HISTORICAL, AND HERMETIC TITLES

Arabic number	Roman numeral	Conventional card title	Alternate English titles*	Romance language titles	Hermetic titles
15	XV	The Devil	Pan, Typhon, Baphomet	Perditorum Raptor (Captor of the Lost), Il Diavolo, Le Diable	Lord of the Gates of Matter, Child of the Forces of Time
16	XVI	The Tower	The House of God, The Blasted Tower, The Lightning-Struck Tower, The Hospital, The Arrow, The Thunderbolt, the Fire, The Lightning-Struck Temple, The Ruined Tower	La Maison Dieu, le Foudre, La Torre, Il Fuoco, La Saetta, La Sagitta	Lord of the Hosts of the Mighty
17	XVII	The Star	The Stars, The Blazing Star, Star of the Magi	Inclitum Sydus (Renowned Star), L'Etoile, La Stelle, Le Stelle	Daughter of the Firmament, Dweller Between the Waters
18	XVIII	The Moon	Twilight	La Lune, La Luna	Ruler of the Flux and Reflux, Child of the Sons of the Mighty

TABLE 1—CONVENTIONAL, HISTORICAL, AND HERMETIC TITLES

Arabic number	Roman numeral	Conventional card title	Alternate English titles*	Romance language titles	Hermetic titles
19	XIX	The Sun	The Blazing Light	Le Soleil, il Sole	Lord of the Fire of the World
20	XX	Judgement (The Aeon)	The Last Judgement, The Angel, Creation, the Awakening of the Dead	Le judgement, L'Ange, L'Angelo, Il Giudizio, La Trompete	The Spirit of the Primal Fire
21	XXI	The World (The Universe)	Time, Crown of the Magi	Le Monde, Il Mondo	The Great One of the Night of Time

Notes on Coventional, Historical, and Hermetic Titles for the Major Arcana

"Standard" titles are those used in the Rider Waite Smith and Thoth decks; titles in parentheses refers to titles used in Aleister Crowley's Thoth deck. Many of the alternate English titles I discovered in Paul Huson's fascinating *Mystical Origins of the Tarot*, Bill Whitcomb's *The Magician's Companion*, and *The History and Practice of Magic* by Paul Christian. Romance language titles can be found in European decks from the fifteenth through nineteenth centuries: the Marseille Tarot, the Tarot de Besançon, decks from Piedmont and Lombardy, and the Leber-Rouen Tarot.

"Hermetic" titles come from the Golden Dawn, where they are given in *Book T—The Tarot*. The term "hermetic" broadly refers to the Hermetic tradition, a syncretistic knowledge cult dating back to the beginning of common era. These Hermetic titles are strictly the work of the Hermetic Order of the Golden Dawn and date back only to the end of the nineteenth century.

Note that throughout the majors I give both the modern trump numbering devised by the Golden Dawn: 08/VIII = Strength and 11/IX=Justice, as well as the traditional numbering (used also by Crowley in his Thoth deck): 08/VIII=Justice and 11/IX=Strength. For an explanation of the switch, see *Explaining the Strength-Justice and the Heh-Tzaddi Switch*.

TABLE 2—ASTROLOGICAL CORRESPONDENCES

Arabic number	Roman numeral	Conventional card title	Zodiacal glyph	Planet, sign, or element	Dates (Tropical)
0	0	The Fool	♎︎♅♉︎	Air or Uranus	
01	I	The Magician	☿	Mercury	
02	II	The High Priestess	☽	Moon	
03	III	The Empress	♀	Venus	
04	IV	The Emperor	♈	Aries	March 21–April 20
05	V	The Hierophant	♉	Taurus	April 21–May 21
06	VI	The Lovers	♊	Gemini	May 22–June 21
07	VII	The Chariot	♋	Cancer	June 22–July 23
08/11	VIII/IX	Strength	♌	Leo	July 24–August 23
09	IX	The Hermit	♍	Virgo	August 24–September 23
10	X	The Wheel of Fortune	♃	Jupiter	
11/08	XI/VIII	Justice	♎	Libra	September 24–October 23
12	XII	The Hanged Man	▽♆	Water or Neptune	
13	XIII	Death	♏	Scorpio	October 23–November 22

TABLE 2—ASTROLOGICAL CORRESPONDENCES

Arabic number	Roman numeral	Conventional card title	Zodiacal glyph	Planet, sign, or element	Dates (Tropical)
14	XIV	**Temperance**	♐	Sagittarius	November 23–December 21
15	XV	**The Devil**	♑	Capricorn	December 22–January 20
16	XVI	**The Tower**	♂	Mars	
17	XVII	**The Star**	♒	Aquarius	January 21–February 19
18	XVIII	**The Moon**	♓	Pisces	February 20–March 21
19	XIX	**The Sun**	☉	Sun	
20	XX	**Judgement**	△∗♀	Fire/Spirit or Pluto	
21	XXI	**The World**	♄	Saturn/Earth	

Notes on Astrological Correspondences for the Major Arcana

Astrological correspondences to tarot have varied widely since occultists first began assigning them to the major arcana in the mid-eighteenth century. The correspondences presented here (and throughout this book) are those settled upon by the Order of the Golden Dawn and its followers, otherwise known as the English School, at the beginning of the twentieth century. The French School or Continental correspondences differ quite substantially, and if you would like to know more about them, see Christine Payne-Towler's very illuminating Astro-Alpha-Numeric chart.

Within the English School itself there are a couple of variations, and these are noted in the "Planet, sign, and element" column:

> Elements → Modern Planets. Whereas the Golden Dawn exclusively assigned attributions with the 7 classical planets, subsequent readers swapped in the modern planets Uranus, Neptune, and Pluto where the Golden Dawn used the air, water, and fire elements.

> Spirit and Earth → To the two final cards, Crowley added the fifth element of "Spirit" and the fourth element of "Earth," so that Judgement/The Aeon and The World/The Universe each have two astrological attributions.

Finally, it's worth just mentioning that the dates given are based on the tropical rather than the sidereal zodiac. The tropical zodiac, based on the seasonal relationship between Sun and Earth and their relative positions, is that most used by Western astrologers. The sidereal zodiac, based on the actual current positions of the stars in the sky, is used primarily by Vedic astrologers.

TABLE 3—TREE OF LIFE CORRESPONDENCES

Arabic Number	Roman numeral	Conventional card title	Hebrew alphabet letter	Hebrew transliteration	Type of Hebrew letter	English letter equivalent
00	0	The Fool	א	Aleph	Mother	A
01	I	The Magician	ב	Beth	Double	B
02	II	The High Priestess	ג	Gimel	Double	G
03	III	The Empress	ד	Daleth	Double	D
04	IV	The Emperor	ה	He	Single	H
05	V	The Hierophant	ו	Vav	Single	V/W
06	VI	The Lovers	ז	Zayin	Single	Z
07	VII	The Chariot	ח	Cheth	Single	Ch

TABLE 3—TREE OF LIFE CORRESPONDENCES

Arabic Number	Hebrew letter meaning	Number equivalent	Gifts and attributes	Sephirothic Path	Sephirothic Path Meanings	Alt Hebrew letter Crowley	Alt. Sephirothic Path Crowley
00	Ox Strength Teach	1	Air—temperate	Kether—Chokmah	Crown—Wisdom	א	Kether—Chokmah
01	House Household ' In'	2	Life & Death	Kether—Binah	Crown—Understanding	ב	Kether—Binah
02	Camel Prize/Reward Lift Up	3	Wisdom & Folly	Kether—Tiphereth	Crown—Beauty	ג	Kether—Tiphereth
03	Door Path, Weakness To move in or out	4	Peace & War	Chokmah—Binah	Wisdom—Understanding	ד	Chokmah—Binah
04	Window To show, reveal	5	Sight	Chokmah—Tiphereth	Wisdom—Beauty	צ	Netzach—Yesod
05	Nail or hook Joining together Making fast	6	Hearing	Chokmah—Chesed	Wisdom—Mercy	ו	Chokmah—Chesed
06	Sword or weapon Axe To cut	7	Smell	Binah—Tiphereth	Understanding—Beauty	ז	Binah—Tiphereth
07	Fence Inner Chamber to separate or protect	8	Speech	Binah—Geburah	Understanding—Severity	ח	Binah—Geburah

TABLE 3—TREE OF LIFE CORRESPONDENCES

Arabic Number	Roman numeral	Conventional card title	Hebrew alphabet letter	Hebrew transliteration	Type of Hebrew letter	English letter equivalent
08/11	VIII/IX	Strength	ט	Teth	Single	T
09	IX	The Hermit	י	Yod	Single	I/Y
10	X	The Wheel of Fortune	כ	Kaph	Double	K
11/08	XI/VIII	Justice	ל	Lamed	Single	L
12	XII	The Hanged Man	מ	Mem	Mother	M
13	XIII	Death	נ	Nun	Single	N

TABLE 3—TREE OF LIFE CORRESPONDENCES

Arabic Number	Hebrew letter meaning	Number equivalent	Gifts and attributes	Sephirothic Path	Sephirothic Path Meanings	Alt Hebrew letter Crowley	Alt. Sephirothic Path Crowley
08/11	Snake Knot To twist or coil	9	Taste	Chesed—Geburah	Mercy—Severity	ט	Chesed—Geburah
09	Closed hand Power To share	10	Sex	Chesed—Tiphereth	Mercy—Beauty	י	Chesed—Tiphereth
10	Palm of hand/ the hand bent To open the hand To receive	20, 500	Riches & Poverty	Chesed—Netzach	Mercy—Victory	כ	Chesed—Netzach
11/08	Ox-goad To urge forward or teach To Learn	30	Work	Geburah—Tiphereth	Severity—Beauty	ל	Geburah—Tiphereth
12	Water Nations People	40, 600	The Earth—cold	Geburah—Hod	Severity—Glory	מ	Geburah—Hod
13	Fish Descendants To propagate	50, 700	Movement	Tiphereth—Netzach	Beauty—Victory	נ	Tiphereth—Netzach

TABLE 3—TREE OF LIFE CORRESPONDENCES

Arabic Number	Roman numeral	Conventional card title	Hebrew alphabet letter	Hebrew transliteration	Type of Hebrew letter	English letter equivalent
14	XIV	Temperance	ס	Samekh	Single	S
15	XV	The Devil	ע	Ayin	Single	O
16	XVI	The Tower	פ	Pe	Double	P
17	XVII	The Star	צ	Tzaddi	Single	Tz
18	XVIII	The Moon	ק	Qoph	Single	Q
19	XIX	The Sun	ר	Resh	Double	R

TABLE 3—TREE OF LIFE CORRESPONDENCES

Arabic Number	Hebrew letter meaning	Number equivalent	Gifts and attributes	Sephirothic Path	Sephirothic Path Meanings	Alt Hebrew letter Crowley	Alt. Sephirothic Path Crowley
14	Prop or support Training (as a plant) To trust	60	Anger	Tiphereth—Yesod	Beauty—Foundation	ס	Tiphereth—Yesod
15	Eye Expression To see	70	Mirth	Tiphereth—Hod	Beauty—Glory	ע	Tiphereth—Hod
16	Mouth Entrance To speak	80, 800	Grace & Indignation	Netzach—Hod	Victory—Glory	פ	Netzach—Hod
17	Fish hook Righteous To pull toward	90, 900	Imagination	Netzach—Yesod	Victory—Foundation	ה	Chokmah—Tiphereth
18	Back of the head Final or last To circle	100	Sleep	Netzach—Malkuth	Victory—Kingdom	ק	Netzach—Malkuth
19	Head Chief Poverty	200	Fertility & Barrenness	Hod—Yesod	Glory—Foundation	ר	Hod—Yesod

TABLE 3—TREE OF LIFE CORRESPONDENCES

Arabic Number	Roman numeral	Conventional card title	Hebrew alphabet letter	Hebrew transliteration	Type of Hebrew letter	English letter equivalent
20	**XX**	Judgement	שׁ	Shin	Mother	Sh
21	**XXI**	The World	ת	Tav	Double	Th

TABLE 3—TREE OF LIFE CORRESPONDENCES

Arabic Number	Hebrew letter meaning	Number equivalent	Gifts and attributes	Sephirothic Path	Sephirothic Path Meanings	Alt Hebrew letter Crowley	Alt. Sephirothic Path Crowley
20	Tooth Ivory To sharpen, devour	300	The Heavens— Hot	Hod— Malkuth	Glory— Kingdom	ש	Hod— Malkuth
21	Mark or cross Seal of ownership To join or bind	400	Power & Servitude	Yesod— Malkuth	Founda-tion—King-dom	ת	Yesod— Malkuth

Notes on the Tree of Life Correspondences for the Major Arcana

As with the astrological correspondences, these Tree of Life correspondences have many variations. They are based, first of all, on which Hebrew letter is assigned to which trump. Crowley switched the attributions of the Emperor and the Star, but other than that the English School attributions are consistent.

The next question is: how do the Hebrew letters join up with the astrological correspondences? With great complexity and variation, is how! These correspondences derive from the *Sefer Yetzirah*, a foundational text of Kabbalah which dates from the first or second century CE. The *Sefer Yetzirah* is a cosmology, a story of creation in which the alphabet IS the instrument of creation. Each letter governs an essential part of Creation as a whole. While there is some agreement about which signs and elements go with which letter, the seven planets are another matter. The astrological Hebrew letter correspondences determine a number of other qualitative correspondences, of which I've only include column J, "Gifts and Attributes," as the others are too entangled to enumerate.

The next question is: where should each Hebrew letter fall on the Tree of Life; which path? The English school is consistent in itself, but it diverges widely from the path assignments of Jewish Kabbalah and earlier versions of Christian Cabala.

Yet another question is: which model of the Tree of Life should you use? The English School uses the version drafted by seventeenth-century Jesuit scholar Athanasius Kircher in 1652; Kircher in turn derived it from Moses ben Jacob Cordovero, a sixteenth-century Jewish mystic. Again, this diverges from previous Trees fairly profoundly.

If you would like to venture into the tangled web of historical Tree of Life correspondences, Stephen Skinner makes a heroic effort to clarify matters in his introduction to *The Complete Magician's Tables* (Llewellyn, 2006). For the purposes of this text, however, we will mostly abide by the choices made by the English School.

A few column notes:

Type of Hebrew letter. There are three types of Hebrew letter. The three "mother" letters are Aleph, Mem, and Shin, corresponding to three elements (excluding earth). "Double" letters traditionally had two sounds, a hard or aspirated sound and a soft or unaspirated sound. Like the planets, they are 7. The remaining "single" letters are 12, and therefore correspond neatly to the twelve zodiacal signs.

Number equivalent. Numbers and letters are intimately connected in Hebrew in a way they are not in other linguistic traditions. This gives rise, among other things, to the mystical science of gematria, which draws out linkages between words whose add up to the same number.

Gifts and Attributes. The idea here is that each of these qualities was brought into being along with its corresponding letter at the creation of the Universe. The assignment of these qualities to Hebrew letters, again, varies greatly within every tradition. Here I have used the ones presented in Bill Whitcomb's *The Magician's Companion* (Llewellyn, 1993), which reflect a consensus in Hermetic magical circles.

Finally, here are very approximate English pronunciations for the sephiroth:
Kether: *KETT-er*
Chokmah: *khokh-MAH*
Binah: *bee-NAH*
Chesed: *KHE-sed*
Geburah: *ge-BOO-rah* or *ge-VOO-rah*
Tiphereth: *ti-PER-et* or *ti-PER-ess*
Netzach: *NET-zakh*
Hod: *Howd*
Yesod: *ye-SOD*
Malkuth: *mal-KOOT* or *mal-KOOS*

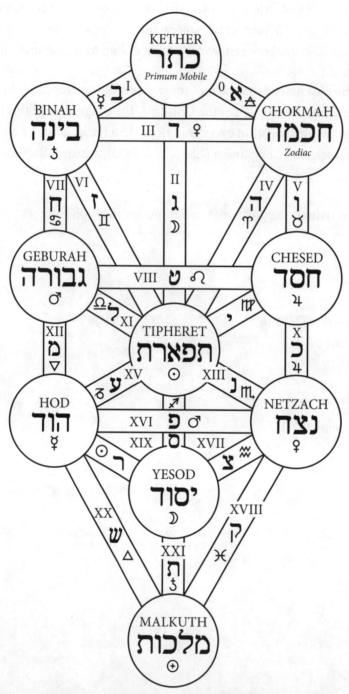

1. This is the tree model, letter and astrological attributions used by the Golden Dawn.
This version of the tree was drafted by seventeenth-century Jesuit scholar Athanasius Kircher,
who derived it from Moses ben Jacob Cordovero, a sixteenth-century Jewish mystic.

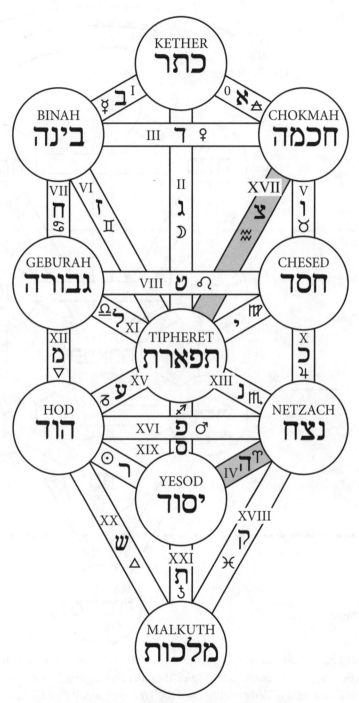

2. Here is the same tree used by the Golden Dawn,
but with Aleister Crowley's variation, in which the letters
Heh and Tzaddi—and therefore the Emperor and the Star—are switched.

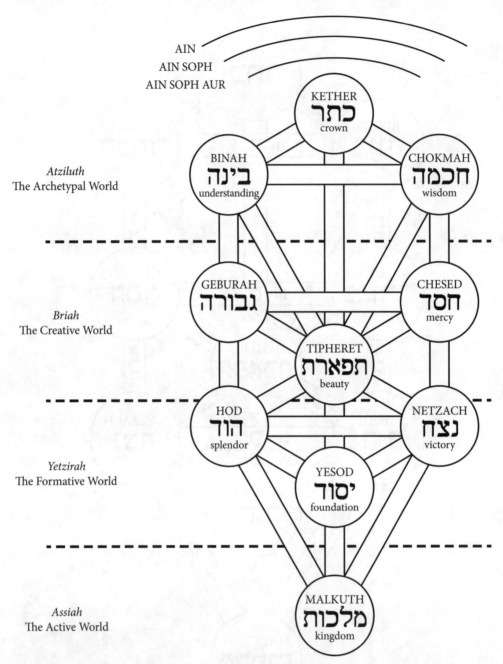

AIN
AIN SOPH
AIN SOPH AUR

KETHER
כתר
crown

Atziluth
The Archetypal World

BINAH
בינה
understanding

CHOKMAH
חכמה
wisdom

Briah
The Creative World

GEBURAH
גבורה

CHESED
חסד
mercy

TIPHERET
תפארת
beauty

HOD
הוד
splendor

NETZACH
נצח
victory

Yetzirah
The Formative World

YESOD
יסוד
foundation

Assiah
The Active World

MALKUTH
מלכות
kingdom

3. The Tree of Life is a cosmology; a model of the emanation of Creation. Emanating from the "three veils" *Ain* ["nothingness"], *Ain Soph* ["limitless nothingness"], and *Ain Soph Aur* ["limitless light"] the light of Kether spills down the Tree, each sephira containing and creating the next. The Four Worlds are an analogue of the Divine Name, Yod-Heh-Vav-Heh, and another representation of the progressive crystallization of matter from the sublime.

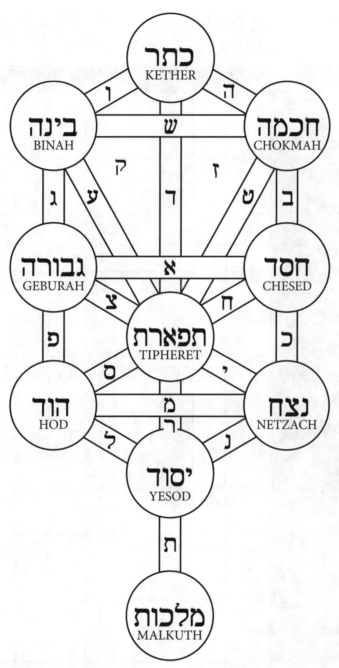

4. This is the tree model conceived by Isaac Luria, the sixteenth-century Jewish rabbi known as the Ari ("the Lion"). It is more widely used in Jewish Kabbalah than Hermetic Qabalah and has a structural elegance lacking in the Kircher tree. The three horizontal paths hold the three elements and mother letters; the seven vertical paths hold the seven planets and double letters; and the twelve diagonal paths hold the twelve planets and single letters.

TABLE 4—ALTERNATE ASTRO-ALPHA-NUMERIC CORRESPONDENCES

English Letter		A	B	G	D	H	V	Z	Ch	T	I
Hebrew Letter (Continental Use of Hebrew)		א	ב	ג	ד	ה	ו	ז	ח	ט	י
Arcana Names	Fool	Magus	Priestess	Empress	Emperor	Pope	Lovers	Chariot	Justice	Hermit	Wheel
Arcana Number	0	1	2	3	4	5	6	7	8	9	10
Sefer Yetzirah (Gra version, ~1800 B.C.) El Gran Tarot Esoterico, Tarot of the Ages		🜁	☽	♂	☉	♈	♉	♊	♋	♌	♍
Old Alexandrian, 600 B.C.-Hermetic Etteilla, Falconnier Tarot		🜁	☽	♀	♃	♈	♉	♊	♋	♌	♍
Continental Tarots ~1880 A.D. Levi, Wirth, Papus		🜁	☽	♀	♃	♈	♉	♊	♋	♌	♍
Marseilles, Spanish Tarot Maxwell's correspondences	Fool △	☉	☽	♀	♃	☿	♐	♂	♎	♓	♑
Pierre Piobb, 1908 A.D.Spanish Variant #1 Dali, Euskalherria	Fool ♏	☉	☽	Earth (♁)	♃	☿	♍	♐	♎	♆	♑
Balbi, Spanish Variant #2	Fool ש ♏	☉	☽	☿	♃	♉	♍	♊	♎	♆	♑

Notes on Alternate Astro-Alpha-Numeric Correspondences for the Major Arcana

The Golden Dawn's system of Hebrew letter attribution and astrological attribution is only one of many. The numerous variations fall outside the scope of this book.

TABLE 4—ALTERNATE ASTRO-ALPHA-NUMERIC CORRESPONDENCES

English Letter	C	L	M	N	S	Ayn	P	Ts	Qk	R	Sch	Th
Hebrew Letter (Continental Use of Hebrew)	כ	ל	מ	נ	ס	ע	פ	צ	ק	ר	ט	ת
Arcana Names	Strength	Hanged Man	Death	Temperance	Devil	Tower	Star	Moon	Sun	Judgement		
Arcana Number	11	12	13	14	15	16	17	18	19	20	21	22
Gra version SephirYetzirah–From ~1800 B.C. El Gran Tarto Esoterico, Tarot of the Ages	♀	♎	▽	♏	♐	♑	☿	♒	♓	♄	Fool △	World ♃
Old Alexandrian, 600 B.C.–Hermetic Etteilla, Falconnier Tarot	♂	♎	▽	♏	♐	♑	☿	♒	♓	♄	World △	Fool ☉
Continental Tarots ~1880 A.D. Levi, Wirth, Papus	♂	♎	▽	♏	♐	♑	☿	♒	♓	♄	Fool △ #0	World ☉ #21
Marseilles, Spanish Tarot Maxwell's correspondences	♌	♈	♄	♒		🜁	♉	♋	♊	♏	World ♍	
Pierre Piobb, 1908 A.D.Spanish Variant #1 Dali, Euskalherria	♌	♅	♄	♒	♈	♈	♀	♋	♊	♓	World ♉	
Balbi, Spanish Variant #2	♌	♓	♄	♒	♈	♈	♀	♋	♅	♐		World ⯓

However, Christine Payne-Towler has conducted comprehensive research on the subject and has kindly permitted me to reproduce her concise representation of the varying correspondences seen here.

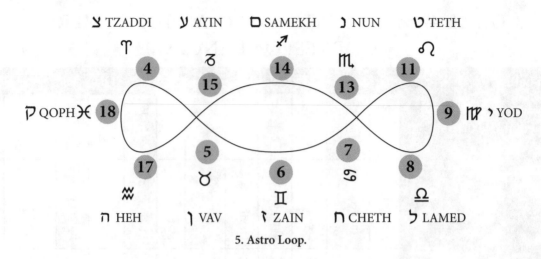

5. Astro Loop.

EXPLAINING THE STRENGTH-JUSTICE
AND THE HEH-TZADDI SWITCH

If you're a tarot reader, you probably already know about the switch of the Strength and Justice major arcana (although if you're a Thoth reader, you call them Lust and Adjustment). You know that on your Rider-Waite-Smith deck Strength is 8, or VIII and Justice is 11, or XI. But you've also noticed that in Marseille decks and in Thoth and in a lot of other decks, Justice is 8 and Strength is 11. Why?

The answer is this: Justice-as-8 and Strength-as-11 is in fact the correct original sequence. But when the Golden Dawn got around to assigning astrological correspondences, they stumbled on this problem:

7 Chariot (Cancer) —> 8 Justice (Libra) —> 9 Hermit (Virgo) —> 11 Strength (Leo) —> 13 Death (Scorpio)

(Notice we left out the Wheel of Fortune and the Hanged Man. That's because the Wheel is associated with planet Jupiter, and the Hanged Man is associated with elemental water. We're dealing only with zodiacal signs here).

As you can see, it's zodiacally out of order. Libra appears before Virgo instead of the other way around. And with those scales all over Justice/Adjustment and the lion imagery all over Strength/Lust, you can't just say OK, fine, Justice goes with Leo and Strength with Libra. The simple solution? Switch the number correspondences instead.

7 Chariot (Cancer) —> **8 Strength** (Leo) —> 9 Hermit (Virgo)—> **11 Justice** (Libra) —> 13 Death (Scorpio)

If you use any Rider Waite Smith or RWS-derived deck, that's what you'll see.

But Crowley didn't want to switch the number correspondences. Instead, he twisted the right side of the loop as you see above. Now, if you follow the twist of the loop, the signs march neatly in their usual zodiacal procession. But if you go around the *outside* of the loop, ignoring the twist, the numbers can still go in their original, pre-Golden Dawn order—7 Chariot, 8 Justice, 9 Hermit and the rest.

And that's what you'll see in any Thoth deck.

But what about the Emperor/Star switch? This one is not so obvious. This time we're not switching the number correspondences based on the zodiacal placements. We're switching the Hebrew letter correspondences based on the zodiacal placements. Unless you are a tarot nerd, or specifically a Golden Dawn or Crowley nerd, you probably don't know about this switch.

Visually, what you see on the left side of the diagram is a loop that switches the positions of Aries [the Emperor] and Aquarius [the Star]. It appears to be an exact balance for the switch between Leo [Strength/Lust] and Libra [Justice/Adjustment].

But esoterically, what's going on? The switch allows you to proceed, going around the outside of the loop, in Hebrew alphabetical order:

Ayin —> Tzaddi —> Qoph —> Heh —> Vav

(We're skipping Pe, Resh, Shin, Tav, Aleph, and Beth because they are planets or elements rather than zodiacal signs). If you know your Hebrew alphabet, you'll see that this sequence actually goes to the end of the alphabet and starts over again, like so:

Ayin —> [Pe] —> Tzaddi —> Qoph —> [Resh] —> [Shin] —> [Tav, end of alphabet] —> [Aleph, beginning of alphabet] —> [Beth] —> Heh —> Vav

Just as with the Strength-Justice twist, this allows you to follow the path going along the loop in correct zodiacal order.

What's so wacky about this diagram is that the twist on the left preserves Hebrew letter order but messes up the numerical order, and the twist on the other side preserves numerical order but messes up Hebrew letter order. Meaning you have to be (1) enough of an occultist that you know astrology, the Hebrew alphabet, and your numerical system well enough simply to perceive the problem, and (2) neurotic enough to be bothered by it at all.

To sum up:

- Using the Emperor/Star switch allows you to assign Heh to the Star and Tzaddi to the Emperor, while preserving zodiacal order.

- Using the Strength/Justice switch allows you assign 8/VIII to Justice and 11/IX to Strength, while preserving zodiacal order.

TABLE 5—COLOR SCALES OF THE GOLDEN DAWN

Arabic Number	Roman numeral		*King Scale*	Queen Scale	Prince Scale	Princess Scale
0	0	The Fool	*Bright pale yellow*	Sky blue	Blue emerald green	Emerald, flecked gold
01	I	The Magician	*Yellow*	Purple	Grey	Indigo, rayed violet
02	II	The High Priestess	*Blue*	Silver	Cold pale blue	Silver, rayed sky blue
03	III	The Empress	*Emerald green*	Sky blue	Early spring green	Bright rose or cerise, rayed pale green
04	IV	The Emperor	*Scarlet*	Red	Brilliant flame	Glowing red
05	V	The Hierophant	*Red orange*	Deep indigo	Deep warm olive	Rich brown
06	VI	The Lovers	*Orange*	Pale mauve	New yellow leather	Reddish grey, inclined to mauve
07	VII	The Chariot	*Amber*	Maroon	Rich bright russet	Dark greenish brown
08/11	VIII/IX	Strength	*Yellow (greenish)*	Deep purple	Grey	Reddish amber
09	IX	The Hermit	*Green (yellowish)*	Slate grey	Green grey	Plum color
10	X	The Wheel of Fortune	*Violet*	Blue	Rich purple	Bright blue, rayed yellow

TABLE 5—COLOR SCALES OF THE GOLDEN DAWN

Arabic Number	Roman numeral		*King Scale*	Queen Scale	Prince Scale	Princess Scale
11/08	XI/VIII	Justice	Emerald green	Blue	Deep blue-green	Plum color
12	XII	The Hanged Man	Deep blue	Sea-green	Deep olive-green	White, flecked purple
13	XIII	Death	Green blue	Dull brown	Very dark brown	Livid in-digo brown
14	XIV	Temperance	Blue	Yellow ·	Green grey	Dark vivid blue
15	XV	The Devil	Indigo	Black	Blue-black	Cold dark grey near-ing black
16	XVI	The Tower	Scarlet	Red	Venetian red	Bright red, rayed azure or emerald
17	XVII	The Star	Violet	Sky blue	Bluish mauve	White, tinged purple
18	XVIII	The Moon	Crimson (ultra violet)	Buff, flecked silver white	Light translucent pinkish brown	Stone color
19	XIX	The Sun	Orange	Gold yellow	Rich amber	Amber, rayed red
20	XX	Judgement	Glowing orange scarlet	Vermilion	Scarlet, flecked gold	Vermilion, flecked crimson and emerald
21	XXI	The World	Indigo	Black	Blue-black	Black, rayed blue

Notes on Color Scale Correspondences for the Major Arcana

According to the Golden Dawn, each major arcana path corresponds to a different color in each of the four worlds of the Tree of Life: Atziluth, the Archetypal World; Briah, the Creative World; Yetzirah, the Formative World; and Assiah, the Active World. In most colored representations of the Tree of Life, the paths of the Tree are given the Atziluthic color (italicized in this table) of their corresponding trump. The ten sephiroth also have four colors apiece for the four worlds, but they are usually represented with their Briatic colors (see Table 5, page 123).

TABLE 6—NATURAL, MAGICAL, MYTHICAL CORRESPONDENCES

Arabic number	Roman numeral	Conventional card title	Zodiacal glyph	Animal	Plant	Perfume/ Incense
0	0	The Fool	△	Eagle, crocodile, birds, butterflies, insects	Aspen, bamboo, linden, almond, pine, papyrus, fern dill, peppermint, lavender	Galbanum, grass, pines/ firs, synthetic aldehydes
01	I	The Magician	☿	Baboon, monkey, ibis, coyote, fox, greyhound, hare, weasel, ape, nightingale, thrush, lark, parrot, mullet, jackal	Marjoram, vervain, almond, aspen, bamboo, caraway, clover, coriander, dill, fennel, lily of the valley, laurel, cinquefoil, horehound, lavender, mint, papyrus, parsley, wildflowers	Cinnamon, mace, citrus peel, bayberries, all odoriferous seeds, mastic, white sandalwood, mace, storax, nutmeg, "all fleeting odors"
02	II	The High Priestess	☽	Deer, camel, dog, boar, cow, bear, cats, watery fowl, dung beetle, herons, owls, shellfish, egg whites, eels, all aquatic creatures	Hazel, pomegranate, moonwort, cypress, cabbage, camellia, coconut, cotton, cucumber, gardenia, jasmine, lettuce, lily, lotus, melons, vines, mushrooms, poppy, potato, turnip, willow, melons	Myrtle, bay, hyssop, olives all leaves, camphor, aloe, myrrh, jasmine, "all sweet and virginal odors"

TABLE 6—NATURAL, MAGICAL, MYTHICAL CORRESPONDENCES

Arabic number	Roman numeral	Gemstone/ metal	Mythic figures	Magical weapon	Musical note	Color correspondences for musical note
0	0	Topaz, chalcedony, aluminum, tin, pumice, clear quartz, all oxides	Hoor-paar-Kraat/ Harpocrates, Zeus, Jupiter as air, Vayu, Valkyries	The Dagger or Fan	E	Yellow
01	I	Quicksilver, marcasite, agate, opal, quartz, coral, emerald, glass/ imitation gems, all metals struck as coins, all metals of mixed color	Mercury, Hermes, Hermes Trismegistus, Odin, Thoth, Hanuman, Loki	The Wand or Caduceus	E	Yellow
02	II	Silver, moonstone, pearl, crystal, chalcedony, selenites	Artemis, Hecate, Chomse, Chandra, Isis, Hathorn, Nut, Demeter, Persephone, Hekate	The Bow and Arrow	G#	Blue

TABLE 6—NATURAL, MAGICAL, MYTHICAL CORRESPONDENCES

Arabic number	Roman numeral	Conventional card title	Zodiacal glyph	Animal	Plant	Perfume/Incense
03	III	The Empress	♀	Bee, dove, pigeon, gazelle, rabbit, calf, nightingale, swan, swallow	Clover, rose, cypress, myrtle, apple, blackberry, buckwheat, cardamom, cherry, corn, daffodil, elder, figs, foxglove, hyacinth, lilac, passion flower, peach, pear, quince, strawberry, thyme, tomato, tulip, valerian, vervain, vanilla	Roses, violets, saffron, all flowers, labdanum, ambergris, musk, sandalwoods, coriander, patchouli, oakmoss, "all soft voluptuous odors"
04	IV	The Emperor	♈	Ram, eagle, hawk, owl	Geranium, oak, thorn, bloodroot	Myrrh, dragon's blood, basil
05	V	The Hierophant	♉	Beaver, bull, tiger	Mallow, sage, hawthorn, linden, dandelion, lily of the valley, "straight vervain"	Costus, storax, mastic

TABLE 6—NATURAL, MAGICAL, MYTHICAL CORRESPONDENCES

Arabic number	Roman Numeral	Gemstone/ metal	Mythic figures	Magical weapon	Musical note	Color correspondences for musical note
03	III	Copper, emerald, turquoise, brass, all green stones	Venus, Aphrodite, Demeter, Gaia, Nephthys, Lalita, Hathor, Freya	The Girdle	F#	Green
04	IV	Bloodstone, topaz, ruby, diaimond	Athena, Shiva, Mars, Minerva, Mentu, Tyr,	The Horns, the Energy	C	Red
05	V	Sapphire, garnet, carnelian, jade, topaz	Shiva, Asar Ameshet Apis, Hera, Hymen, Bacchus, Parsifal, the Trinity	The Labor of Preparation [The Throne & Altar]	C#	Red Orange

TABLE 6—NATURAL, MAGICAL, MYTHICAL CORRESPONDENCES

Arabic Number	Roman numeral	Conventional card title	Zodiacal glyph	Animal	Plant	Perfume/ Incense
06	VI	The Lovers	♊	Magpie, all hybrids	Nut trees, orchids, "bending vervain"	Mastic, Worm-wood, lavender, bergamot
07	VII	The Chariot	♋	Crab, sphinx, turtle, dog, horse, rabbit, beetle	Lotus, cypress, olive, comfrey	Camphor, onycha, labdanum
08	VIII	Strength	♌	Lion, serpent	Sun-flower, Citrus, bay, palm, cycla-men	Frankin-cense

TABLE 6—NATURAL, MAGICAL, MYTHICAL CORRESPONDENCES

Arabic Number	Roman Numeral	Gemstone/ metal	Mythic figures	Magical weapon	Musical note	Color correspondences for musical note
06	VI	Agate, emerald, topaz, tourmaline, calcite, rose quartz, alexandrite	Aphrodite, Inanna, Venus, Eros, Amor, Cupid All twin gods (Rekht/Merti, Castor/Pollux, Apollo as soothsayer, Janus, Hoor-paar-Kratt as Horus + Harpocrates	The Tripod	D	Orange
07	VII	Amber, Emerald, sapphire, chalcedony, antique silver	Khephra, Nermod, Mercury and Apollo as messengers, Shiva, Ezekiel, Elijah, Osiris	The Furnace [The Cup or Grail]	D#	
08	VIII	Onyx, diamond, jasper, cat's eye	Pasht, Sekhet, Mau, Ra-Hoor-Khuit, Demeer, Venus, Anuket, Hebe	The Discipline [The Phoenix wand]	E	Yellow

TABLE 6—NATURAL, MAGICAL, MYTHICAL CORRESPONDENCES

Arabic Number	Roman numeral	Conventional card title	Zodiacal glyph	Animal	Plant	Perfume/ Incense
09	IX	The Hermit	♍	Bear, cat, pig, squirrel	Beech, chestnut, mimosa, walnut, aster, hyacinth, violet, snowdrop, narcissus, calamint	Sandalwood, narcissus
10	X	The Wheel of Fortune	♃	Eagle, owl, deer, hens, cuckoo, pheasant, dolphin, whale, elephant, sheep, all domestic animals	Oak, anise, elm, beech clove, ash, alkanet, pistachio, pineapples, rhubarb, cinnamon, fruit trees, leeks, dandelion, fig, hyssop, maple, nutmeg, grains, wines, mastic, mints	Nutmeg, cloves, storax, all odoriferous fruits Saffron, mace, ash, balm of Gilead, nutmeg, cinnamon, cloves, oud, "all expansive odors"
11	XI	Justice	♎	Hare, elephant, spider	Ash, aloe, mugwort	Galbanum

TABLE 6—NATURAL, MAGICAL, MYTHICAL CORRESPONDENCES

Arabic Number	Roman Numeral	Gemstone/metal	Mythic figures	Magical weapon	Musical note	Color correspondences for musical note
09	IX	Carnelian, zircon, peridot, bloodstone, sardonyx, aluminum, mercury	Cronos, Hermes, Mercury, Isis, Nephthys, Narcissus, Adonis, Baldur	The Lamp and Wand; the Bread	F	Yellow Green
10	X	Tin, sapphire, amethyst, lapis lazuli, silver, marble, gold, zinc	Fortuna, Jupiter, Zeus, Brahma, Indra, Njord	The Scepter	G#	Blue
11	XI	Sapphire, peridot, agate, carnelian, cat's eye	Themis, Pallas Athena, Maat, Dike, Nemesis	The Cross of Equilibrium	F#	Green

TABLE 6—NATURAL, MAGICAL, MYTHICAL CORRESPONDENCES

Arabic Number	Roman numeral	Conventional card title	Zodiacal glyph	Animal	Plant	Perfume/ Incense
12	XII	The Hanged Man	▽	Eagle, snake, scorpion, fish, water fowl, dolphin	Lotus, ash, all water plants, willow, comfrey	Myrrh, iris (orris root), gardenia, jasmine, vanilla
13	XIII	Death	♏	Scorpion, eagle, phoenix, bat, panther, wolf, vulture, khephra beetle	Aspen, myrtle, elder, yew, blackthorn, cactus, scorpion grass	Opoponax (sweet myrrh), benzoin
14	XIV	Temperance	♐	Elk, horse, centaur, dog	Lime, mulberry, oak, birch, rush, pimpernel	Lign-aloe (agarwood), oud

TABLE 6—NATURAL, MAGICAL, MYTHICAL CORRESPONDENCES

Arabic Number	Roman Numeral	Gemstone/ metal	Mythic figures	Magical weapon	Musical note	Color correspondences for musical note
12	XII	Silver, pearl, moonstone, crystal, beryl, aquamarine, sulfates	Tum Ptah Auromoth, Poseidon, Neptune, Prometheus, Odin, Attis, Schemcha-sai	The Cup & Cross of Suffering; the sacramental wine	G#	Blue
13	XIII	Aquamarine, beryl, am-ethyst, snake-stone, amber, bloodstone	Mars, Ares, Apep, Khephra, Hades, Pluto, Thanatos, Hypnos	The Pain of the Obligation; The Oath	G	Blue Green
14	XIV	Jacinth, topaz, beryl, am-ethyst	Diana, Artemis/ Apollo, Iris, Nemesis, Ares	The Arrow	G#	Blue

TABLE 6—NATURAL, MAGICAL, MYTHICAL CORRESPONDENCES

Arabic Number	Roman numeral	Conventional card title	Zodiacal glyph	Animal	Plant	Perfume/ Incense
15	XV	The Devil	♑	Elephant, mountain goat, dog, dolphin, ass	Birch, willow, elm, Thistle, poppy, sweet woodruff, thyme, hemp, dock	Benzoin musk, civet, benzoin
16	XVI	The Tower	♂	Wolf, bear, crow, screech owl, vulture, scorpion, kestrels, pike, sturgeon, wasps, all stinging insects	Rue, wormwood, pepper, cumin, chili, ginger, asafoetida, capers, hoseradish, garlic, leek, onion, mustard, radish, hops, pennyroyal, tobacco, hellebore, thistle, radish, nettle, chestnut, all thorny and lacrimatory plants	Sandalwood, cypress, agarwood, all odoriferous wood pepper, dragon's blood, benzoin, "all hot pungent odors"
17	XVII	The Star	♒	Otter, eagle, peacock	Olive, fir, skullcap, moss, fruit trees, dracunculus plants	Euphorbium Galbanum

TABLE 6—NATURAL, MAGICAL, MYTHICAL CORRESPONDENCES

Arabic Number	Roman Numeral	Gemstone/ metal	Mythic figures	Magical weapon	Musical note	Color correspondences for musical note
15	XV	Ruby, onyx, chrysoprase, turquoise, black diamond	Lucifer, Seth, Beelzebub, Agni, Pan, Dionysus, Khem, Priapus, Bacchus	The Secret Force, the Lamp	A	Blue Violet
16	XVI	Iron, garnet, diamond, ruby, lodestone, bloodstone, jasper	Horus, Krishna, Odin, war gods, Shiva, Zeus, Thor, Mars, Ares	The Sword	C	Red
17	XVII	Chalcedony, amethyst, garnet, jasper, crystal, quartz, turquoise	Juno, Athena as artisan, Ganymede, Ahepi, aroueris, Ishtar, Astarte, Isis	The Censer or Aspergillus	A#	Violet

TABLE 6—NATURAL, MAGICAL, MYTHICAL CORRESPONDENCES

Arabic Number	Roman numeral	Conventional card title	Zodiacal glyph	Animal	Plant	Perfume/ Incense
18	XVIII	The Moon	♓	Crab, dog, jackal, crayfish, horse, rabbit, fish, dolphin	Hazel, fig, willow, heartwort	Red storax Ambergris
19	XIX	The Sun	☉	Deer, lion, crocodile, horse, snake, dolphin, swan, ox/bull, rooster, peacock,sparrowhawk, salamanders, hummingbird	Sunflower, cypress, angelica, bay laurel, carnation, chamomile, chrysanthemum, date, eucalyptus, juniper, ginseng, hazel, heliotrope, juniper, lemon, lime, marigold, oak, olive, peony, oranges, pineapple, sesame, sugarcane, tea, walnut, witchhazel, all yellow flowers	Frankincense, mastic, benzoin, storax, labdanum, ambergris, musk, pepper, sandalwood,` cinnamon, amber, saffron, cloves, and "all brilliant odors"
20	XX	Judgement	△		Red poppy, hibiscus, nettles, pepper, garlic, mustard, warm spices, marigold, sunflower	Frankincense, citruses, cedar, warming spices, "all fiery odors"

TABLE 6—NATURAL, MAGICAL, MYTHICAL CORRESPONDENCES

Arabic Number	Roman Numeral	Gemstone/ metal	Mythic figures	Magical weapon	Musical note	Color correspondences for musical note
18	XVIII	Amethyst, ruby, pearl, coral, moonstone	Anubis, Hecate, Vishnu as fish, Neptune, Poseidon, Khephra, Christ, Oannes	The Twilight of the Place, the Magic Mirror	B	Red violet
19	XIX	Gold, diamond, tiger's eye, chrysolite, sunstone, rubies	Apollo, Helios, Hyperion, Ra, Krishna, Legba, Vishnu	The Lamen, The Bow & Arrow	D	Orange
20	XX	Fire opal, malachite, gold, iron, brass, all nitrates	Agni, Hades, Vulcan, Pluto, Harpocrates, Horus	The Wand or Lamp, the Pyramid of Fire, the Thurible	C	Red

TABLE 6—NATURAL, MAGICAL, MYTHICAL CORRESPONDENCES

Arabic Number	Roman numeral	Conventional card title	Zodiacal glyph	Animal	Plant	Perfume/ Incense
21	XXI	The World	♄	Basilisk, toad, snake, flies, carrion birds, all black creatures, all nocturnal creatures, all creatures living in holes.	Aconite, cypress, yew, beet, beech, belladonna, comfrey, fern, hemlock, ivy, lobelia, morning glory, mosses, oleander, patchouli, poplar, tamarind, wolfsbane, rye, nightshade, rue	Pepperwort, all odoriferous roots, asafoetida, sulfur, civet, musk, "all dark or unpleasant odors," narcotic drugs

TABLE 6—NATURAL, MAGICAL, MYTHICAL CORRESPONDENCES

Arabic Number	Roman Numeral	Gemstone/metal	Mythic figures	Magical weapon	Musical note	Color correspondences for musical note
21	XXI	Lead, onyx, jet, marble, hematite, lapis lazuli, black opal, golden marcasite	Brahma, Pan, Gaea, Vidar, Saturn. Sebek, Tamogunam	The Sickle	A	Blue Violet

Notes on Natural, Magical, and Mythical Correspondences for the Major Arcana

Natural correspondences have strong ties to astrological correspondences: planet, sign, and element. So a card like the The Emperor, which is associated with Ares (fiery sign ruled by Mars) will share many correspondences with Tower, which is associated with Mars, and Judgement, which is associated with fire. Although any such table is bound to be incomplete unless it includes every species in the natural world, I've tried to include enough correspondences that you can get a sense of the rationale behind the correspondences—for example, Martial flora and fauna will tend to be prickly, fiery, aggressive, or sharp-tasting.

Source texts for natural and magico-mythical correspondences are legion, but here are some that I've used for this chart, and which you may find good starting points for your own explorations:

Liber 777, by Aleister Crowley

Llewellyn's Complete Book of Correspondences, by Sandra Kynes

The Complete Magician's Tables, by Stephen Skinner

The Rulership Book, by Rex E. Bills

Cunningham's Encyclopedia of Magical Herbs, by Scott Cunningham

The Magician's Companion, by Bill Whitcomb,

Ritual and Magical Uses of Perfumes, by Richard and Iona Miller

For musical note correspondences:

Qabalistic Tarot, by Robert Wang

The Western Mysteries, by David Allen Hulse

The seven planetary musical note and color correspondences can be done in two ways: according to the planet's *path* on the Tree of Life (so, Mercury is associated with the path of the Magician, from Kether to Binah, whose Atziluthic color is yellow and whose note is E) or according to the planet's *sephira* on the Tree of Life (so, Mercury is associated with the sephira Hod, whose Briatic color is orange and whose note is D). The Atziluthic path colors are given in this table.

The Briah/sephiroth alternates (some of which happen to be the same as the Atziluthic paths) are:

Saturn = Binah = A =Blue Violet

Jupiter = Chesed = G# = Blue

Mars = Geburah = C = Red

Sun = Tiphereth = E = Yellow

Venus = Netzach = F# = Green

Mercury = Hod = D = Orange

Moon = Yesod = A# = Violet

TABLE 7—NUMEROLOGICAL REDUCTION

0	The Fool				
01	The Magician	10	The Wheel of Fortune	19	The Sun
02	The High Priestess	11/08	Justice	20	Judgement
03	The Empress	12	The Hanged Man	21	The World
04	The Emperor	13	Death		
05	The Hierophant	14	Temperance		
06	The Lovers	15	The Devil		
07	The Chariot	16	The Tower		
08/11	Strength	17	The Star		
09	The Hermit	18	The Moon		

Notes on Numerological Correspondences for the Major Arcana

Many readers use numerological reduction in the calculation of their "birth cards" and "year cards." For example, if your birthday's April 1, 1980, you'd add 4+1+1+9+8+0 for a total of 23, which reduces to 5, so your birth card would be the Hierophant. You'd substitute the current year to find your year card.

You can learn more about this technique in Mary Greer's *Tarot for Your Self* (New Page, 1984).

CORRESPONDENCES
FOR THE 4 SUITS

TABLE 1—NOMENCLATURE AND PHYSICAL CORRESPONDENCES

	Wands	Cups	Swords	Pentacles
Alternate English names	Batons, Rods, Staves, Scepters	Chalices	Daggers, Athames	Coins, Disks
Playing card equivalent	Clubs	Hearts	Spades	Diamonds
Names in French, Spanish, Italian, German	Bâtons/Sceptres, Bastos/Cetros, Bastoni/Scettri, Staben/Zepter	Coupes, Copas, Coppe, Kelche	Épées, Espadas, Spade, Schwerter	Deniers, Oros, Denari/Dischi, Scheiben/Münzen
Traditional Professions	Peasants/agricultural workers	Clerics	Knights/aristocracy	Merchants
Elemental glyph	△	▽	△	▽
Elements	Fire	Water	Air	Earth
Quality from Aristotle's *Metaphysics* (4th c. BCE)	Dry/Hot	Wet/Cold	Hot/Wet	Cold/Dry
Bodily fluid From Hippocrates (5th c. BCE)	Yellow bile	Phlegm	Blood	Black bile
Modern physiology	Body temperature, nervous system, immune system	Bodily fluids	Lungs and breath	Solid parts: flesh, muscle, bones, organs
Temperament from Galen	Choleric (active, enthusiastic)	Phlegmatic (brooding)	Sanguine (irritable, volatile)	Melancholic (sluggish)
Sense	Sight	Taste	Smell	Touch

TABLE 2—ASTROLOGICAL, SPATIOTEMPORAL, AND MYTHICAL CORRESPONDENCES

	Wands	Cups	Swords	Pentacles
Elemental glyph	△	▽	△	▽
Elements	Fire	Water	Air	Earth
Astrological glyphs	♈♌♐	♋♏♓	♎♒♊	♑♉♍
Zodiacal signs	Aries, Leo, Sagittarius	Cancer, Scorpio, Pisces	Libra, Aquarius, Gemini	Capricorn, Taurus, Virgo
Northern Hemisphere Cardinal Directions	South	West	East	North
Times of Day	Noon	Sunset	Dawn	Midnight
Season	Summer	Fall	Spring	Winter
Celebration	Litha	Mabon	Ostara	Yule
Southern Hemisphere Standard flip (north-south only)	North	West	East	South
Tetragrammaton letter	י	ה	ו	ה
Kabbalistic World	Atziluth	Briah	Yetzirah	Assiah
Faculty of the Soul from Plato	Imagination	Opinion	Intelligence	Demonstration
Powers of the Sphinx	To Will	To Dare	To Know	To Keep silent
Powers of the Sphinx Latin	Velle	Audere	Scire	Tacere
Deity From Empedocles	Zeus	Nestis [prob. Persephone]	Hera	Aidoneus [Hades]
Elemental beings	Salamanders	Undines	Sylphs	Gnomes
Archangels	Michael	Gabriel	Raphael	Auriel
Egyptian deities	Horus, Sekhet	Nut, Isis, Hathor, Ptah	Shu, Tefnut	Geb, Nephthys

TABLE 2—ASTROLOGICAL, SPATIOTEMPORAL, AND MYTHICAL CORRESPONDENCES

	Wands	Cups	Swords	Pentacles
Greek deities	Hestia, Prometheus, Ares	Poseidon, Tethys, Amphitrite	Zeus, Hermes, Aeolus	Demeter, Kore, Gaia
Roman deities	Vulcan, Pluto	Neptune	Jupiter, Aeolus, Mercury	Ceres, Faunus, Proserpina
Hindu deities	Agni	Soma	Marut	Prisni
Evangelists	Mark	John	Matthew	Luke
Kerubic Beast	Lion	Eagle	Man	Ox

TABLE 3—NATURAL CORRESPONDENCES

	Wands	Cups	Swords	Pentacles
Elemental glyph	△	▽	△	▽
Elements	Fire	Water	Air	Earth
Plants and Herbs	Nettles, garlic, ginger, pepper, rue, tobacco, wormwood, asa-foetida, cinnamon, mustard, onion, sunflower, orange, marigold, chrysan-themum, rosemary, cumin, all seeds	Cabbage, cardamom, coconut, gardenia, iris, jasmine, lotus, willow, grape, comfrey, all leaves	Almond, anise, caraway, hazel, lavender, marjoram, papyrus, pine, rice, sage, laurel, linden, pine, ivy, fern, bamboo, all flowers	Cotton, cypress, fern, patchouli, pea, turnip, vervain, mandrake, elder, oak, pomegranate, maple, clove, all roots
Animals	Horse, lion, tiger, ram, eagle, falcon, firefly, scorpion, phoenix	Moose, beaver, fish, snake, otter, hare, crane, dove, duck, swan, frog, crocodile, dolphin	Gazelle, eagle, falcon, hawk, all birds, insects	Bear, cattle, el-ephant, armadillo, tortoise, crow, goat, hippo, mole, pig, worms, rodents
Gemstones & metals	Gold, iron, brass, steel diamond, ruby, pyrite, fire opal, bloodstone, sardonyx, red coral, carnelian, garnet, sunstone, flint, asbestos	Silver, copper, amethyst, aquama-rine, labradorite, lapis lazuli, moon-stone, rose quartz, sapphire, blue topaz, turquoise, pearl, coral, crystal, beryl, all transparent stones	Mercury, aluminum, tin Agate, blue lace agate, moldovite, pumice, clear quartz	Lead, amber, cat's eye, emerald, hematite, jade, malachite, peridot, black tourmaline, jet, all dark stones
Perfume	Frankincense, citruses, hot spices, cedar	Myrrh, florals, ambers and sweet resins (rose, jasmine, ylang ylang), vanilla, gardenia, orris root	Galbanum, pines, greens, aldehydes	Storax, vetiver, woods (sandal-wood, agarwood/ oud, patchouli) and animalics civet, musk, castoreum)

Notes on Suit Correspondences

For our purposes, suit correspondences are tied to and dependent on the four elements: fire, water, air, and earth. The rest of the fourfold correspondences—mythical, natural, astrological, kabbalistic and so forth—stem from these original elemental correspondences. (The suit of Swords is associated with birds and insects *because* it is associated with the element of air, not because birds and swords were independently connected in tarot.) For that reason, I've repeated the elemental correspondences in each of these three tables.

There are other ways of assigning the elemental correspondences to the four suits. In the most common variation, Wands are associated with Air and Swords with Fire. If you prefer that attribution, then switch columns 1 and 3 throughout all three tables. (In all systems, Cups are associated with Water.)

You'll notice that throughout this book, the elements are always presented in the same sequence: (1) Fire, (2) Water, (3) Air, and (4) Earth. This is the sequence used across the board in Golden Dawn-based magical traditions, and relates to the descent of creation on the Tree of Life through the Four Worlds—from the most supernal and fiery to the most crystallized and earthen.

You'll also notice that throughout this book I refer to Pentacles rather than Disks or Coins, though the latter terms are widespread and maybe even more common than "pentacles" worldwide. This is in deference to the fact that the majority of modern, English-speaking tarot readers have some familiarity with the Rider Waite Smith deck, where pentacles were first established as a suit emblem in accordance with the work of the nineteenth-century occultist Eliphas Lévi.

Further references:

Llewellyn's Complete Book of Correspondences, by Sandra Kynes (Llewellyn, 2016)
The Way of Four: Create Elemental Balance in Your Life, by Deborah Lipp (Llewellyn, 2004)

CORRESPONDENCES FOR THE 40 NUMERIC MINOR ARCANA (ACE–10)

TABLE 1—NOMENCLATURE, ASTROLOGY, AND DECANS

Suit	Hermetic title (Thoth/*Golden Dawn)*	Planet ruling decan*	Zodiac	Planetary glyph	Zodiacal glyph
2 of Wands	Dominion	Mars	0°–9° Aries	♂	♈
3 of Wands	Virtue/ *Established Strength*	Sun	10°–19° Aries	☉	♈
4 of Wands	Completion/ *Perfected Work*	Venus	20°–29° Aries	♀	♈

TABLE 1—NOMENCLATURE, ASTROLOGY, AND DECANS

Suit	Dates	Decan image from the Picatrix	Decan signification from the Picatrix	Decan image from Agrippa's 3 Books of Occult Philosophy	Decan signification from Agrippa
2 of Wands	Mar. 21–Mar. 30	A black man, with a large and restless body, having red eyes and with an axe in his hand, girded in white cloth.	Strength, high rank, wealth without shame	A black man, standing and cloathed in a white garment, girdled about, of a great body, with reddish eyes, and great strength, and like one that is angry.	Boldness, fortitude, loftiness and shamelesness
3 of Wands	Mar. 31–Apr. 10	A woman dressed in green clothes, lacking one leg.	High rank, nobility, wealth, rulership	A woman, outwardly clothed with a red garment, and under it a white, spreading abroad over her feet.	Nobleness, height of a kingdom, and greatness of dominion
4 of Wands	Apr. 11–Apr. 20	A restless man, holding in his hands a gold bracelet, wearing red clothing, who wishes to do good, but is not able to do it.	Subtlety, subtle mastery, new things, instruments	A white man, pale, with reddish hair, and clothed with a red garment, who carrying on the one hand a golden bracelet, and holding forth a wooden staff, is restless, and like one in wrath, because he cannot perform that good he would.	Wit, meekness, joy, and beauty

TABLE 1—NOMENCLATURE, ASTROLOGY, AND DECANS

Suit	Hermetic title (Thoth/*Golden Dawn)*	Planet ruling decan*	Zodiac	Planetary glyph	Zodiacal glyph
5 of Disks	Worry/*Material Trouble*	Mercury	0°–9° Taurus	☿	♉
6 of Disks	Success/*Material Success*	Moon	10°–19° Taurus	☽	♉
7 of Disks	Failure/*Success Unfulfilled*	Saturn	20°–29° Taurus	♄	♉

TABLE 1—NOMENCLATURE, ASTROLOGY, AND DECANS

Suit	Dates	Decan image from the Picatrix	Decan signification from the Picatrix	Decan image from Agrippa's 3 Books of Occult Philosophy	Decan signification from Agrippa
5 of Disks	Apr. 21–Apr. 30	A woman with curly hair, who has one son wearing clothing looking like flame, and she is wearing garments of the same sort.	Plowing, working on the land, sciences, geometry, sowing, building	A naked man, an Archer, Harvester or Husbandman.	To sow, plough, build, people, and divide the earth, according to the rules of Geometry
6 of Disks	May 1–May 10	A man with a body like a camel, who has cow's hooves on his fingers, and he is covered by a linen cloth. He desires to work the land, sow, and build.	Nobility, power, rewarding the people.	A naked man, holding in his hand a key.	Power, nobility, and dominion over people
7 of Disks	May 11–May 20	A man of reddish complexion with large white teeth exposed outside of his mouth, and a boy like an elephant with long legs, and with him one horse, one dog and one calf.	Sloth, poverty, misery, dread	A man in whose hand is a Serpent, and a dart.	Necessity and profit, and also misery & slavery

TABLE 1—NOMENCLATURE, ASTROLOGY, AND DECANS

Suit	Hermetic title (Thoth/*Golden Dawn*)	Planet ruling decan*	Zodiac	Planetary glyph	Zodiacal glyph
8 of Swords	Interference/ *Shortened Force*	Jupiter	0°–9° Gemini	♃	♊
9 of Swords	Cruelty/*Despair and Cruelty*	Mars	10°–19° Gemini	♂	♊
10 of Swords	Ruin	Sun	20°–29° Gemini	☉	♊

TABLE 1—NOMENCLATURE, ASTROLOGY, AND DECANS

Suit	Dates	Decan image from the Picatrix	Decan signification from the Picatrix	Decan image from Agrippa's 3 Books of Occult Philosophy	Decan signification from Agrippa
8 of Swords	May 21–May 30	A beautiful woman, a mistress of stitching, two calves and two horses.	Writing, computation and number, giving and taking, the sciences	A man in whose hand is a rod, and he is, as it were, serving another.	Wisdom, and the knowledge of numbers and arts in which there is no profit
9 of Swords	Jun. 1–Jun. 10	A man whose face is like an eagle and his head is covered by linen cloth; clothed and protected by a coat of leaden mail, and on his head is an iron helmet above which is a silk crown, and in his hand he has a bow and arrows.	Oppression, evils, and subtlety	A man in whose hand is a pipe, and another being bowed down, digging the earth	Infamous and dishonest agility, as that of jesters and jugglers; it also signifies labors and painful searching.
10 of Swords	Jun. 11–Jun. 20	A man clothed in mail, with a bow, arrows, and quiver.	Audacity, honesty, division of labor, and consolation	A man seeking for arms, and a fool holding in the right hand a bird, and in his left a pipe.	Forgetfulness, wrath, boldness, jests, scurrilities, and unprofitable words

TABLE 1—NOMENCLATURE, ASTROLOGY, AND DECANS

Suit	Hermetic title (Thoth/*Golden Dawn)*	Planet ruling decan*	Zodiac	Planetary glyph	Zodiacal glyph
2 of Cups	Love	Venus	0°–9° Cancer	♀	♋
3 of Cups	Abundance	Mercury	10°–19° Cancer	☿	♋
4 of Cups	Luxury/*Blended Pleasure*	Moon	20°–29° Cancer	☽	♋

TABLE 1—NOMENCLATURE, ASTROLOGY, AND DECANS

Suit	Dates	Decan image from the Picatrix	Decan signification from the Picatrix	Decan image from Agrippa's 3 Books of Occult Philosophy	Decan signification from Agrippa
2 of Cups	Jun. 21–Jul. 1	A man whose fingers and head are distorted and slanted, and his body is similar to a horse's body; his feet are white, and he has fig leaves on his body.	Instruction, knowledge, love, subtlety and mastery	A young virgin, adorned with fine clothes, and having a crown on her head.	Acuteness of senses, subtlety of wit, and the love of men
3 of Cups	Jul. 2–Jul. 12	A woman with a beautiful face, and on her head she has a crown of green myrtle, and in her hand is a stem of the water lily, and she is singing songs of love and joy.	Games, wealth, joy, and abundance	A man clothed in comely apparel, or a man and woman sitting at the table and playing.	Riches, mirth, gladness, and the love of women
4 of Cups	Jul. 13–Jul. 20	A celhafe* with a snake in his hand, who has golden chains before him. *probably a turtle	Running, riding, and acquisition by means of war, lawsuits, and conflict	A man, a hunter with his lance and horn, bringing out dogs for to hunt.	The contention of men, the pursuing of those who fly, the hunting and possessing of things by arms and brawlings.

TABLE 1—NOMENCLATURE, ASTROLOGY, AND DECANS

Suit	Hermetic title (Thoth/*Golden Dawn)*	Planet ruling decan*	Zodiac	Planetary glyph	Zodiacal glyph
5 of Wands	Strife	Saturn	0°–9° Leo	♄	♌
6 of Wands	Victory	Jupiter	10°–19° Leo	♃	♌
7 of Wands	Valor	Mars	20°–29° Leo	♂	♌

TABLE 1—NOMENCLATURE, ASTROLOGY, AND DECANS

Suit	Dates	Decan image from the Picatrix	Decan signification from the Picatrix	Decan image from Agrippa's 3 Books of Occult Philosophy	Decan signification from Agrippa
5 of Wands	Jul. 21– Aug. 1	A man wearing dirty clothes, and … the image of a rider looking to the north, and his body looks like the body of a bear and the body of a dog.	Strength, generosity, and victory	A man riding on a Lion.	Boldness, violence, cruelty, wickedness, lust and labors to be sustained
6 of Wands	Aug. 2– Aug. 10	A man who wears a crown of white myrtle on his head, and he has a bow in his hand … the ascension of a man who is ignorant and base.	Beauty, riding, the ascension of a man who is ignorant and base, war and naked swords	An image with hands lifted up, and a man on whose head is a crown; he hath the appearance of an angry man, and one that threateneth, having in his right hand a sword drawn out of the scabbard, and in his left a buckler.	Hidden contentions, and unknown victories, & upon base men, and upon the occasions of quarrels and battles
7 of Wands	Aug. 11– Aug. 22	A man who is old and black and ugly, with fruit and meat in his mouth and holding a copper jug in his hand.	Love and delight and food trays and health	A young man in whose hand is a whip, and a man very sad, and of an ill aspect.	Love and society, and the loss of one's right for avoiding strife

TABLE 1—NOMENCLATURE, ASTROLOGY, AND DECANS

Suit	Hermetic title (Thoth/*Golden Dawn*)	Planet ruling decan*	Zodiac	Planetary glyph	Zodiacal glyph
8 of Disks	Prudence	Sun	0°–9° Virgo	☉	♍
9 of Disks	Gain/*Material Gain*	Venus	10°–19° Virgo	♀	♍
10 of Disks	Wealth	Mercury	20°–29° Virgo	☿	♍

TABLE 1—NOMENCLATURE, ASTROLOGY, AND DECANS

Suit	Dates	Decan image from the Picatrix	Decan signification from the Picatrix	Decan image from Agrippa's 3 Books of Occult Philosophy	Decan signification from Agrippa
8 of Disks	Aug. 23–Sep. 1	A young girl covered with an old woolen cloth, and in her hand is a pomegranate.	Sowing, plowing, the germination of plants, gathering grapes, good living	The figure of a good maid, and a man casting seeds.	Getting of wealth, ordering of diet, plowing, sowing, and peopling
9 of Disks	Sep. 2–Sep. 11	A man of beautiful color, dressed in leather, and over his garment of leather is another garment of iron.	Petitions, requests, and again, tribute and denying justice	A black man clothed with a skin, and a man having a bush of hair, holding a bag.	Gain, scraping together of wealth and covetousness
10 of Disks	Sep. 12–Sep. 22	A white man, with a great body, wrapped in white linen, and with him is a woman holding in her hand black oil.	Debility, age, infirmity, sloth, injury to limbs and the destruction of people	A white woman and deaf, or an old man leaning on a staff.	Weakness, infirmity, loss of members, destruction of trees, and depopulation of lands

TABLE 1—NOMENCLATURE,
ASTROLOGY, AND DECANS

Suit	Hermetic title (Thoth/*Golden Dawn*)	Planet ruling decan*	Zodiac	Planetary glyph	Zodiacal glyph
2 of Swords	Peace/*Peace Restored*	Moon	0°–9° Libra	☽	♎
3 of Swords	Sorrow	Saturn	10°–19° Libra	♄	♎
4 of Swords	Truce/*Rest from Strife*	Jupiter	20°–29° Libra	♃	♎

TABLE 1—NOMENCLATURE, ASTROLOGY, AND DECANS

Suit	Dates	Decan image from the Picatrix	Decan signification from the Picatrix	Decan image from Agrippa's 3 Books of Occult Philosophy	Decan signification from Agrippa
2 of Swords	Sep. 23–Oct. 2	A man with a lance in his right hand, and in his left hand he holds a bird hanging by its feet.	Justice, truth, good judgment, complete justice for the people and weak persons, and doing good for beggars	An angry man, in whose hand is a pipe, and the form of a man reading in a book.	Justifying and helping the miserable and weak against the powerful and wicked
3 of Swords	Oct. 3–Oct. 12	A black man, a bridegroom having a joyous journey.	Tranquility, joy, abundance and good living	Two men furious and wrathful and a man in a comely garment, sitting in a chair.	Indignation against the evil, and quietness and security of life with plenty of good things
4 of Swords	Oct. 13–Oct. 22	A man riding a donkey with a wolf in front of him.	Evil works, sodomy, adultery, singing, joy and flavors	A violent man holding a bow, and before him a naked man, and also another man holding bread in one hand, and a cup of wine in the other.	Wicked lusts, singings, sports and gluttony

TABLE 1—NOMENCLATURE, ASTROLOGY, AND DECANS

Suit	Hermetic title (Thoth/*Golden Dawn*)	Planet ruling decan*	Zodiac	Planetary glyph	Zodiacal glyph
5 of Cups	Disappointment/ *Loss in Pleasure*	Mars	0°–9° Scorpio	♂	♏
6 of Cups	Pleasure	Sun	10°–19° Scorpio	☉	♏
7 of Cups	Debauch/ *Illusionary Success*	Venus	20°–29° Scorpio	♀	♏

TABLE 1—NOMENCLATURE, ASTROLOGY, AND DECANS

Suit	Dates	Decan image from the Picatrix	Decan signification from the Picatrix	Decan image from Agrippa's 3 Books of Occult Philosophy	Decan signification from Agrippa
5 of Cups	Oct. 23–Nov. 1	A man with a lance in his right hand and in his left hand he holds the head of a man.	Settlement, sadness, ill will and hatred	A woman of good face and habit, and two men striking her.	Comeliness, beauty, and strifes, treacheries, deceits, detractations, and perditions
6 of Cups	Nov. 2–Nov. 11	A man riding a camel, holding a scorpion in his hand.	Knowledge, modesty, settlement, and of speaking evil of one another	A man naked, and a woman naked, and a man sitting on the earth, and before him two dogs biting one another.	Impudence, deceit, and false dealing, and for to lend mischief and strife amongst men
7 of Cups	Nov. 12–Nov. 22	A horse and a rabbit.	Evil works and flavors, and forcing sex upon unwilling women	A man bowed downward upon his knees, and a woman striking him with a staff.	Drunkenness, fornication, wrath, violence, and strife

TABLE 1—NOMENCLATURE, ASTROLOGY, AND DECANS

Suit	Hermetic title (Thoth/*Golden Dawn*)	Planet ruling decan*	Zodiac	Planetary glyph	Zodiacal glyph
8 of Wands	Swiftness	Mercury	0°–9° Sagittarius	☿	♐
9 of Wands	Strength/*Great Strength*	Moon	10°–19° Sagittarius	☽	♐
10 of Wands	Oppression	Saturn	20°–29° Sagittarius	♄	♐

TABLE 1—NOMENCLATURE, ASTROLOGY, AND DECANS

Suit	Dates	Decan image from the Picatrix	Decan signification from the Picatrix	Decan image from Agrippa's 3 Books of Occult Philosophy	Decan signification from Agrippa
8 of Wands	Nov. 23–Dec. 2	The bodies of three men and one body is yellow, another white and the third is red.	Heat, heaviness, growth in plains and fields, sustenance and division	A man armed with a coat of mail, and holding a naked sword in his hand.	Boldness, malice, and liberty
9 of Wands	Dec. 3–Dec. 12	A man leading cows and in front of him he has an ape and a bear.	Fear, lamentations, grief, sadness, misery and troubles	A woman weeping, and covered with clothes.	Sadness and fear of his own body
10 of Wands	Dec. 13–Dec. 22	A man with a cap on his head, who is murdering another man.	Evil desires, adverse and evil effects, and fickleness in these and evil wishes, hatred, dispersion, and evil conduct	A man like in colour to gold, or an idle man playing with a staff.	Following our own wills, and obstinacy in them, and activeness for evil things, contentions, and horrible matters

TABLE 1—NOMENCLATURE, ASTROLOGY, AND DECANS

Suit	Hermetic title (Thoth/*Golden Dawn)*	Planet ruling decan*	Zodiac	Planetary glyph	Zodiacal glyph
2 of Disks	Change/ *Harmonious Change*	Jupiter	0°–9° Capricorn	♃	♑
3 of Disks	Work/*Material Works*	Mars	10°–19° Capricorn	♂	♑
4 of Disks	Power/*Earthly Power*	Sun	20°–29° Capricorn	☉	♑

TABLE 1—NOMENCLATURE, ASTROLOGY, AND DECANS

Suit	Dates	Decan image from the Picatrix	Decan signification from the Picatrix	Decan image from Agrippa's 3 Books of Occult Philosophy	Decan signification from Agrippa
2 of Disks	Dec. 21–Dec. 30	A man with a reed in his right hand and a hoopoe bird in his left.	Happiness, joy, and bringing things to an end that are sluggish, weak, and proceeding poorly	A woman, and a man carrying full bags.	To go forth and to rejoice, to gain and to lose with weakness and baseness
3 of Disks	Dec. 31–Jan. 9	A man with a common ape in front of him.	Seeking to do what cannot be done and to attain what cannot be	Two women, and a man looking towards a bird flying in the air.	Requiring those things which cannot be done, searching after those things which cannot be known
4 of Disks	Jan. 10–Jan. 19	A man holding a book which he opens and closes, and before him is the tail of a fish.	Wealth and the accumulation of money and increase and embarking on trade and pressing on to a good end	A woman chaste in body, and wise in her work, and a banker gathering his money together on the table.	To govern in prudence, in covetousness of money, and in avarice

TABLE 1—NOMENCLATURE, ASTROLOGY, AND DECANS

Suit	Hermetic title (Thoth/*Golden Dawn)*	Planet ruling decan*	Zodiac	Planetary glyph	Zodiacal glyph
5 of Swords	Defeat	Venus	0°–9° Aquarius	♀	♒
6 of Swords	Science, *Earned Success*	Mercury	10°–19° Aquarius	☿	♒
7 of Swords	Futility/*Unstable Effort*	Moon	20°–29° Aquarius	☽	♒

TABLE 1—NOMENCLATURE, ASTROLOGY, AND DECANS

Suit	Dates	Decan image from the Picatrix	Decan signification from the Picatrix	Decan image from Agrippa's 3 Books of Occult Philosophy	Decan signification from Agrippa
5 of Swords	Jan. 20–Jan. 29	A man whose head is mutilated and he holds a peacock in his hand.	Misery, poverty, and slavery	A prudent man, and of a woman spinning.	The thought and labor for gain, in poverty and baseness
6 of Swords	Jan. 30–Feb. 8	A man who looks like a king, who permits much to himself and abhors what he sees.	Beauty and position, having what is desired, completion, detriment and debility	A man with a long beard.	Understanding, meekness, modesty, liberty and good manners
7 of Swords	Feb. 9–Feb. 18	A man having a mutilated head, and an old woman is with him.	Abundance, accomplishing of will, giving offense	A black and angry man.	Insolence and impudence

TABLE 1—NOMENCLATURE, ASTROLOGY, AND DECANS

Suit	Hermetic title (Thoth/*Golden Dawn*)	Planet ruling decan*	Zodiac	Planetary glyph	Zodiacal glyph
8 of Cups	Indolence/*Abandoned Success*	Saturn	0°–9° Pisces	♄	♓
9 of Cups	Happiness/*Material Happiness*	Jupiter	10°–19° Pisces	♃	♓
10 of Cups	Satiety/*Perpetual Success*	Mars	20°–29° Pisces	♂	♓

TABLE 1—NOMENCLATURE, ASTROLOGY, AND DECANS

Suit	Dates	Decan image from the Picatrix	Decan signification from the Picatrix	Decan image from Agrippa's 3 Books of Occult Philosophy	Decan signification from Agrippa
8 of Cups	Feb. 19–Feb. 28	A man with two bodies, who looks as though he is giving a gesture of greeting with his hands.	Peace and humility, debility, many journeys, misery, seeking wealth, miserable life	A man carrying burdens on his shoulder, and well clothed.	Journeys, change of place, and in carefulness of getting wealth and clothes
9 of Cups	Mar. 1–Mar. 10	A man upside down with his head below and his feet raised up, and in his hand is a tray from which the food has been eaten.	Great reward, and strong will in things that are high, serious and thoughtful	A woman of a good countenance, and well adorned.	To desire and put oneself on about high and great matters
10 of Cups	Mar. 11–Mar. 20	A sad man full of evil thoughts, thinking of deception and treachery, and before him is a woman with a donkey climbing atop her, and in her hand is a bird.	Advancement and lying with women with a great appetite, and of quiet and seeking rest	A man naked, or a youth, and nigh him a beautiful maid, whose head is adorned with flowers.	Rest, idleness, delight, fornication, and embracings of women

Notes on Nomenclature, Astrology, and Decan Correspondences for the Numeric Minor Arcana

Regarding the Hermetic titles: The form of these titles is actually "Lord of …"—e.g., the 8 of Wands is the "Lord of Swiftness." In a number of cases, I've listed two titles. The second, in italics, is the Golden Dawn's original formulation. The first is the streamlined form used by Aleister Crowley for the Thoth deck; all Thoth-based decks follow Crowley's naming conventions, so these titles tend to be more widely in circulation.

Regarding the decans: As you may know, each zodiac sign occupies 30° of the zodiac. Decans are ten-degree segments of the zodiac; therefore, there are three decans per sign. In the minor arcana, each sign is represented by three cards, one for each decan. And when you see a "planet in sign" designation on minor arcana in the Golden Dawn tradition, that refers to which planet rules, or governs, the decan associated with that card. So, for example, "Mars in Aries" on the 2 of Wands means that the planet Mars rules the first decan, (ten degrees) of Aries. For further insights into interpretation, you can look at the associated majors, The Tower [Mars] and The Emperor [Aries] (as seen in the following table). In traditional astrology, the 36 decans or "faces" and the spirits they housed were thought to hold great influence over earthly affairs. The Golden Dawn did not explicitly associate its imagery for the numeric minor arcana with any of the traditional images associated with the decans. But when you compare the images and meanings provided in ancient astrological texts with the images and meanings presented on the cards, some very compelling parallels arise. Austin Coppock's *36 Faces* offers a thorough comparison of tarot and decanic imagery.

If you'd like many, many more *astronomical* correspondences such as which stars and constellations correspond to which cards, they can be found in the Golden Dawn's *Book T*.

Regarding the decan images: *The Picatrix* is an eleventh-century Arabic text on magic and astrology that was later translated into Latin. The text used here is drawn from John Michael Greer's and Christopher Warnock's translation from the Latin (*The Picatrix: Liber Atratus* edition, 2010–2011, Adocentyn Press) and is used with permission. You can learn more about the Picatrix and classical astrology at Chris Warnock's highly educational website, www.renaissanceastrology.com. Many other astrological texts present images of the decans as well, from Agrippa's *Three Books of Occult Philosophy* to the Sanskrit *Yavanajataka* and *Liber Hermetis*. Each set of 36 images differs in small or large ways from the next. It's worth remembering that these images are products of their time; sometimes the views reflected in them should be taken with a grain of salt.

TABLE 2—ASSOCIATED MAJOR ARCANA BY PLANET AND SIGN

Card	Planetary glyph	Planet	Associated Planetary Major	Zodiacal glyph	Sign	Associated Zodiacal Major
2 of Wands	♂	Mars	The Tower	♈	Aries	The Emperor
3 of Wands	☉	Sun	The Sun	♈	Aries	The Emperor
4 of Wands	♀	Venus	The Empress	♈	Aries	The Emperor
5 of Pentacles	☿	Mercury	The Magician	♉	Taurus	The Hierophant
6 of Pentacles	☽	Moon	The High Priestess	♉	Taurus	The Hierophant
7 of Pentacles	♄	Saturn	The World	♉	Taurus	The Hierophant
8 of Swords	♃	Jupiter	The Wheel of Fortune	♊	Gemini	The Lovers
9 of Swords	♂	Mars	The Tower	♊	Gemini	The Lovers
10 of Swords	☉	Sun	The Sun	♊	Gemini	The Lovers
2 of Cups	♀	Venus	The Empress	♋	Cancer	The Chariot
3 of Cups	☿	Mercury	The Magician	♋	Cancer	The Chariot
4 of Cups	☽	Moon	The High Priestess	♋	Cancer	The Chariot
5 of Wands	♄	Saturn	The World	♌	Leo	Strength
6 of Wands	♃	Jupiter	The Wheel of Fortune	♌	Leo	Strength
7 of Wands	♂	Mars	The Tower	♌	Leo	Strength
8 of Pentacles	☉	Sun	The Sun	♍	Virgo	The Hermit
9 of Pentacles	♀	Venus	The Empress	♍	Virgo	The Hermit
10 of Pentacles	☿	Mercury	The Magician	♍	Virgo	The Hermit

TABLE 2—ASSOCIATED MAJOR ARCANA BY PLANET AND SIGN

Card	Planetary glyph	Planet	Associated Planetary Major	Zodiacal glyph	Sign	Associated Zodiacal Major
2 of Swords	☽	Moon	The High Priestess	♎	Libra	Justice
3 of Swords	♄	Saturn	The World	♎	Libra	Justice
4 of Swords	♃	Jupiter	The Wheel of Fortune	♎	Libra	Justice
5 of Cups	♂	Mars	The Tower	♏	Scorpio	Death
6 of Cups	☉	Sun	The Sun	♏	Scorpio	Death
7 of Cups	♀	Venus	The Empress	♏	Scorpio	Death
8 of Wands	☿	Mercury	The Magician	♐	Sagittarius	Temperance
9 of Wands	☽	Moon	The High Priestess	♐	Sagittarius	Temperance
10 of Wands	♄	Saturn	The World	♐	Sagittarius	Temperance
2 of Pentacles	♃	Jupiter	The Wheel of Fortune	♑	Capricorn	The Devil
3 of Pentacles	♂	Mars	The Tower	♑	Capricorn	The Devil
4 of Pentacles	☉	Sun	The Sun	♑	Capricorn	The Devil
5 of Swords	♀	Venus	The Empress	♒	Aquarius	The Star
6 of Swords	☿	Mercury	The Magician	♒	Aquarius	The Star
7 of Swords	☽	Moon	The High Priestess	♒	Aquarius	The Star
8 of Cups	♄	Saturn	World	♓	Pisces	The Moon
9 of Cups	♃	Jupiter	Wheel of Fortune	♓	Pisces	The Moon
10 of Cups	♂	Mars	Tower	♓	Pisces	The Moon

TABLE 3—COMBINED ACES

	A	B	C	D	E	F	G	H
1	Suit	Hermetic title (Thoth/ *Golden Dawn*)	Elemental glyph	Zodiacal signs by calendar	Zodiacal majors by calendar	Dates	Zodiacal signs by element	Zodiacal majors by element
2	Ace of Wands	The Root of the Powers of Fire	△	♋♌♍	The Chariot Strength The Hermit	Jun. 19– Sep. 17	♈, ♌, ♐	The Emperor Strength Temperance
3	Ace of Cups	The Root of the Powers of the Waters	▽	♎♏♐	Justice Death Temperance	Sep. 18– Dec. 17	♋, ♏, ♓	The Chariot Death The Moon
4	Ace of Swords	The Root of the Powers of the Air	△	♑♒♓	The Devil The Star The Moon	Dec. 18– Mar. 19	♎, ♒, ♊	Justice, The Star The Lovers
5	Ace of Pen-tacles	The Root of the Powers of Earth	▽	♈♉♊	The Emperor The Hiero-phant The Lovers	Mar. 20– Jun. 18	♑, ♉, ♍	The Devil The Hiero-phant The Hermit

Notes on Associated Major Arcana Correspondences for the Numeric Minor Arcana

The practice of associating minor arcana with their corresponding major arcana does not originate with the Golden Dawn. For me it was a personal practice that began in 2015, at which time I made the acquaintance of M. M. Meleen and was delighted to discover that she was building these associations into her minor arcana for the Tabula Mundi deck. To date it is still the only deck I know of that makes these connections explicit in a stunning, visual way; if you wish to study the minor-major correspondences, the Tabula Mundi deck is a must.

Knowing that the 5 of Cups has something to do with the Tower and Death adds an extra layer of interpretation and depth. Not every pairing of majors and minor is so transparent, but all are evocative. All reward further contemplation, especially alongside a study of the decans.

The four aces of each suit don't correspond to clear planetary and zodiacal majors, but you could think of them as being connected to all the majors that match their element. Thus the Ace of Wands is connected with all fiery majors. You could also think of them as being connected to the same majors as the page or princess cards (see round diagram of correspondences on p. 143, and court card correspondences).

TABLE 4—SABIAN SYMBOLS

	Hermetic title (Thoth/ *Golden Dawn)*	Decan no.	Zodiac	Sabian Symbols
2 of Wands	Dominion	1	0°–9° Aries	0–1 deg Aries: A Woman Just Risen From The Sea; A Seal Is Embracing Her 1–2 deg Aries: A Comedian Reveals Human Nature 2–3 deg Aries: The Cameo Profile Of A Man, Suggesting The Shape Of His Country 3–4 deg Aries: Two Lovers Strolling On A Secluded Walk 4–5 deg Aries: A Triangle With Wings 5–6 deg Aries: A Square, With One Of Its Sides Brightly Illumined 6–7 deg Aries: A Man Succeeds In Expressing Himself Simultaneously In Two Realms 7–8 deg Aries: A Large Woman's Hat With Streamers Blown By An East Wind 8–9 deg Aries: A Crystal Gazer 9–10 deg Aries: A Teacher Gives New Symbolic Forms To Traditional Images
3 of Wands	Virtue/ *Established Strength*	2	10°–19° Aries	10–11 deg Aries: The Ruler Of A Nation 11–12 deg Aries: A Triangularly Shaped Flight Of Wild Geese 12–13 deg Aries: An Unexploded Bomb Reveals An Unsuccessful Social Protest 13–14 deg Aries: A Serpent Coiling Near A Man And A Woman 14–15 deg Aries: An Indian Weaving A Ceremonial Blanket 15–16 deg Aries: Nature Spirits Are Seen At Work In The Light Of Sunset 16–17 deg Aries: Two Dignified Spinsters Sitting In Silence 17–18 deg Aries: An Empty Hammock Stretched Between Two Trees 18–19 deg Aries: The "Magic Carpet" Of Oriental Imagery 19–20 deg Aries: A Young Girl Feeding Birds In Winter

TABLE 4—SABIAN SYMBOLS

	Hermetic title (Thoth/ *Golden Dawn*)	Decan no.	Zodiac	Sabian Symbols
4 of Wands	Completion/ *Perfected Work*	3	20°–29° Aries	20–21 deg Aries: A Pugilist Enters The Ring 21–22 deg Aries: The Gate To The Garden Of All Fulfilled Desires 22–23 deg Aries: A Pregnant Woman In Light Summer Dress 23–24 deg Aries: Blown Inward By The Wind, The Curtains Of An Open Window Take The Shape Of A Cornucopia 24–25 deg Aries: The Possibility For Man To Gain Experience At Two Levels Of Being 25–26 deg Aries: A Man Possessed Of More Gifts Than He Can Hold 26–27 deg Aries: Through Imagination A Lost Opportunity Is Regained 27–28 deg Aries: A Large Audiences Confronts The Performer Who Disappointed Its Expectations 28–29 deg Aries: The Music Of The Spheres 29–30 deg Aries: A Duck Pond And Its Brood
5 of Pentacles	Worry/ *Material Trouble*	4	0°–9° Taurus	0–1 deg Taurus: A Clear Mountain Stream 1–2 deg Taurus: An Electrical Storm 2–3 deg Taurus: Natural Steps Lead To A Lawn Of Clover In Bloom 3–4 deg Taurus: The Pot Of Gold At The End Of The Rainbow 4–5 deg Taurus: A Widow At An Open Grave 5–6 deg Taurus: Cantilever Bridge Across A Deep Gorge 6–7 deg Taurus: The Woman Of Samaria At The Ancestral Well 7–8 deg Taurus: A Sleigh On Land Uncovered By Snow 8–9 deg Taurus: A Fully Decorated Christmas Tree 9–10 deg Taurus: A Red Cross Nurse

TABLE 4—SABIAN SYMBOLS

	Hermetic title (Thoth/ *Golden Dawn*)	Decan no.	Zodiac	Sabian Symbols
6 of Pentacles	Success/ *Material Success*	5	10°–19° Taurus	10–11 deg Taurus: A Woman Watering Flowers In Her Garden. 11–12 deg Taurus: A Young Couple Window Shopping 12–13 deg Taurus: A Porter Carrying Heavy Baggage 13–14 deg Taurus: On The Beach, Children Play While Shellfish Grope At The Edge Of The Water 14–15 deg Taurus: Head Covered With A Rakish Silk Hat, Muffled Against The Cold, A Man Braves A Storm 15–16 deg Taurus: An Old Teacher Fails To Interest His Pupils In Traditional Knowledge 16–17 deg Taurus: A Symbolical Battle Between "Swords" And "Torches" 17–18 deg Taurus: A Woman Airing An Old Bag Through The Open Window Of Her Room 18–19 deg Taurus: A New Continent Rising Out Of The Ocean 19–20 deg Taurus: Wisps Of Winglike Clouds Streaming Across The Sky
7 of Pentacles	Failure/ *Success Unfulfilled*	6	20°–29° Taurus	20–21 deg Taurus: A Finger Pointing To A Line In An Open Book 21–22 deg Taurus: White Dove Flying Over Troubled Waters 22–23 deg Taurus: A Jewelry Shop Filled With Valuable Gems 23–24 deg Taurus: An Indian Warrior Riding Fiercely, Human Scalps Hanging From His Belt 24–25 deg Taurus: A Vast Public Park 25–26 deg Taurus: A Spanish Gallant Serenades His Beloved 26–27 deg Taurus: An Old Indian Woman Selling The Artifacts Of Her Tribe To Passerby 27–28 deg Taurus: A Woman, Past Her "Change Of Life," Experiences A New Love 28–29 deg Taurus: Two Cobblers Working At A Table 29–30 deg Taurus: A Peacock Parading On The Terrace Of An Old Castle

TABLE 4—SABIAN SYMBOLS

	Hermetic title (Thoth/ *Golden Dawn)*	Decan no.	Zodiac	Sabian Symbols
8 of Swords	Interference/ *Shortened Force*	7	0°–9° Gemini	0–1 deg Gemini: A Glass-Bottomed Boat Reveals Undersea Wonders 1–2 deg Gemini: Santa Claus Furtively Filling Stockings Hanging In Front Of Fireplace 2–3 deg Gemini: The Garden Of The Tuileries In Paris 3–4 deg Gemini: Holly And Mistletoe Reawaken Old Memories Of Christmas 4–5 deg Gemini: A Revolutionary Magazine Asking For Action 5–6 deg Gemini: Workmen Drilling For Oil 6–7 deg Gemini: A Well With Bucket And Rope Under The Shade Of Majestic Trees 7–8 deg Gemini: Aroused Strikers Surround A Factory 8–9 deg Gemini: A Quiver Filled With Arrows 9–10 deg Gemini: An Airplane Performing A Nose Dive
9 of Swords	Cruelty/ *Despair and Cruelty*	8	10°–19° Gemini	10–11 deg Gemini: Newly Opened Lands Offer The Pioneer New Opportunities For Experience 11–12 deg Gemini: A Negro Girl Fights For Her Independence In The City 12–13 deg Gemini: A Famous Pianist Giving A Concert Performance 13–14 deg Gemini: Bridging Physical Space And Social Distinctions, Two Men Communicate Telepathically 14–15 deg Gemini: Two Dutch Children Talking To Each Other, Exchanging Their Knowledge 15–16 deg Gemini: A Woman Activist In An Emotional Speech Dramatizing Her Cause 16–17 deg Gemini: The Head Of A Robust Youth Changes Into That Of A Mature Thinker 17–18 deg Gemini: Two Chinese Men Converse In Their Native Tongue In An American City 18–19 deg Gemini: A Large Archaic Volume Reveals A Traditional Wisdom 19–20 deg Gemini: A Modern Cafeteria Displays An Abundance Of Food, Products Of Various Regions

TABLE 4—SABIAN SYMBOLS

	Hermetic title (Thoth/*Golden Dawn*)	Decan no.	Zodiac	Sabian Symbols
10 of Swords	Ruin	9	20°–29° Gemini	20–21 deg Gemini: A Tumultuous Labor Demonstration 21–22 deg Gemini: Dancing Couples In A Harvest Festival 22–23 deg Gemini: Three Fledglings In A Nest High In A Tree 23–24 deg Gemini: Children Skating Over A Frozen Village Pond 24–25 deg Gemini: A Gardener Trimming Large Palm Trees 25–26 deg Gemini: Frost-Covered Trees Against Winter Skies 26–27 deg Gemini: A Gypsy Emerging From The Forest Wherein Her Tribe Is Encamped 27–28 deg Gemini: Through Bankruptcy, Society Gives To An Overburdened Individual The Opportunity To Begin Again 28–29 deg Gemini: The First Mockingbird Of Spring 29–30 deg Gemini: A Parade Of Bathing Beauties Before Large Beach Crowds
2 of Cups	Love	10	0°–9° Cancer	0–1 deg Cancer: On A Ship The Sailors Lower An Old Flag And Raise A New One 1–2 deg Cancer: A Man On A Magic Carpet Hovers Over A Large Area Of Land 2–3 deg Cancer: A Man Bundled In Fur Leads A Shaggy Deer 3–4 deg Cancer: A Cat Arguing With A Mouse 4–5 deg Cancer: At A Railroad Crossing, An Automobile is Wrecked By A Train 5–6 deg Cancer: Game Birds Feathering Their Nests 6–7 deg Cancer: Two Nature Spirits Dancing Under the Moonlight 7–8 deg Cancer: A Group Of Rabbits Dressed in Human Clothes Walk As If On Parade 8–9 deg Cancer: A Small Naked Girl Bends Over A Pond Trying To Catch A Fish 9–10 deg Cancer: A Large Diamond In The First Stages Of The Cutting Process

TABLE 4—SABIAN SYMBOLS

	Hermetic title (Thoth/ *Golden Dawn)*	Decan no.	Zodiac	Sabian Symbols
3 of Cups	Abundance	11	10°–19° Cancer	10–11 deg Cancer: A Clown Caricaturing Well-Known Personalities 11–12 deg Cancer: A Chinese Woman Nursing A Baby Whose Aura Reveals Him To Be The Reincarnation Of A Great Teacher 12–13 deg Cancer: A Hand With A Prominent Thumb Is Held Out For Study 13–14 deg Cancer: A Very Old Man Facing A Vast Dark Space To The Northeast 14–15 deg Cancer: In A Sumptuous Dining Hall Guests Relax After Partaking Of A Huge Banquet 15–16 deg Cancer: A Man Studying A Mandala In Front Of Him, With The Help Of A Very Ancient Book 16–17 deg Cancer: The Unfoldment Of Multilevel Potentialities Issuing From An Original Germ 17–18 deg Cancer: A Hen Scratching The Ground To Find Nourishment For Her Progeny 18–19 deg Cancer: A Priest Performing A Marriage Ceremony 19–20 deg Cancer: Venetian Gondoliers Giving A Serenade

TABLE 4—SABIAN SYMBOLS

	Hermetic title (Thoth/ *Golden Dawn*)	Decan no.	Zodiac	Sabian Symbols
4 of Cups	Luxury/ *Blended Pleasure*	12	20°–29° Cancer	20–21 deg Cancer: A Famous Singer Is Proving Her Virtuosity During An Operatic Performance 21–22 deg Cancer: A Young Woman Awaiting A Sailboat 22–23 deg Cancer: The Meeting Of A Literary Society 23–24 deg Cancer: A Woman And Two Men Castaways On A Small Island Of The South Seas 24–25 deg Cancer: A Willful Man Is Overshadowed By A Descent Of Superior Power 25–26 deg Cancer: Guests Are Reading In The Library Of A Luxurious Home 26–27 deg Cancer: A Violent Storm in A Canyon Filled With Expensive Homes 27–28 deg Cancer: An Indian Girl Introduces Her White Lover To Her Assembled Tribe 28–29 deg Cancer: A Greek Muse Weighing Newborn Twins In Golden Scales 29–30 deg Cancer: A Daughter of The American Revolution

TABLE 4—SABIAN SYMBOLS

	Hermetic title (Thoth/ *Golden Dawn*)	Decan no.	Zodiac	Sabian Symbols
5 of Wands	Strife	13	0°–9° Leo	0–1 deg Leo: Blood Rushes To A Man's Head As His Vital Energies Are Mobilized Under The Spur Of Ambition 1–2 deg Leo: An Epidemic Of Mumps 2–3 deg Leo: A Middle-Aged Woman, Her Long Hair Flowing Over Her Shoulders And In A Braless Youthful Garment 3–4 deg Leo: A Formally Dressed Elderly Man Stands Near Trophies He Brought Back From A Hunting Expedition 4–5 deg Leo: Rock Formations Tower Over A Deep Canyon 5–6 deg Leo: A Conservative, Old-Fashioned Lady Is Confronted By A "Hippie" Girl 6–7 deg Leo: The Constellations Of Stars Shine Brilliantly In The Night Sky 7–8 deg Leo: A Communist Activist Spreading His Revolutionary Ideals 8–9 deg Leo: Glass Blowers Shape Beautiful Vases With Their Controlled Breathing 9–10 deg Leo: Early Morning Dew Sparkles As Sunlight Floods The Field

TABLE 4—SABIAN SYMBOLS

	Hermetic title (Thoth/ *Golden Dawn*)	Decan no.	Zodiac	Sabian Symbols
6 of Wands	Victory	14	10°–19° Leo	10–11 deg Leo: Children Play On A Swing Hanging From The Branches Of A Huge Oak Tree 11–12 deg Leo: An Evening Party Of Adults On A Lawn Illumined By Fancy Lanterns 12–13 deg Leo: An Old Sea Captain Rocking Himself On The Porch Of His Cottage 13–14 deg Leo: A Human Soul Seeking Opportunities For Outward Manifestation 14–15 deg Leo: A Pageant, With Its Spectacular Floats, Moves Along A Street Crowded With Cheering People 15–16 deg Leo: The Storm Ended, All Nature Rejoices In Brilliant Sunshine 16–17 deg Leo: A Volunteer Church Choir Singing Religious Hymns 17–18 deg Leo: A Chemist Conducts An Experiment For His Students 18–19 deg Leo: A Houseboat Party 19–20 deg Leo: Zuni Indians Perform A Ritual To The Sun

TABLE 4—SABIAN SYMBOLS

	Hermetic title (Thoth/ *Golden Dawn)*	Decan no.	Zodiac	Sabian Symbols
7 of Wands	Valor	15	20°–29° Leo	20–21 deg Leo: Intoxicated Chickens Dizzily Flap Their Wings Trying To Fly 21–22 deg Leo: A Carrier Pigeon Fulfilling Its Mission 22–23 deg Leo: In A Circus The Bareback Rider Displays Her Dangerous Skill 23–24 deg Leo: Totally Concentrated Upon Inner Spiritual Attainment, A Man Is Sitting In A State Of Complete Neglect Of Bodily Appearance And Cleanliness 24–25 deg Leo: A Large Camel Is Seen Crossing A Vast And Forbidding Desert 25–26 deg Leo: After The Heavy Storm, A Rainbow 26–27 deg Leo: The Luminescence Of Dawn In The Eastern Sky 27–28 deg Leo: Many Little Birds On A Limb Of A Big Tree 28–29 deg Leo: A Mermaid Emerges From The Ocean Waves Ready For Rebirth In Human Form 29–30 deg Leo: An Unsealed Letter

TABLE 4—SABIAN SYMBOLS

	Hermetic title (Thoth/ *Golden Dawn*)	Decan no.	Zodiac	Sabian Symbols
8 of Pentacles	Prudence	16	0°–9° Virgo	0–1 deg Virgo: In A Portrait, The Significant Features Of A Man's Head Are Artistically Emphasized 1–2 deg Virgo: A Large White Cross Dominates The Landscape 2–3 deg Virgo: Two Guardian Angels 3–4 deg Virgo: Black And White Children Play Together Happily 4–5 deg Virgo: A Man Becoming Aware Of Nature Spirits And Normally Unseen Spiritual Agencies 5–6 deg Virgo: A Merry-Go-Round 6–7 deg Virgo: A Harem 7–8 deg Virgo: A Five-Year-Old Child Takes A First Dancing Lesson 8–9 deg Virgo: An Expressionist Painter At Work 9–10 deg Virgo: Two Heads Looking Out And Beyond The Shadows
9 of Pentacles	Gain/ *Material Gain*	17	10°–19° Virgo	10–11 deg Virgo: In Her Baby A Mother Sees Her Deep Longing For A Son Answered 11–12 deg Virgo: After The Wedding, The Groom Snatches The Veil Away From His Bride 12–13 deg Virgo: A Powerful Statesman Overcomes A State Of Political Hysteria 13–14 deg Virgo: An Aristocratic Family Tree 14–15 deg Virgo: A Fine Lace Handkerchief, Heirloom From Valorous Ancestors 15–16 deg Virgo: In The Zoo, Children Are Brought Face To Face With An Orangutan 16–17 deg Virgo: A Volcanic Eruption 17–18 deg Virgo: An Ouija Board 18–19 deg Virgo: A Swimming Race 19–20 deg Virgo: A Caravan Of Cars Headed To The West Coast

TABLE 4—SABIAN SYMBOLS

	Hermetic title (Thoth/ *Golden Dawn*)	Decan no.	Zodiac	Sabian Symbols
10 of Pentacles	Wealth	18	20°–29° Virgo	20–21 deg Virgo: A Girls' Basketball Team 21–22 deg Virgo: A Royal Coat Of Arms Enriched With Precious Stones 22–23 deg Virgo: A Lion Tamer Displays His Skill And Character 23–24 deg Virgo: Mary And Her Little Lamb 24–25 deg Virgo: A Flag At Half-Mast In Front Of A Public Building 25–26 deg Virgo: A Boy With A Censer Serves The Priest Near The Altar 26–27 deg Virgo: A Group Of Aristocratic Ladies Meet Ceremonially At A Court's Function 27–28 deg Virgo: A Baldheaded Man Who Has Seized Power 28–29 deg Virgo: A Seeker After Occult Knowledge Is Reading An Ancient Scroll Which Illumines His Mind 29–30 deg Virgo: Totally Intent Upon Completing An Immediate Task, A Man Is Deaf To Any Allurement

TABLE 4—SABIAN SYMBOLS

	Hermetic title (Thoth/ *Golden Dawn)*	Decan no.	Zodiac	Sabian Symbols
2 of Swords	Peace/*Peace Restored*	19	0°–9° Libra	0–1 deg Libra: In A Collection Of Perfect Specimens Of Many Biological Forms, A Butterfly Displays The Beauty Of Its Wings, Its Body Impaled By A Fine Dart 1–2 deg Libra: The Transmutation Of The Fruits Of Past Experiences Into The Seed—Realizations Of The Forever Creative Spirit 2–3 deg Libra: The Dawn Of A New Day Reveals Everything Changed 3–4 deg Libra: Around A Campfire A Group Of Young People Sit In Spiritual Communion 4–5 deg Libra: A Man Revealing To His Students The Foundation Of An Inner Knowledge Upon Which A "New World" Could Be Built 5–6 deg Libra: A Man Watches His Ideals Taking A Concrete Form Before His Inner Vision 6–7 deg Libra: A Woman Feeding Chickens And Protecting Them From The Hawks 7–8 deg Libra: A Blazing Fireplace In A Deserted Home 8–9 deg Libra: Three "Old Masters" Hanging On The Wall Of A Special Room In An Art Gallery 9–10 deg Libra: Having Passed Through Narrow Rapids, A Canoe Reaches Calm Waters

TABLE 4—SABIAN SYMBOLS

	Hermetic title (Thoth/ *Golden Dawn)*	Decan no.	Zodiac	Sabian Symbols
3 of Swords	Sorrow	20	10°–19° Libra	10–11 deg Libra: A Professor Peering Over His Glasses At His Students 11–12 deg Libra: Miners Are Surfacing From A Deep Coal Mine 12–13 deg Libra: Children Blowing Soap Bubbles 13–14 deg Libra: In The Heat Of The Noon Hour A Man Takes A Siesta 14–15 deg Libra: Circular Paths 15–16 deg Libra: After A Storm A Boat Landing Stands In Need Of Reconstruction 16–17 deg Libra: A Retired Sea Captain Watches Ships Entering And Leaving The Harbor 17–18 deg Libra: Two Men Placed Under Arrest 18–19 deg Libra: A Gang Of Robbers In Hiding 19–20 deg Libra: A Rabbi Performing His Duties
4 of Swords	Truce/*Rest from Strife*	21	20°–29° Libra	20–21 deg Libra: A Sunday Crowd Enjoying The Beach 21–22 deg Libra: A Child Giving Birds A Drink At A Fountain 22–23 deg Libra: Chanticleer's Voice Heralds Sunrise 23–24 deg Libra: A Butterfly With A Third Wing On Its Left Side 24–25 deg Libra: The Sight Of An Autumn Leaf Brings To A Pilgrim The Sudden Revelation Of The Mystery Of Life And Death 25–26 deg Libra: An Eagle And A Large White Dove Change Into Each Other 26–27 deg Libra: An Airplane Sails, High In The Clear Sky 27–28 deg Libra: A Man Becoming Aware Of Spiritual Forces Surrounding And Assisting Him 28–29 deg Libra: Mankind's Vast And Enduring Effort To Reach For Knowledge Transferable From Generation To Generation 29–30 deg Libra: Three Mounds Of Knowledge On A Philosopher's Head

TABLE 4—SABIAN SYMBOLS

	Hermetic title (Thoth/ *Golden Dawn*)	Decan no.	Zodiac	Sabian Symbols
5 of Cups	Disappoint-ment/*Loss in Pleasure*	22	0°–9° Scorpio	0–1 deg Scorpio: A Crowded Sightseeing Bus On A City Street 1–2 deg Scorpio: A Delicate Bottle Of Perfume Lies Broken, Releasing Its Fragrance 2–3 deg Scorpio: A House-Raising Party In A Small Village Enlists The Neighbors' Cooperation 3–4 deg Scorpio: A Youth Carries A Lighted Candle In A Devotional Ritual 4–5 deg Scorpio: A Massive Rocky Shore Resist The Pounding Of The Sea 5–6 deg Scorpio: The Gold Rush Tears Men Away From Their Native Soil 6–7 deg Scorpio: Deep-Sea Divers 7–8 deg Scorpio: A Calm Lake Bathed In Moonlight 8–9 deg Scorpio: A Dentist At Work 9–10 deg Scorpio: A Fellowship Supper Reunites Old Comrades

TABLE 4—SABIAN SYMBOLS

	Hermetic title (Thoth/ *Golden Dawn)*	Decan no.	Zodiac	Sabian Symbols
6 of Cups	Pleasure	23	10°–19° Scorpio	10–11 deg Scorpio: A Drowning Man is Being Rescued 11–12 deg Scorpio: An Official Embassy Ball 12–13 deg Scorpio: An Inventor Performs A Laboratory Experiment 13–14 deg Scorpio: Telephone Lineman At Work Installling New Connections 14–15 deg Scorpio: Children Playing Around Five Mounds Of Sand 15–16 deg Scorpio: A Girl's Face Breaking Into A Smile 16–17 deg Scorpio: A Woman, Fecundated By Her Own Spirit, Is "Great With Child" 17–18 deg Scorpio: A Path Through Woods Brilliant With Multicolored Splendor 18–19 deg Scorpio: A Parrot Repeats The Conversation He Has Overheard 19–20 deg Scorpio: A Woman Draws Away Two Dark Curtains Closing The Entrance To A Sacred Pathway

TABLE 4—SABIAN SYMBOLS

	Hermetic title (Thoth/ *Golden Dawn)*	Decan no.	Zodiac	Sabian Symbols
7 of Cups	Debauch/ *Illusionary Success*	24	20°–29° Scorpio	20–21 deg Scorpio: Obeying His Conscience, A Soldier Resists Orders 21–22 deg Scorpio: Hunters Shooting Wild Ducks 22–23 deg Scorpio: A Rabbit Metamorphoses Into A Nature Sprit 23–24 deg Scorpio: After Having Heard An Inspired Individual Deliver His "Sermon On The Mount," Crowds Are Returning Home 24–25 deg Scorpio: An X-Ray Photograph 25–26 deg Scorpio: American Indians Making Camp After Moving Into A New Territory 26–27 deg Scorpio: A Military Band Marches Noisily On Through The City Streets 27–28 deg Scorpio: The King Of The Fairies Approaching His Domain 28–29 deg Scorpio: An Indian Squaw Pleading To The Chief For The Lives Of Her Children 29–30 deg Scorpio: Children In Halloween Costumes Indulge In Various Pranks

TABLE 4—SABIAN SYMBOLS

	Hermetic title (Thoth/ *Golden Dawn)*	Decan no.	Zodiac	Sabian Symbols
8 of Wands	Swiftness	25	0°–9° Sagittarius	0–1 deg Sagittarius: Retired Army Veterans Gather To Reawaken Old Memories 1–2 deg Sagittarius: White-capped Waves Display The Power Of Wind Over Sea 2–3 deg Sagittarius: Two Men Playing Chess 3–4 deg Sagittarius: A Little Child Learning To Walk With The Encouragement Of His Parents 4–5 deg Sagittarius: An Old Owl Sits Alone On The Branch Of A Large Tree 5–6 deg Sagittarius: A Game Of Cricket 6–7 deg Sagittarius: Cupid Knocks At The Door Of A Human Heart 7–8 deg Sagittarius: Within The Depths Of The Earth New Elements Are Being Formed 8–9 deg Sagittarius: A Mother Leads Her Small Child Step By Step Up A Steep Stairway 9–10 deg Sagittarius: A Theatrical Representation Of A Golden-Haired Goddess Of Opportunity

TABLE 4—SABIAN SYMBOLS

	Hermetic title (Thoth/ *Golden Dawn*)	Decan no.	Zodiac	Sabian Symbols
9 of Wands	Strength/ *Great Strength*	26	10°–19° Sagittarius	10–11 deg Sagittarius: In The Left Section Of An Archaic Temple, A Lamp Burns In A Container Shaped Like A Human Body 11–12 deg Sagittarius: A Flag Turns Into An Eagle; The Eagle Into A Chanticleer Saluting The Dawn 12–13 deg Sagittarius: A Widow's Past Is Brought To Light 13–14 deg Sagittarius: The Great Pyramid And The Sphinx 14–15 deg Sagittarius: The Ground Hog Looking For Its Shadow On Ground Hog Day 15–16 deg Sagittarius: Sea Gulls Fly Around A Ship In Expectation Of Food 16–17 deg Sagittarius: An Easter Sunrise Service Draws A Large Crowd 17–18 deg Sagittarius: Children Playing On The Beach, Their Heads Protected By Sunbonnets 18–19 deg Sagittarius: Pelicans Menaced By The Behavior And Refuse Of Men Seek Safer Areas For Bringing Up Their Young 19–20 deg Sagittarius: In An Old-Fashioned Northern Village Men Cut The Ice Of A Frozen Pond For Use During The Summer

TABLE 4—SABIAN SYMBOLS

	Hermetic title (Thoth/ *Golden Dawn*)	Decan no.	Zodiac	Sabian Symbols
10 of Wands	Oppression	27	20°–29° Sagittarius	20–21 deg Sagittarius: A Child And A Dog Wearing Borrowed Eyeglasses 21–22 deg Sagittarius: A Chinese Laundry 22–23 deg Sagittarius: A Group Of Immigrants As They Fulfill The Requirements Of Entrance Into The New Country 23–24 deg Sagittarius: A Bluebird Perched On The Gate Of A Cottage 24–25 deg Sagittarius: A Chubby Boy On A Hobby-Horse 25–26 deg Sagittarius: A Flag Bearer In A Battle 26–27 deg Sagittarius: A Sculptor At His Work 27–28 deg Sagittarius: An Old Bridge Over A Beautiful Stream Is Still In Constant Use 28–29 deg Sagittarius: A Fat Boy Mowing The Lawn Of His House On An Elegant Suburban Street 29–30 deg Sagittarius: The Pope Blessing The Faithful

TABLE 4—SABIAN SYMBOLS

	Hermetic title (Thoth/ *Golden Dawn)*	Decan no.	Zodiac	Sabian Symbols
2 of Pentacles	Change/ *Harmonious Change*	28	0°–9° Capricorn	0–1 deg Capricorn: An Indian Chief Claims Power From The Assembled Tribe 1–2 deg Capricorn: Three Rose Windows In A Gothic Church, One Damaged By War 2–3 deg Capricorn: A Human Soul, In Its Eagerness For New Experiences, Seeks Embodiment 3–4 deg Capricorn: A Group Of People Outfitting A Large Canoe At The Start Of A Journey By Water 4–5 deg Capricorn: Indians On The Warpath. While Some Men Row A Well-Filled Canoe, Others In It Perform A War Dance 5–6 deg Capricorn: Ten Logs Lie Under An Archway Leading To Darker Woods 6–7 deg Capricorn: A Veiled Prophet Speaks, Seized By The Power Of A God 7–8 deg Capricorn: In A Sunlit Home Domesticated Birds Sing Joyously 8–9 deg Capricorn: An Angel Carrying A Harp 9–10 deg Capricorn: An Albatross Feeding From The Hand Of A Sailor

TABLE 4—SABIAN SYMBOLS

	Hermetic title (Thoth/ *Golden Dawn*)	Decan no.	Zodiac	Sabian Symbols
3 of Pentacles	Work/ *Material Works*	29	10°–19° Capricorn	10–11 deg Capricorn: A Large Group Of Pheasant On A Private Estate 11–12 deg Capricorn: An Illustrated Lecture On Natural Science Reveals Little-Known Aspects Of Life 12–13 deg Capricorn: A Fire Worshipper Meditates On The Ultimate Realities Of Existence 13–14 deg Capricorn: An Ancient Bas-Relief Carved In Granite Remains A Witness To A Long-Forgotten Culture 14–15 deg Capricorn: In A Hospital, The Children's Ward Is Filled With Toys 15–16 deg Capricorn: School Grounds Filled With Boys And Girls In Gymnasium Suits 16–17 deg Capricorn: A Repressed Woman Finds A Psychological Release In Nudism 17–18 deg Capricorn: The Union Jack Flag Files From A British Warship 18–19 deg Capricorn: A Five-Year-Old Child Carrying A Bag Filled With Groceries 19–20 deg Capricorn: A Hidden Choir Is Singing During A Religious Service

TABLE 4—SABIAN SYMBOLS

	Hermetic title (Thoth/ *Golden Dawn)*	Decan no.	Zodiac	Sabian Symbols
4 of Pentacles	Power/ *Earthly Power*	30	20°–29° Capricorn	20–21 deg Capricorn: A Relay Race 21–22 deg Capricorn: By Accepting Defeat Gracefully, A General Reveals Nobility Of Character 22–23 deg Capricorn: A Soldier Receiving Two Awards For Bravery In Combat 23–24 deg Capricorn: A Woman Entering A Convent 24–25 deg Capricorn: A Store Filled With Precious Oriental Rugs 25–26 deg Capricorn: A Nature Sprit Dancing In The Iridescent Mist Of A Waterfall 26–27 deg Capricorn: Pilgrims Climbing The Steep Steps Leading To A Mountain Shrine 27–28 deg Capricorn: A Large Aviary 28–29 deg Capricorn: A Woman Reading Tea Leaves 29–30 deg Capricorn: A Secret Meeting Of Men Responsible For Executive Decisions In World Affairs
5 of Swords	Defeat	31	0°–9° Aquarius	0–1 deg Aquarius: An Old Adobe Mission In California 1–2 deg Aquarius: An Unexpected Thunderstorm 2–3 deg Aquarius: A Deserter From The Navy 3–4 deg Aquarius: A Hindu Yogi Demonstrates His Healing Powers 4–5 deg Aquarius: A Council Of Ancestors Is Seen Implementing The Efforts Of A Young Leader 5–6 deg Aquarius: A Masked Figure Performs Ritualistic Acts In A Mystery Play 6–7 deg Aquarius: A Child Is Seen Being Born Out Of An Egg 7–8 deg Aquarius: Beautifully Gowned Wax Figures On Display 8–9 deg Aquarius: A Flag Is Seen Turning Into An Eagle 9–10 deg Aquarius: A Man Who Had For A Time Become The Embodiment Of A Popular Ideal Is Made To Realize That As A Person He Is Not This Ideal

TABLE 4—SABIAN SYMBOLS

	Hermetic title (Thoth/ *Golden Dawn)*	Decan no.	Zodiac	Sabian Symbols
6 of Swords	Science/ *Earned Success*	32	10°–19° Aquar-ius	10–11 deg Aquarius: During A Silent Hour, A Man Receives A New Inspiration Which May Change His Life 11–12 deg Aquarius: On A Vast Staircase Stand People Of Different Types, Graduated Upward 12–13 deg Aquarius: A Barometer 13–14 deg Aquarius: A Train Entering A Tunnel 14–15 deg Aquarius: Two Lovebirds Sitting On A Fence And Singing Happily 15–16 deg Aquarius: A Big Businessman At His Desk 16–17 deg Aquarius: A Watchdog Stands Guard, Protecting His Master And His Possessions 17–18 deg Aquarius: A Man's Secret Motives Are Being Publicly Unmasked 18–19 deg Aquarius: A Forest Fire Is Being Subdued By The Use Of Water, Chemicals And Sheer Muscular Energy 19–20 deg Aquarius: A Large White Dove Bearing A Message

TABLE 4—SABIAN SYMBOLS

	Hermetic title (Thoth/ *Golden Dawn*)	Decan no.	Zodiac	Sabian Symbols
7 of Swords	Futility/ *Unstable Effort*	33	20°–29° Aquarius	20–21 deg Aquarius: A Disappointed And Disillusioned Woman Courageously Faces A Seemingly Empty Life 21–22 deg Aquarius: A Rug Is Placed On The Floor Of A Nursery To Allow Children To Play In Comfort And Warmth 22–23 deg Aquarius: A Big Bear Sitting Down And Waving All Its Paws 23–24 deg Aquarius: A Man, Having Overcome His Passions, Teaches Deep Wisdom In Terms Of His Experience 24–25 deg Aquarius: A Butterfly With The Right Wing More Perfectly Formed 25–26 deg Aquarius: A Garage Man Testing A Car's Battery With A Hydrometer 26–27 deg Aquarius: An Ancient Pottery Bowl Filled With Fresh Violets 27–28 deg Aquarius: A Tree Felled And Sawed To Ensure A Supply Of Wood For The Winter 28–29 deg Aquarius: A Butterfly Emerging From A Chrysalis 29–30 deg Aquarius: Deeply Rooted In The Past Of A Very Ancient Culture, A Spiritual Brotherhood In Which Many Individual Minds Are Merged Into The Glowing Light Of A Unanimous Consciousness Is Revealed To One Who Has Emerged Successfully From His Metamorphosis

TABLE 4—SABIAN SYMBOLS

	Hermetic title (Thoth/ *Golden Dawn*)	Decan no.	Zodiac	Sabian Symbols
8 of Cups	Indolence/ *Abandoned Success*	34	0°–9° Pisces	0–1 deg Pisces: In A Crowded Marketplace Farmers And Middlemen Display A Great Variety Of Products 1–2 deg Pisces: A Squirrel Hiding From Hunters 2–3 deg Pisces: Petrified Tree Trunks Lie Broken On Desert Sand 3–4 deg Pisces: Heavy Car Traffic On A Narrow Isthmus Linking Two Seashore Resorts 4–5 deg Pisces: A Church Bazaar 5–6 deg Pisces: A Parade Of Army Officers In Full Dress 6–7 deg Pisces: Illumined By A Shaft Of Light, A Large Cross Lies On Rocks Surrounded By Sea 7–8 deg Pisces: A Girl Blowing A Bugle 8–9 deg Pisces: A Jockey Spurs His Horse, Intent On Outdistancing His Rivals 9–10 deg Pisces: An Aviator Pursues His Journey, Flying Through Ground-Obscuring Clouds
9 of Cups	Happiness/ *Material Happiness*	35	10°–19° Pisces	10–11 deg Pisces: Men Traveling A Narrow Path, Seeking Illumination 11–12 deg Pisces: In The Sanctuary Of An Occult Brotherhood, Newly Initiated Members Are Being Examined And Their Character Tested 12–13 deg Pisces: An Ancient Sword, Used In Many Battles, Is Displayed In A Museum 13–14 deg Pisces: A Lady Wrapped In A Large Stole Of Fox Fur 14–15 deg Pisces: An Officer Instructing His Men Before A Simulated Assault Under A Barrage Of Live Shells 15–16 deg Pisces: In The Quiet Of His Study A Creative Individual Experiences A Flow Of Inspiration 16–17 deg Pisces: An Easter Parade 17–18 deg Pisces: In A Gigantic Tent, Villagers Witness A Spectacular Performance 18–19 deg Pisces: A Master Instructing His Disciple 19–20 deg Pisces: A Table Set For An Evening Meal

TABLE 4—SABIAN SYMBOLS

	Hermetic title (Thoth/ *Golden Dawn*)	Decan no.	Zodiac	Sabian Symbols
10 of Cups	Satiety/ *Perpetual Success*	36	20°–29° Pisces	20–21 deg Pisces: Under The Watchful And Kind Eye Of A Chinese Servant, A Girl Fondles A Little White Lamb 21–22 deg Pisces: A Prophet Carrying Tablets Of The New Law Is Walking Down The Slopes Of Mount Sinai 22–23 deg Pisces: A "Materializing" Medium Giving A Seance 23–24 deg Pisces: On A Small Island Surrounded By The Vast Expanse Of The Sea, People Are Seen Living In Close Interaction 24–25 deg Pisces: A Religious Organization Succeeds In Overcoming The Corrupting Influence Of Perverted Practices and Materialized Ideals 25–26 deg Pisces: Watching The Very Thin Moon Crescent Appearing At Sunset, Different People Realize That The Time Has Come To Go Ahead With Their Different Projects 26–27 deg Pisces: The Harvest Moon Illumines A Clear Autumnal Sky 27–28 deg Pisces: A Fertile Garden Under The Full Moon Reveals A Variety Of Full-Grown Vegetables 28–29 deg Pisces: Light Breaking Into Many Colors As It Passes Through A Prism 29–30 deg Pisces: A Majestic Rock Formation Resembling A Face Is Idealized By A Boy Who Takes It As His Ideal Of Greatness, And As He Grows Up, Begins To Look Like It.

Notes on the Sabian Symbol Correspondences for the Numeric Minor Arcana

Although the Sabian Symbols have no direct connection with the Golden Dawn correspondences featured in this book, they date from a similar era. They were conceived—or by some accounts, *received*—by California spiritualists Elsie Wheeler and Marc Edmund Jones in 1925. Each symbol corresponds with a zodiacal degree; so 10 Sabian Symbols correspond to each decan (or minor arcana card) and 30 to each sign.

Like the *Picatrix* images, they are products of their time and are best consumed with the requisite grain of salt. But they are marvelously evocative, and I've found them useful for extending interpretive meanings around a given card.

TABLE 5— GEOMETRY, KABBALAH, AND SYMBOLISM OF 1 THROUGH 10

Number	Geometric forms of number	Number correspondences	Tree of Life sephira	Planet
1	Monad, the point	Everything & Nothing	Kether	*Primum Mobile*; in modern astrology, Pluto
2	Duad or dyad, the line	Yin/Yang, Heaven/Earth	Chokmah	Zodiac; in modern astrology, Neptune
3	Triad, triangle, plane	Father/Son/Holy Spirit; Mother/Maiden/Crone, Trinities	Binah	Saturn
4	Tetrad, square, triangular pyramid, solid	Elements, seasons, directions, the world of matter, Apostles, Archangels, Humors, Tetragrammaton, Tetramorph	Chesed	Jupiter

TABLE 5— GEOMETRY, KABBALAH, AND SYMBOLISM OF 1 THROUGH 10

Number	Traditional meaning	Color associated with Number on the Tree of Life	Deities associated with number	Papus's dialectic	Number significations
1	Crown	White	Creator gods	Commencement of Commencement	Wholeness, immortality, unity. Potential, conception, initiative. Independence, creativity, will.
2	Wisdom	Grey	Father and sky gods	Opposition of Commencement	Electrical charge, balance, mirror, equilibrium, opposition, the Other, the "gaze", self-consciousness. Choice, crossroads
3	Understanding	Black	Mother and chthonic goddesses; time	Equilibrium of Commencement	Collaboration, community. Manifestation, action, movement.
4	Mercy	Blue	Ruler gods	Commencement of Opposition	Order, solidity, stability, the family, accomplishment, stillness.

TABLE 5— GEOMETRY, KABBALAH, AND SYMBOLISM OF 1 THROUGH 10

Number	Geometric forms of number	Number correspondences	Tree of Life sephira	Planet
5	Pentad, pentagram, square pyramid	Spirit + Matter, Tattwas, Chinese elements	Geburah	Mars
6	Hexad, hexagram octahedron (6 points, 8 faces), cube (6 faces)	As above, so below, union of male and female	Tiphereth	Sun
7	Heptad, heptagram	Planets, days of the week, chakras, musical whole notes	Netzach	Venus
8	Octad, octahedron (8 faces)	ba gua, 8-spoked wheel of Wicca, 8-channel model of consciousness	Hod	Mercury
9	Nonad, enneagram	3 x 3, number of magic	Yesod	Moon
10	Decad, decagram	Digits, decans, sephiroth	Malkuth	Earth

TABLE 5— GEOMETRY, KABBALAH, AND SYMBOLISM OF 1 THROUGH 10

Number	Traditional meaning	Color associated with Number on the Tree of Life	Deities associated with number	Papus's dialectic	Number significations
5	Severity	Red	War gods	Opposition of Opposition	Disruption—freedom from cycle of matter, creativity, risk
6	Beauty	Yellow	Solar and sacrificial gods	Equilibrium of Opposition	Harmony, beauty, love, reconciliation of opposites, well-being, responsibility, purpose
7	Victory	Green	Love and Beauty goddesses	Commencement of Equilibrium	Imagination, secrets, quests, enchantment, mystery, ego
8	Glory	Orange	Knowledge gods	Opposition of Equilibrium	Order, discipline, accomplishment, leadership, success, mastery
9	Foundation	Purple	Lunar goddesses	Equilibrium of Equilibrium	Magic, psychic ability, power, completion, idealism
10	Kingdom	Russet—Olive—Citrine—Black	Harvest goddesses	Uncertainty	Renewal

Notes on Geometry, Kabbalah, and Numeric
Symbolism Correspondences for the Numeric Minor Arcana

The planetary and numerical correspondences are particularly useful for those pursuing planetary magic. The geometric forms in the second column—polygons and solids—form the mystical core of sacred geometry. (See Stephen Skinner's remarkable *Sacred Geometry : Deciphering the Code*). For a wonderful visual and written re-imagining of the Tree of Life, planetary, and deity information in columns 4 through 8, see Alan Moore's remarkable talismanic work, the graphic novel *Promethea*. Column 9 deals with the dialectic of nineteenth-century French esotericist "Papus," which provides a 3x3 structure for thinking about numeric progression and is widely used in interpreting minor arcana.

The planetary correlations used by the Golden Dawn assign the seven classical planets to sephiroth 2 through 9. To the highest sephira, Kether, they assigned the "Primum Mobile"—the movement of the universe, causing all celestial bodies to move. To Chokmah, the second sephira, they assigned the zodiac itself, the great band of constellations. The lowest sephira, Malkuth, corresponded to the earth itself.

As for the final column, I've provided just a few of the numeric associations with 1 through 10, but any numerology text, as well as the reader's own common sense and intuition, will provide additional inspiration.

TABLE 6—COLOR SCALES OF THE GOLDEN DAWN

Number	Sephira	Planetary association	Atziluth "King Scale" "Knight Scale" in Thoth	Briah "Queen Scale"	Yetzirah "Emperor Scale" "Prince Scale" in Thoth	Assiah "Empress Scale" "Princess Scale"
			Yod (Fire) △	Heh (Water) ▽	Vav (Air) △	Heh (Earth) ▽
			Wands	Cups	Swords	Pentacles
1	Kether	The "Primum Mobile"	Brilliance	White brilliance	White brilliance	White flecked gold
2	Chokmah	The Zodiac	Pure Soft Blue	Grey	Blue pearl grey, like mother of pearl	White flecked red, blue, and yellow
3	Binah	Saturn	Crimson	Black	Dark brown	Grey flecked pink
4	Chesed	Jupiter	Deep Violet	Blue	Deep purple	Deep azure flecked yellow
5	Geburah	Mars	Orange	Scarlet red	Bright scarlet	Red flecked black
6	Tiphereth	Sun	Clear Pink Rose	Yellow (gold)	Rich salmon	Gold amber
7	Netzach	Venus	Amber	Emerald	Bright yellow green	Olive flecked gold
8	Hod	Mercury	Violet Purple	Orange	Red-russet	Yellow-brown flecked white
9	Yesod	Moon	Indigo	Violet	Very dark purple	Citrine flecked azure
10	Malkuth	Earth	Yellow	Citrine, Olive, Russet and Black	Citrine, olive, russet and black–but flecked with gold	Black rayed yellow

Notes on Color Scale Correspondences for the Numeric Minor Arcana

You'll note that colors run thematically in rows—all fives have a reddish hue, which is characteristic of Geburah, the sephira of Severity, associated with Mars. To find the color associated with a numeric minor, check the suit column against the numeric row—for example, the 2 of Swords is bluish mother of pearl.

The planetary associations come from Kircher's model of the Tree of Life, as used by the Golden Dawn.

CORRESPONDENCES
FOR THE
16 COURT CARDS

TABLE 1—NOMENCLATURE, ASTROLOGY, AND CORRESPONDING MINORS

Suit and Rank	Golden Dawn Hermetic title	Elemental glyph	Elemental title	Zodiacal modality	Zodiacal glyph
King of Wands *Knight of Wands (Thoth)*	Lord of the Flame and the Lightning King of the Spirits of Fire King of the Salamanders	△△	Fire of Fire	Mutable	♐
Queen of Wands	Queen of the Thrones of Flame Queen of the Salamanders	▽△	Water of Fire	Cardinal	♈
Knight of Wands *Prince of Wands (Thoth)*	Prince of the Chariot of Fire Prince and Emperor of Salamanders	△△	Air of Fire	Fixed	♌
Page of Wands *Princess of Wands (Thoth)*	Princess of the Shining Flame The Rose of the Palace of Fire Princess and Empress of the Salamanders Throne of the Ace of Wands	▽△	Earth of Fire		♋♌♍

TABLE 1—NOMENCLATURE, ASTROLOGY, AND CORRESPONDING MINORS

Suit and Rank	Zodiac	Corresponding Majors	Dates	Corresponding Minors	Corresponding Minors Hermetic Titles
King of Wands *Knight of Wands (Thoth)*	20°–29° Scorpio III 0°–19° Sagittarius I & II	[Death] Temperance/Art	November 12– December 12	7 of Cups 8 of Wands 9 of Wands	Debauch/ Illusionary Success Swiftness Strength/Great Strength
Queen of Wands	20°–29° Pisces III 0°–19° Aries I & II	[The Moon] The Emperor	March 11– April 10	10 of Cups 2 of Wands 3 of Wands	Satiety/Perpetual Success Dominion Virtue/Estab- lished Strength
Knight of Wands *Prince of Wands (Thoth)*	20°–29° Cancer III 0°–19° Leo I & II	[The Chariot] Strength	July 13– August 11	4 of Cups 5 of Wands 6 of Wands	Luxury/Blended Pleasure Strife Victory
Page of Wands *Princess of Wands (Thoth)*	0°–29° Cancer 0°–29° Leo 0°–29° Virgo	The Chariot Strength/Lust The Hermit	June 21– September 22	2 of Cups 3 of Cups 4 of Cups 5 of Wands 6 of Wands 7 of Wands 8 of Disks 9 of Disks 10 of Disks	Love Abundance Luxury/Blended Pleasure Strife Victory Valor Prudence Gain/Material Gain Wealth

TABLE 1—NOMENCLATURE, ASTROLOGY, AND CORRESPONDING MINORS

Suit and Rank	Golden Dawn Hermetic title	Elemental glyph	Elemental title	Zodiacal modality	Zodiacal glyph
King of Cups *Knight of Cups (Thoth)*	Lord of the Waves and the Waters King of the Hosts of the Sea King of Undines and of Nymphs	△▽	Fire of Water	Mutable	♓
Queen of Cups	Queen of the Thrones of the Waters Queen of Nymphs and Undines	▽▽	Water of Water	Cardinal	♋
Knight of Cups *Prince of Cups (Thoth)*	Prince of the Chariot of the Waters Prince and Emperor of Nymphs and Undines	△▽	Air of Water	Fixed	♏
Page of Cups *Princess of Cups (Thoth)*	Princess of the Waters Lotus of the Palace of Floods Princess and Empress of Nymphs and Undines Throne of the Ace of Cups	▽▽	Earth of Water		♎♏♐

TABLE 1—NOMENCLATURE, ASTROLOGY, AND CORRESPONDING MINORS

Suit and Rank	Zodiac	Corresponding Majors	Dates	Corresponding Minors	Corresponding Minors Hermetic Titles
King of Cups *Knight of Cups (Thoth)*	20°–29° Aquarius III 0°–19° Pisces I & II	[The Star] The Moon	February 9– March 10	7 of Swords 8 of Cups 9 of Cups	Futility Indolence/ Abandoned Success Happiness/ Material Happiness
Queen of Cups	20°–29° Gemini III 0°–19° Cancer I & II	[The Lovers] The Chariot	June 11– July 12	10 of Swords 2 of Cups 3 of Cups	Ruin Love Abundance
Knight of Cups *Prince of Cups (Thoth)*	20°–29° Libra III 0°–19° Scorpio I & II	[Justice/ Adjustment] Death	October 13– November 11	4 of Swords 5 of Cups 6 of Cups	Truce/Rest from Strife Disappointment/ Loss in Pleasure Pleasure
Page of Cups *Princess of Cups (Thoth)*	0°–29° Libra 0°–29° Scorpio 0°–29° Sagittarius	Justice/ Adjustment Death Temperance/Art	September 23– December 20	2 of Swords 3 of Swords 4 of Swords 5 of Cups 6 of Cups 7 of Cups 8 of Wands 9 of Wands 10 of Wands	Peace/Peace Restored Sorrow Truce/Rest from Strife Disappointment/ Loss in Pleasure Pleasure Debauch/ Illusionary Success Swiftness Strength/Great Strength Oppression

TABLE 1—NOMENCLATURE, ASTROLOGY, AND CORRESPONDING MINORS

Suit and Rank	Golden Dawn Hermetic title	Elemental glyph	Elemental title	Zodiacal modality	Zodiacal glyph
King of Swords *Knight of Swords* *(Thoth)*	Lord of the Winds and the Breezes King of the Spirit of Air King of Sylphs and Sylphides	△△	Fire of Air	Mutable	Ⅱ
Queen of Swords	Queen of the Thrones of Air Queen of the Sylphs and Sylphides	▽△	Water of Air	Cardinal	♎
Knight of Swords *Prince of Swords* *(Thoth)*	Prince of the Chariots of the Winds Prince and Emperor of Sylphs and Sylphides	△△	Air of Air	Fixed	♒
Page of Swords *Princess of Swords* *(Thoth)*	Princess of the Rushing Winds Lotus of the Palace of Air Princess and Empress of the Sylphs and Sylphides Throne of the Ace of Swords	▽△	Earth of Air		♑♒♓

TABLE 1—NOMENCLATURE, ASTROLOGY, AND CORRESPONDING MINORS

Suit and Rank	Zodiac	Corresponding Majors	Dates	Corresponding Minors	Corresponding Minors Hermetic Titles
King of Swords *Knight of Swords (Thoth)*	20°–29° Taurus III 0°–19° Gemini I & II	[The Hierophant] The Lovers	May 11–June 10	7 of Disks 8 of Swords 9 of Swords	Failure/Success Unfulfilled Interference/ Shortened Force Cruelty/Despair and Cruelty
Queen of Swords	20°–29° Virgo III 0°–19° Libra I & II	[The Hermit] Justice/Adjust-ment	September 12–October 12	10 of Disks 2 of Swords 3 of Swords	Wealth Peace/Peace Restored Sorrow
Knight of Swords *Prince of Swords (Thoth)*	20°–29° Capricorn III 0°–19° Aquarius I & II	[The Devil] The Star	January 10–February 8	4 of Disks 5 of Swords 6 of Swords	Power/Earthly Power Defeat Science/Earned Success
Page of Swords *Princess of Swords (Thoth)*	0°–29° Capricorn 0°–29° Aquarius 0°–29° Pisces	The Devil The Star The Moon	December 21–March 20	2 of Disks 3 of Disks 4 of Disks 5 of Swords 6 of Swords 7 of Swords 8 of Cups 9 of Cups 10 of Cups	Change/ Harmonious Change Work/Material Works Power/Earthly Power Defeat Science, Earned Success Futility/Unstable Effort Indolence/ Abandoned Success Happiness/Material Happiness Satiety/Perpetual Success

TABLE 1—NOMENCLATURE, ASTROLOGY, AND CORRESPONDING MINORS

Suit and Rank	Golden Dawn Hermetic title	Elemental glyph	Elemental title	Zodiacal modality	Zodiacal glyph
King of Pentacles *Knight of Disks (Thoth)*	Lord of the Wide and Fertile Land King of the Spirits of Earth King of the Gnomes	△▽	Fire of Earth	Mutable	♍
Queen of Pentacles *Queen of Disks (Thoth)*	Queen of the Thrones of Earth Queen of Gnomes	▽▽	Water of Earth	Cardinal	♑
Knight of Pentacles *Prince of Disks (Thoth)*	Prince of the Chariot of Earth Prince and Emperor of the Gnomes	△▽	Air of Earth	Fixed	♉
Page of Pentacles *Princess of Disks (Thoth)*	Princess of the Echoing Hills Rose of the Palace of Earth Princess and Empress of the Gnomes Throne of the Ace of Pentacles	▽▽	Earth of Earth		♈♉♊

TABLE 1—NOMENCLATURE, ASTROLOGY, AND CORRESPONDING MINORS

Suit and Rank	Zodiac	Corresponding Majors	Dates	Corresponding Minors	Corresponding Minors Hermetic Titles
King of Pentacles *Knight of Disks (Thoth)*	20°–29° Leo III 0°–19° Virgo I & II	[Strength/Lust] The Hermit	August 11– September 11	7 of Wands 8 of Disks 9 of Disks	Valor Prudence Gain/Material Gain
Queen of Pentacles *Queen of Disks (Thoth)*	20°–29° Sagittarius III 0°–19° Capricorn I & II	[Temperance/Art] The Devil	December 13– January 9	10 of Wands 2 of Disks 3 of Disks	Oppression Change/Harmonious Change Work/Material Works
Knight of Pentacles *Prince of Disks (Thoth)*	20°–29° Aries III 0°–19° Taurus I & II	[The Emperor] The Hierophant	April 11– May 10	4 of Wands 5 of Disks 6 of Disks	Completion/Perfected Work Worry/Material Trouble Success/Material Success
Page of Pentacles *Princess of Disks (Thoth)*	0°–29° Aries 0°–29° Taurus 0°–29° Gemini	The Emperor The Hierophant The Lovers	March 21– June 20	2 of Wands 3 of Wands 4 of Wands 5 of Disks 6 of Disks 7 of Disks 8 of Swords 9 of Swords 10 of Swords	Dominion Virtue/Established Strength Completion/Perfected Work Worry/Material Trouble Success/Material Success Failure/Success Unfulfilled Interference/Shortened Force Cruelty/Despair and Cruelty Ruin

Notes on Nomenclature, Astrology, and Associated
Minor Arcana Correspondences for the Court Cards

When it comes to court cards, tarot has a big problem with nomenclature. After centuries of Continental decks happily using King, Queen, Knight, and Page/Valet/Knave, disagreement erupted in the English School. In the Golden Dawn's tarot system, Queens remained Queens. Pages became Princesses, only to once again emerge as Pages in the Rider Waite Smith deck.

As for the two male ranks, confusion is rife. As in the European traditions preceding the Golden Dawn, there were one figure on horseback (traditionally the Knight), and one throned or seated figure (traditionally the King). But the Golden Dawn believed the more active, youthful, horsed figure should be the leader of the suit, rather than the more established, seated ruler. Therefore, the King-like figure became the rider, the figure on horseback, and gave him the title of Knight. Even more confusingly, they maintained the title of "King" in the Hermetic designation. So the erstwhile King of Wands became, in the Golden Dawn tradition: "The Knight of Wands—Lord of the Flame and the Lightning; King of the Spirits of Fire." Confused yet?!

As for the former "Knight of Wands" on horseback, he became the seated or throned "Prince of Wands." His confusing Hermetic title? "The Prince of the Chariot of Fire: King of Wands!" (Even more confusingly, in the four color scales devised by the Golden Dawn, the "Prince Scale" is often referred to as the "Emperor Scale.") Accordingly, "Knight" and "Prince" were the terms Aleister Crowley and Lady Frieda Harris would much later use in the Thoth deck, painted between 1938 and 1943.

All of this was laid out in *Book T* (around 1888), some twenty years before the publication of the Rider Waite Smith deck in 1909. When the Rider Waite Smith deck came out, the traditional ranks—King, Queen, Knight, Page—were restored. A seated, older King heads up each suit and a youthful, active Knight rides through on horseback, just as they did in the Continental tarots. But to this day argument persists—is the RWS Knight-on-horseback *really* the Golden Dawn's Prince (corresponding to elemental Air)? Or is he the Golden Dawn's Knight (corresponding to elemental Fire)? You will find compelling arguments on both sides.

For the most part, readers have concluded that the kingly knight on horseback of the Golden Dawn and the Thoth deck corresponds to the seated, throned King of Rider Waite Smith. But if you look at the Knight of Pentacles (corresponding to Prince) in the Rider Waite Smith and the Knight of Disks (corresponding to King) in the Thoth deck, it is hard not to entertain the opposite point of view—that a Knight is a Knight is a Knight.

Finally, it is worth noting that in the Golden Dawn's conception of the courts, they did not represent a static family. The ruling Prince became the active Knight or King; the Princess grows to become the Queen in an endless repeating cycle. Rather than father and son, mother and daughter, it can be helpful (or maybe, just more confusing) to think of the male courts as aspects of each other—roles that they play—and the same goes for the female courts.

Ultimately, the only thing you can do is choose a set of attributions and stick with it as best you can. In practice, I have found that Wands courts tend to generally line up with fire signs (Aries, Leo, Sagittarius), but that any more specific matching (say, King of Wands to Sagittarius) doesn't work out that well.

Regarding the zodiacal attributions, you'll notice that the twelve King, Queen, and Knight cards represent the twelve zodiacal signs—but they are staggered. The Queen of Wands governs the last decan of Pisces and the first two decans of Aries. By overlapping signs, these twelve courts knit together the wheel of the year. The Pages, by contrast, each govern a full season. For a much fuller clarification of how this (and many other confusing court card points) works, Lon Milo Duquette's *Understanding Aleister Crowley's Thoth Tarot* is incomparable, and very accessible; although it concentrates on the Thoth deck, most of the material applies to the Golden Dawn system as a whole.

You may also notice that unlike the tables for the major and the numeric minor arcana, this court card table doesn't include a "Golden Dawn" color scales section. Although there is no specific color correspondence table for the courts, tradition dictates that the colors are loosely thematic by element: all Wands courts look warm and fiery, all Cups courts look cool and watery. For a more specific application of esoteric color theory, consider my colleague M. M. Meleen's Tabula Mundi Colores Arcus deck, which ties *every* card, including courts, to a carefully reasoned esoteric color scheme.

TABLE 2—ASTROLOGICAL CORRESPONDENCES IN CHRONOLOGICAL ORDER

Suit	Zodiac modality	Zodiacal glyph	Zodiac	Dates
Queen of Wands	Cardinal	♈	20°–29° Pisces 0°–19° Aries	March 11– April 10
Knight of Pentacles	Fixed	♉	20°–29° Aries 0°–19° Taurus	April 11– May 10
King of Swords	Mutable	♊	20°–29° Taurus 0°–19° Gemini	May 11– June 10
Queen of Cups	Cardinal	♋	20°–29° Gemini 0°–19° Cancer	June 11– July 12
Knight of Wands	Fixed	♌	20°–29° Cancer 0°–19° Leo	July 13– August 11
King of Pentacles	Mutable	♍	20°–29° Leo 0°–19° Virgo	August 11– September 11
Queen of Swords	Cardinal	♎	20°–29° Virgo 0°–19° Libra	September 12– October 12
Knight of Cups	Fixed	♏	20°–29° Libra 0°–19° Scorpio	October 13– November 11
King of Wands	Mutable	♐	20°–29° Scorpio 0°–19° Sagittarius	November 12– December 12
Queen of Pentacles	Cardinal	♑	20°–29° Sagittarius 0°–19° Capricorn	December 13– January 9
Knight of Swords	Fixed	♒	20°–29° Capricorn 0°–19° Aquarius	January 10– February 8
King of Cups	Mutable	♓	20°–29° Aquarius 0°–19° Pisces	February 9– March 10

TABLE 2—ASTROLOGICAL CORRESPONDENCES IN CHRONOLOGICAL ORDER

Suit	Season	Zodiacal glyph	Zodiac	Dates
Page of Pentacles	Spring (Northern hemisphere) Fall (Southern hemisphere)	♈♉♊	0°–29° Aries 0°–29° Taurus 0°–29° Gemini	March 21– June 20
Page of Wands	Summer (Northern hemisphere) Winter (Southern hemisphere)	♋♌♍	0°–29° Cancer 0°–29° Leo 0°–29° Virgo	June 21– September 22
Page of Cups	Fall (Northern hemisphere) Spring (Southern hemisphere)	♎♏♐	0°–29° Libra 0°–29° Scorpio 0°–29° Sagittarius	September 23– December 20
Page of Swords	Winter (Northern hemisphere) Summer (Southern hemisphere)	♑♒♓	0°–29° Capricorn 0°–29° Aquarius 0°–29° Pisces	December 21– March 20

Notes on Chronological Astrology Correspondences for the Court Cards

The Golden Dawn followed ancient Egyptian cultural practice in starting the new year at 0° Leo rather than 0° Aries. That gave a special significance to both the Knight of Wands and the 5 of Wands. But 0° Aries, the "Aries point," remains the common referent for the start of spring in most modern esoteric traditions.

The chronological correspondences for court cards are actually only half the story—the Golden Dawn also assigned each court card dominion over a particular section of the Earth. It's beyond the scope of this reference, but you can find out more by search for "Tree of Life Projected as a Solid Sphere."

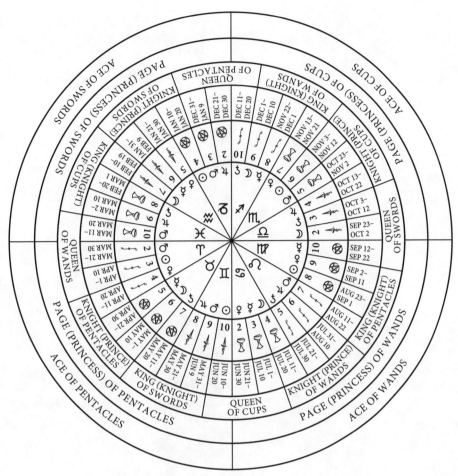

6. Round diagram of decans and minor arcana.

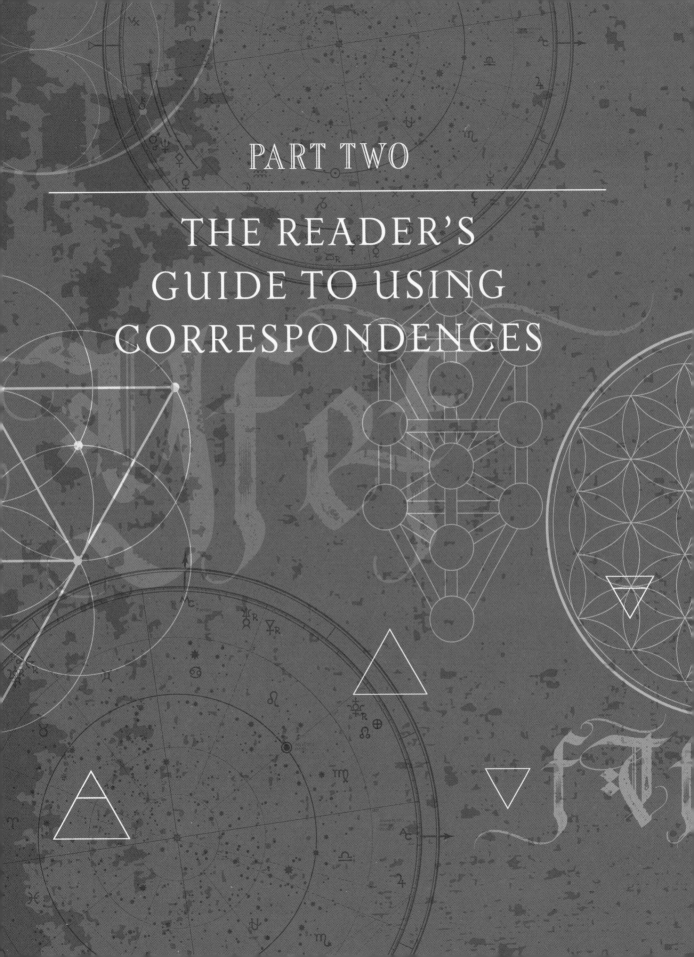

PART TWO

THE READER'S GUIDE TO USING CORRESPONDENCES

ONE

USING ELEMENTAL CORRESPONDENCES

Head in the Clouds,
Mud on Your Boots!

The concept of a universe rooted in four (or five) elements stretches back into antiquity in both Eastern and Western traditions. Starting with Empedocles in 450 BCE, the elemental quartet (often accompanied by a special fifth, Aether or Spirit) has marched down to us essentially un-changed. It was Aristotle who assigned them the qualities of dry, hot, wet, and cold. Hippocrates correlated them to the four temperaments of ancient medicine: choleric, sanguine, phlegmatic, melancholic.

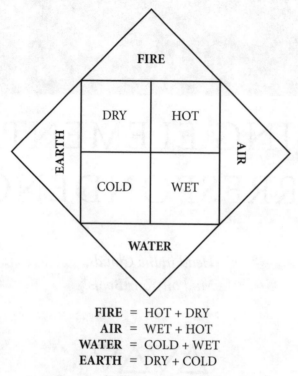

FIRE = HOT + DRY
AIR = WET + HOT
WATER = COLD + WET
EARTH = DRY + COLD

7. Four Qualities, Four Elements diagram.

By the time European occult enthusiasts had their turn with the elements in the eighteenth and nineteenth centuries, they were ready to link them to every other set of four they could think of: the seasons, the directions, the divine names of God, and, of course, the four suits of the tarot.

You won't be surprised to learn that there was and is plenty of debate about which suit went with which element (especially when it comes to fire and air), but here's what a majority agree on:

△ **Fire = Hot + Dry = Wands**
▽ **Water = Cold + Wet = Cups**
△ **Air = Hot + Wet = Swords**
▽ **Earth = Cold + Dry = Pentacles**

You'll notice I'm presenting the four elements in a consistent order: Fire, Water, Air, and Earth. That's because the Kabbalistic theory of the Four Worlds underlies much of the framework of the Western magical tradition. In that theory, which is a theory of creation, the four elements emerge in that order. You also see it in the astrological calendar, where the four cardinal signs emerge in this order over the course of the year (Aries/Fire, Cancer/Water, Libra/Air, Capricorn/Earth).

ELEMENTAL SYMBOLS—
OR, ALL ABOUT THOSE TRIANGLES

If you have trouble remembering which is which, just remember that it's all about gravity. Earth and Water point downward, because they're loyal subjects of gravity. Fire and Air point upward because they're always trying to escape it. That line across the middle in Air and Earth? It's like the ground, the line where air and earth always meet but never cross. Also, the line in Air makes it look like an A, as in Air.

If the gravity analogy doesn't work for you, how about polarity? Fire and Air point up, toward the North Pole; Earth and Water point down, toward the South Pole.

TRADITIONAL ELEMENTAL DIGNITY:
FROM "STRONG" TO "WEAK"

The Golden Dawn's method works on the principle of allies and enemies, along lines that stretch back deep into time.

"SAME" ALLIES, OR "ALL IN THE FAMILY"

When cards of the same suit flock together, they reinforce each other. Wands strengthen other wands; cups strengthen other cups. A pair of same-element cards is a strong combination, and three-of-a-kind is even more powerful. The combined effect of cards in the same suit is considered more powerful than the effect two cards of "friendly" but different suits have:

"FRIENDLY" ALLIES (ALSO KNOWN AS SHARED POLARITY)

Fire + Air

Remember when we talked about gravity? Notice how we've got two triangles both pointing *up and away*. Traditionally, Air and Fire are considered *active* because they fight the pull of gravity (I guess). They're also considered *masculine,* which makes me roll my eyes but that's esoterics for you—whenever there's two of anything, one is going to be the girl and one is going to the boy. Vive la différence.

Fire's Hot and Dry according to our little table, and Air is Hot and Wet. So Fire and Air enjoy each other's company in their Mutual Hotness Admiration Society. Air feeds Fire. Fire gives Air a lift.

Water + Earth

Now the triangles are pointing *down*, in their heavy, "*passive*," "receptive," "feminine"[1] way. Water (Cold and Wet) and Earth (Cold and Dry) are Sisters of Chill. Cold sinks, heat rises, right? Earth holds Water. Water makes earth moldable.

We can think of it in a more lyrical way, if we personify the elements.

Fire hungers, Air feeds it.
Air wants to disperse, Fire expands it.
Water wants to join together, Earth holds it.
Earth thirsts, Water quenches it.

Neutral or Complementary, Elements

Although the Golden Dawn's MacGregor Mathers considered the Fire-Earth and Air-Water relationships just as 'friendly' as the shared-polarity relationship above, later acolytes considered them neutral, or at best complementary—slightly supportive without having a strong effect, and today's users of elemental dignity do too.[2]

How do we remember which elements are complementary? Well, just as the strong allies above share a relationship with gravity (or temperature) the complements share a relationship with moisture.

Earth + Fire

Water and Air are both Wet, according to our chart. You can imagine them combining, like bubbles in a glass of water until they return to their own places.

Earth and Fire are both Dry. Think of fire in a kiln or sun-baked flats—they interact but remain essentially unchanged by one another.

....

1   Before I use up my entire scare-quote quota, let's recall that all correspondences dwell in the realm of metaphor. Although there is certainly a history of sexist stereotyping and even misogyny in the terms, they are evolving as we speak. The qualities they describe can be as value-neutral as we care to make them.

2   I find this in Mary Greer and Anthony Louis, but I have yet to find the original Golden Dawn source text.

In metaphorical terms, Wet elements can be shaped and influenced; Dry elements have self-determination and boundaries.

CONTRARY ELEMENTS

It's not hard to remember that water and fire are enemies. What happens if you pour water over a match? What happens to a puddle in the hot sun? Each can destroy the other, and whichever one has the advantage in terms of sheer amount will win.

Now are air and earth really enemies? The air simply passes over the earth, right? Forever touching, they never join. But just as with water and fire, each can be used to eliminate the other. Imagine a hole in the ground. What's it full of? Air. How can you remove the air? Fire will just burn itself out, and the ground will simply absorb water. The only thing that will fill that hole of air is earth. And what's the first tool you reach for to banish dirt from your home? It's probably a vacuum cleaner—your very own household air elemental-for-hire, and the ancient enemy of dirt.

Symbol Combination	Element names	Relationship	Qualities they share
△ △	Fire / Fire	Strong	Hot + Dry
▽ ▽	Water / Water	Strong	Cold + Wet
△ △	Air / Air	Strong	Hot + Wet
▽ ▽	Earth / Earth	Strong	Cold + Dry
△ ▽	Fire / Air	Friendly	Hot
▽ ▽	Water/Earth	Friendly	Cold
△ ▽	Fire / Earth	Neutral	Dry
△ ▽	Air / Water	Neutral	Wet
△ ▽	Fire / Water	Contrary	None
△ ▽	Air / Earth	Contrary	None

8. 2 of Pentacles "▽ Earth", 2 of Swords "△ Air" (Pictorial Key Tarot).

EXERCISE: READING IN PAIRS

STEP 1: INTERPRET THE ELEMENTS

We know Earth and Air are unfriendly to each other. Cold, dry earth governs the realm of things. Hot, wet air lives in the world of thoughts.

STEP 2: INTERPRET THE CARDS

The 2 of Pentacles wants to create tangible change, coins jangling in his pocket! But the 2 of Swords is at the beginning of a mental journey. She wants to assess, consider, and weigh her options. They're at an impasse.

Now you try.

9. 8 of Cups "▽ Water", 7 of Wands "△ Fire" (Pictorial Key Tarot).

Step 1: Interpret the Elements
How will cold, wet water relate to hot, dry wands?

How will emotions interact with the will?

Step 2: Interpret the cards
Challenges surface in both cards. How does the 7 of Wands react to adversity? What about the 8 of Cups?

Reading in Triads
*"A card is strong or weak, well-dignified or ill-dignified, according to the cards which are next to it on either side. Cards of **opposite natures** [my emphasis], on either side, strengthen it greatly either for good or evil, according to their nature. Cards of the suits answer to its contrary element, on either side, weaken it greatly for good or evil."*—Book T.

The Golden Dawn used elemental dignity as a way of selecting which cards took priority in their multi-card spreads. You can find many, many resources both online and in print for learning how to read this basic unit of interpretation-by-dignity. They don't all agree on the specifics, but practically everyone puts the emphasis on the central card, and how its meaning is affected by the others. So there are two parts to reading the spread: first, determine how strongly the central card is affected—its dignity. Second, interpret it "according to its nature" and that of the surrounding cards—a strongly affected, "well-dignified" 10 of Swords might be very evil indeed!

The conventional way to read elemental dignities for three cards is to read the outer two as a pair, and then proceed to the central card. That's easy when the outer two are the same—it's not so different from reading pairs.

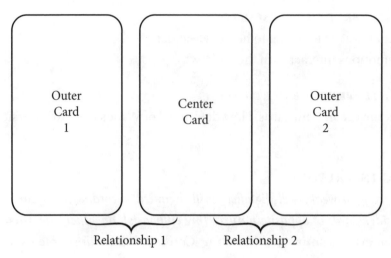

10. Outer Card-Center Card-Outer Card diagram.

There are only four possible types of relationship a central card can have with its neighbors when the neighbors are the same:

Relationship 1	Center card is	Relationship 2	Example:
SAME	strong	SAME	Air-Air-Air
FRIENDLY	strong	FRIENDLY	Fire-Air-Fire
NEUTRAL	moderate	NEUTRAL	Water-Air-Water
CONTRARY	weak	CONTRARY	Earth-Air-Earth

11. 3 of Cups, 5 of Pentacles, 4 of Cups (Mystical Tarot).

STEP 1: DETERMINE THE RELATIONSHIPS

Here we have two outer cards corresponding with Water and a central card corresponding with Earth. Water, we know, is friendly with Earth. So this should be a strong relationship and well dignified.

STEP 2: INTERPRET "ACCORDING TO THEIR NATURE"

The two cups cards are looking pretty benign, and we've determined they have a strong effect on the central card, whose nature is not so fortunate. So we might conclude that despite some very trying times and a sense of isolation or even poverty, the querent will come to feel less alone; indeed to feel that he/she truly has "enough." Help is on the way, as long as s/he has eyes to see it!

But what about when the two outer cards are not the same? Here's where things get tricky, like a room full of strong-willed leaders debating not only who will win the argument, but what the argument is even about.

Let's have a look at the different ways the card relationships could work out.

Relationship 1	Center card is	Relationship 2	Example:	Relationship between outer cards is:
SAME	strong	FRIENDLY	Water-Water-Water	FRIENDLY
SAME	strong	NEUTRAL	Water-Water-Air	NEUTRAL
NEUTRAL	weak	CONTRARY	Air-Water-Fire	FRIENDLY
FRIENDLY	moderate	CONTRARY	Earth-Water-Fire	NEUTRAL
FRIENDLY	moderate	NEUTRAL	Earth-Water-Air	CONTRARY

Since we're talking about all kinds of relationships, let's do an example with actual people in it and see what happens. We'll use the outer cards to represent the people, and the central card to represent the relationship between them.

12. Queen of Pentacles, 8 of Cups, King of Swords (Pictorial Key Tarot).

STEP 1. DETERMINE THE RELATIONSHIPS

The central card is Water. That means on the left we've got Earth + Water, a **friendly** combination. On the right we've got Water + Air, a **neutral** combination. And do the two outer cards relate to each other? Earth and Air are **contrary** elements which get along so poorly they cancel each other out.

STEP 2. INTERPRET "ACCORDING TO THEIR NATURE"

The earthy, hands-on, gentle Queen of Disks and the über-analytical, I-love-the-sound-of-my-own-voice King of Swords may be attempting a relationship, but it's not going anywhere. Their contrary natures allow the watery central card to take priority, and the 8 of Cups has boots made for walking. Maybe the Queen will leave first, maybe the King; maybe they'll both abscond simultaneously. One thing's for sure—no one's sticking around.

NATURAL ELEMENT BLENDING:
STEP OUTSIDE AND LOOK AROUND

Traditional elemental dignity has a certain appeal: it's a tested system with clear rules, and there are many texts and sites where you can explore it. Ultimately, however, it's only some ideas someone came up with 125 years ago or so. Sometimes it can feel limiting to resort to such an old-school approach with its cut-and-dried casting of friends and enemies.

The truth is that we witness the elements blending naturally all around us every day. Mist rises off the damp ground in the morning, as Earth and Water give way to Water and Air. Just this morning I used bellows on the coals in my wood stove, bringing Air to the aid of Fire. Even those ancient "enemies," Water and Fire, combine in the steam from your teakettle, or in oceanic hot springs. Earth and Air reach for each other in desert winds and on clifftops.

We can use these natural phenomena in imaginative ways for our own readings, to suggest qualities which might not otherwise come to mind.

13. 5 of Wands, 4 of Pentacles (Pictorial Key Tarot).

Fire + Earth = VOLCANO

What is a volcano? It's an earthen phenomenon, a projection of the earth's crust. Within or beneath it, fire works on its brethren, turning rock to magma, water to vapor, heating air. When the pressure builds sufficiently, it overcomes the holding structure of the crust and erupts.

Here we can see the earthen forces of containment in the 4 of Pentacles and the forces of pressure and expansion in the 5 of Wands. How long can the two remain in balance before they explode? How long can the king hoard his coin before the rebellious peasantry revolts? How long can we control our behavior before our true feelings erupt?

Will all combinations of Fire and Earth result in a volcano? I suppose it's a question of how far you want to go with your interpretive imagination. Let's try another pair.

14. 8 of Wands and 2 of Pentacles (Steampunk Tarot).

The 8 of Wands has qualities of speed or swiftness. The 2 of Pentacles has qualities of infinite change. How might these two combine into something like volcanic energy? In what ways do a volcano represent speed and change?

Have changes in your life ever come about with astonishing quickness? What did it feel like? Was it catastrophic? Did it make way for lush new growth, the way volcanic ash fertilizes the surrounding terrain?

Earth and Fire can combine in many other ways: pottery kilns, glassware, forest fires, matches. Choose any you like and search out their qualities in the cards. Together, they form powerful metaphors for element-based reading.

	Fire	Water	Air	Earth
Fire	stars lava	underwater vents, radiators	oxygen-fueled burners, stovetops	volcanoes coals and embers forest and brush fires
Water	baths, steam hot springs	currents tides rain on puddles, lakes, bodies of water	clouds bubbles mist and fog high humidity	tidal pools wetlands and marshes seashores riverbanks
Air	desert winds hair dryers lightning	hurricanes blizzards whirlpools fountains	breezes cyclones trade winds	atmosphere tornadoes and dust devils
Earth	wood stoves kilns radiant floors	marshes gardens	cliffs and treetops caves and tunnels occlusions	strata fossils ores and minerals

15. 7 of Cups, 4 of Swords (Pictorial Key Tarot).

Here's one more example to try: How might the emotions of Water and the intellect of Air combine in a "cloudy" way? What might the visionary 7 of Cups and the at-ease 4 of Swords dream up together?

4 DIRECTIONS, 4 SEASONS, 4 STAGES OF GROWTH

One of the greater controversies when we play matchy-match with the number four is which cardinal direction each suit corresponds to, and which season. Ask twenty-four different tarot readers and you'll get twenty-four different answers (although if you ask two million tarot readers, you'll still only get twenty-four different answers because there are only twenty-four possible ways of assigning the suits). The tables in part one show some of the most common variants. It's no surprise that there's so little agreement regarding directional correspondences. How can we agree that Wands = Fire = South = Hot/Dry = Summer when half the world, the Southern Hemisphere, experiences winter as its warmest season?

Nevertheless, once you've settled on your choice of correspondences, you can use them to inform your readings in interesting ways. For example, using this fairly common Northern Hemisphere set of attributions, we might say:

Fire = Wands = Summer = South = a time to explore outdoors, take risks, seek out adventure
Water = Cups = Autumn = West = a time to harvest one's efforts, seek closure and completion
Earth = Pentacles = Winter = North = a time to hibernate, pursue indoor activities, rest
Air = Swords = Spring = East = a time to emerge, make new plans, start fresh.

A reading with a great many Pentacles would suggest it is time to look within, take stock, and inventory your assets.

Because there are so many controversies in assigning the four cardinal directions, I've personally started thinking about the elemental sequence as something that reflects the natural cycle of vegetative growth on our planet, no matter where you live.

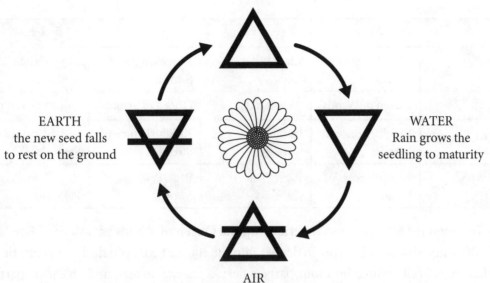

FIRE
The sun warms a seed,
awakens it to a sprout

WATER
Rain grows the
seedling to maturity

EARTH
the new seed falls
to rest on the ground

AIR
brings bees and birds to pollinate;
disseminates the next generation of seed

16. Natural element cycle graphic.

It may be just my view, but it's certainly helped me understand the suit of Wands as a realm of ambition, new ideas, and the will to live. The suit of Cups is the emotional nourishment we need to thrive, the suit of Swords is the ability to break down and re-mobilize our resources, and the suit of Pentacles represents long-term investments in our legacy—whether that's a child, a brainchild, or a portfolio of assets.

ELEMENTS & THE COURTS

Here's a grid that will probably be looking rather familiar by now.

	△ FIRE	▽ WATER	△ AIR	▽ EARTH
FIRE △	King/Knight of Wands	King/Knight of Cups	King/Knight of Swords	King/Knight of Pentacles
WATER ▽	Queen of Wands	Queen of Cups	Queen of Swords	Queen of Pentacles
AIR △	Knight/Prince of Wands	Knight/Prince of Cups	Knight/Prince of Swords	Knight/Prince of Pentacles
EARTH ▽	Page/Princess of Wands	Page/Princess of Cups	Page/Princess of Swords	Page/Princess of Pentacles

It's common for esotericists to describe, say, the Queen of Wands as "Water of Fire," but in a sense that's just shorthand. If you go deeper into the source texts, you find an assumption that each element is itself divided into four parts: a fiery, a watery, an airy, and an earthy part. That means Her Flaming Majesty is properly known as "the Watery part of Fire" … but what does that even *mean*? How can fire have a watery part of anything?

Stepping back from literal thinking for a moment, let's talk conceptually. First, let's make it easy for ourselves:

Fire = CREATIVITY
Water = EMOTIONS
Air = INTELLECT
Earth = MATERIAL MATTERS

What if we simply plug in these conceptual keywords where the elements go?

Queen of Wands: the Watery part of Fire = the EMOTIONAL side of CREATIVITY.

Fine, but what does the "emotional side of creativity" mean? If you're a creative person, chances are you've experienced this. Ever written a poem because you were in love? Composed a song? Drawn a portrait or cherished a photo because of how you felt? So has the Queen of Wands. She's also been a courtesan, a literary agent, and a salon hostess. Feelings about people ignite her creative fire, and heaven help you if you piss her off.

17. Queen of Wands (Steampunk Tarot).

Knight of Pentacles: Air of Earth = the INTELLECTUAL SIDE of MATERIAL MATTERS.

Here we have someone who *thinks* about *things*—not feelings but real things.

What does he do for a living? Where can he apply his awesome skills of professional worrying, disaster prevention, and smart design?

What does he do to relax (if he ever relaxes)? Where can he go to contemplate *things*?

Which of his personality traits drive his partner up a wall?

18. Knight of Pentacles (Pictorial Key Tarot).

BLENDING THE ELEMENTS OF THE COURT

Above, we covered the way natural elements might combine in the world we know—clouds, volcanoes, sandstorms. We used literal imagery to think figuratively, and we can do the same thing with court cards using the court correspondences.

Each elemental family may have four distinct parts: fiery, watery, and so on; nevertheless their suit identity is their core identity. The importance of the suit outweighs the importance of the rank (which is something you can say at your next family reunion if you really want to baffle people). Mother, uncle, sister, grandson—doesn't matter, they're all family first and foremost.

So the Page of Cups, Earth of Water, is not half-Earth and half-Water. She's mostly Water, like the rest of her family, but with a bit of the cool, dry earthiness (self-determination, or pragmatism, if you want to interpret that) all pages/princesses share. If we want to construct a metaphorical world for her abode, we might expect it to be primarily watery with a bit of earth mixed in. We might expect the Knight of Pentacles to enjoy caves—great masses of rock with a little bit of air inside—and the Queen of Swords to live high up in the clouds (air, with a bit of water mixed in).

As an imaginative exercise, what better way to get to know the Page of Cups, the Princess of Water, the Lotus of the Palace of the Floods, than to visit her where she lives?

19. Page of Cups (Animal Totem Tarot).

You're standing on a strand where the sand meets the sea; the moist ground is shifting beneath your bare feet. The air is still but you can smell salt. Gulls congregate, fish multiply, the very air is teeming with life. What do you like about being here? What makes you uncomfortable? Who lives here? The presiding spirit of this place comes to greet you. What's she like? Quiet or commanding? Why does she love it here? What message would she want you to take away? I don't know about you, but when she talks to me she's soft-spoken and dreamy, and I have to strain to hear.

Where does Air of Fire, the Knight or Prince of Wands, live? I don't know for sure, but chances are it's hot, dry, and breezy. Do you have to look hard to find him, or does he seek you out? Once you've met him, is he shy or outgoing? Sunny or cool? His moods are infectious—how does he leave you feeling?

20. Knight of Wands (Pictorial Key Tarot).

A final note about Court and Element correspondences

I should mention that there is ALL KINDS of confusion surrounding the male courts of the Golden Dawn tradition. You probably already know that Waite's men are Kings and Knights, while Crowley's are Knights and Princes. There is a lot of debate as to whether Crowley's Knight is a Waite King or a Waite Knight. Same goes for the Prince.

Now Crowley was quite clear about his elemental assignations. Knights are Fire, Princes are Air. But as far as the Waite Kings and Knights go, there is a good argument for the King equating to Fire and an equally good one for him equating to Air. I've long considered the Waite King to correspond with Fire and the Thoth Knight. The majority of tarot authors concur. But I'm increasingly seeing very good arguments for corresponding the Waite King with Air and the Thoth Prince.

In the end, it comes down to the same advice that holds true for all correspondence work. Pick your set of correspondences, have a reason for your choice, and stick with it. Even if you make up your own set of correspondences, it's the personal investment you put into it that makes it happen.

BALANCE VS. FOCUS

"What does it mean if I have a lot of one element? Does that mean I'm out of balance? Or does it mean that I'm just focused?"

"What about if all four elements turned up? Does that mean I'm well-rounded, or scattered?"

"What if one element is missing? Is that like a vitamin deficiency? If there's no cups in my reading, am I emotionless?"

Most readers have mulled over questions like these at one point or another. It's easy to find texts that will suggest what it means if you have mostly Wands, or no Pentacles. And there's a tradition stretching back into cartomantic history as to what three queens might signify, or four. A lot of these interpretations are rooted in a literal, one-to-one relationship of meanings; if you have no pentacles, you have no work. ("Thanks a lot!" says your client.) I agree with Anthony Louis, who suggests steering clear of using suits/elements to determine the subject of a reading. Not having any Cups doesn't mean you have no emotions, but it might mean you're looking at that the subject in question in a non-emotional way.

Traditional elemental dignities give us a way of looking at tarot suits in a way that makes a missing element easier to interpret. A hard sword like the 9 of Swords (Air) is a lot more potent without the grounding, contrary influence of Earth in the form of a Pentacle. Having a bit of every suit in your reading simply means that none has undue influence over the situation; it's like a neutral pH.

Natural element blending can give us similar clues. A reading dominated by Cups and Pentacles, Earth and Water, might tell us conditions are favorable for growth, like a fertile plot of land.

POSTSCRIPT: WHERE ARE THE MAJOR ARCANA?!

I've deliberately written this chapter without using the major arcana. Why? Simply because the major correspondences aren't quite as clear cut. Some think the Fool is Air, others think he's Uranus. Most everybody thinks the Wheel of Fortune corresponds to Jupiter, but is Jupiter Air or Fire? (Never mind the Continental system of correspondences presented in Major Arcana Table 4, which uses completely different planetary attributions.)

21. Ace of Swords, Emperor, 7 of Cups (Mystical Tarot).

So in parting, here's a nice spread of three using the Emperor (whom practically everyone ascribes to Aries, and therefore Fire) to play with. It's looking like Mr. Decider is poised between conclusive action (Ace of Swords/Air) and dreaming about his many options some more (7 of Cups/Water). Using traditional elemental dignity or natural element blending, which do you think will prevail?

TWO

USING ASTROLOGICAL CORRESPONDENCES

*"The sign of life eternal
is writ on earth and sky."*
—John of Damascus

Astrology is a complex and technical field, much more so than you'd expect from merely looking up your sun sign in the newspaper. By simply mastering the basic vocabulary of elements, planets, and signs, you can add a rich layer of meaning to your card interpretations.

THE ELEMENTAL-ZODIACAL CONNECTION

If elemental correspondences are the most common correspondences used in tarot, then astrological correspondences are next in line. That makes sense, right? Fire, Water, Air, and Earth are central to the way we view the world around us, but they are also woven through our view of the heavens. In astrology, as you probably know, each element governs three zodiacal signs. As above, so below.

This allows you to apply elemental dignities to the major arcana as we learned to do in the previous chapter.

The Emperor	♈	△ Fire	Aries
Strength	♌	△ Fire	Leo
Temperance	♐	△ Fire	Sagittarius
The Chariot	♋	▽ Water	Cancer
Death	♏	▽ Water	Scorpio
The Moon	♓	▽ Water	Pisces
Justice	♎	△ Air	Libra
The Star	♒	△ Air	Aquarius
The Lovers	♊	△ Air	Gemini
The Devil	♑	▽ Earth	Capricorn
The Hierophant	♉	▽ Earth	Taurus
The Hermit	♍	▽ Earth	Virgo

But that's just twelve of the twenty-two majors. How does astrology apply to the remaining 10 majors?

Starting with the French occultist Etteilla (Jean-Baptiste Alliette) in the eighteenth century, one generation after another would take their turn at assigning astrological correspondences to the major arcana of the tarot. But it wasn't until the Golden Dawn had a go at it in the early twentieth century that *every single card*—all the court cards, all the aces through tens as well as the majors—received a separate astrological attribution. And each type of card gets its own *type* of correspondence, so:

Major Arcana: ELEMENT **or** PLANET **or** SIGN (e.g., Fool = Air, Empress = Venus, Death = Scorpio)

Aces: ELEMENT (for example, Ace of Wands = Fire)

2 through 10 Minors: PLANET *in* SIGN (for example, 6 of Swords = Mercury in Aquarius)

Court Cards: SIGN (for example, Queen of Pentacles = Capricorn).

Let's have a quick look at how each of these attributions works, and then we'll move on to applying them in actual interpretation.

ASTROLOGY AND THE
MAJOR ARCANA: HOW IT WORKS

Consider this:

 4 elements ($\triangle \triangledown \triangle \triangledown$)
 7 classical planets ($\odot$ ☽ ☿ ♀ ♂ ♃ ♄)
 12 signs (♈ ♉ ♊ ♋ ♌ ♍ ♎ ♏ ♐ ♑ ♒ ♓)

 _____

 23

4 + 7 + 12 = 23, which is really close to 22 … and what do we have twenty-two of? That's right, major arcana *and* Hebrew letters, but we'll get to that in chapter 4). So if you're an occultist and you want to line up the 23 astrological components with your twenty-two major arcana, you need to lose one. What do you do? You can't drop any of the twelve signs. You can't drop any of the seven classical planets. (Traditional astrology developed before the discovery of Uranus, Neptune, and Pluto, so many tarot systems don't include them. There are systems that do, though, and for users of modern astrology I include those associations too.) That's nineteen signs and planets which are non-negotiable.

But the elements: Fire, Water, Air, … *Earth*—why do we need Earth? Earth is everywhere. Earth is matter, the physical world we know. We are made of earth. We can assume earth is always present, so let's set it aside.

We get:

 3 elements ($\triangle \triangledown \triangle$)
 7 planets ($\odot$ ☽ ☿ ♀ ♂ ♃ ♄)
 12 signs (♈ ♉ ♊ ♋ ♌ ♍ ♎ ♏ ♐ ♑ ♒ ♓)

 _____

 22

There's more than one way to assign the astrological components to the majors. The two most commonly used styles are the English and Continental or French schools. I've included attributions for both in the tables at the front of the book, but for the purposes of this discussion we'll stick with English school/Golden Dawn correspondences.

Conventional card title	Glyph	Type	Planet, sign, or element
The Fool	△	element	Air [Uranus*]
The Magician	☿	planet	Mercury
The High Priestess	☽	planet	Moon
The Empress	♀	planet	Venus
The Emperor	♈	sign	Aries
The Hierophant	♉	sign	Taurus
The Lovers	♊	sign	Gemini
The Chariot	♋	sign	Cancer
Strength	♌	sign	Leo
The Hermit	♍	sign	Virgo
The Wheel of Fortune	♃	planet	Jupiter
Justice	♎	sign	Libra
The Hanged Man	▽	element	Water [Neptune*]
Death	♏	sign	Scorpio
Temperance	♐	sign	Sagittarius
The Devil	♑	sign	Capricorn
The Tower	♂	planet	Mars
The Star	♒	sign	Aquarius
The Moon	♓	sign	Pisces
The Sun	☉	planet	Sun
Judgement	△	element	Fire [Pluto*]
The World	♄	planet	Saturn

[*Modern astrological correspondences using the three outer planets: Uranus, Neptune, and Pluto. The Golden Dawn system uses only the seven classical planets.]

ASTROLOGY AND THE MINORS:
HOW IT WORKS (OR, WHAT IS THIS WORD
"DECAN" YOU KEEP SAYING?)

In astrology, the major arcana are associated with elements, signs, and planets. But if we want to talk about the minor arcana, we're going to need to know about decans. You probably already know that the zodiac is a band of constellations forming a great circle in the sky above us—a 360° circle. We divide the sky into twelve sections of 30° each, and each of those sections is a zodiacal signs: Aries, Taurus, Gemini, and so on. So far so good.

But we can further subdivide each sign into three sections of 10° each. Each of these subsections is a decan, so there are thirty-six decans in total. We have sixteen court cards and forty numeric (Ace through 10) minors. So how is this going to work?

36 decans ÷ 16 court cards = 2.25 decans per card. What? But,

36 decans ÷ 12 court cards = 3 decans per card, four left over.

      So three decans are assigned to each court card—except the four pages.

36 decans ÷ 40 numeric minors = .75 decans per card. Ugh! But,

36 decans ÷ 36 numeric minors = 1 decan per card, with four left over.

      So one decan is assigned to each numeric minor—except the four aces.

As you already know, each zodiacal sign has a different character. A Taurus is not a Virgo is not a Gemini. But would you believe that since the earliest studies of the heavens, astrologers have believed each decan also has a different character? Each has its own presiding spirit, as you'll see in the decan images presented in Minor Arcana Table 1. Each decan is ruled by a different classical planet. So the first decan of Taurus is a bit different from the second decan, and the second is different from the third. And when we talk about the 5, 6, and 7 of Pentacles, those subtle shades of Taurus will start to become clear.

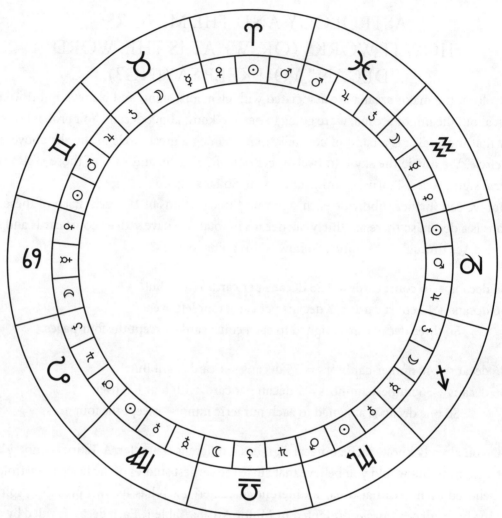

22. Diagram of decans and zodiacal signs.

ASTROLOGY AND THE COURT CARDS: HOW IT WORKS

Now, let's talk about court cards. Each court card—knight, queen, and king—is associated with three decans. If you're wondering about the Pages, don't worry … we'll talk about Pages later.

Now you'd think it's great that one sign equals three decans, so obviously each Knight, Queen, and King lines up with one sign and its three decans. Right? Wrong! In their wisdom, the Golden Dawn decided each court card covers the *last* decan of one sign and the *first two* decans of the next. So the Queen of Wands isn't just Aries. She's Aries with a bit of Pisces mixed in. And the Knight of Cups is Scorpio with a bit of Libra mixed in. They're complex, like people, and together they weave the zodiac as one.

Suit	Zodiacal modality	Zodiacal glyph	Zodiac	Dates
Queen of Wands	Cardinal	♈	20°–29° Pisces 0°–19° Aries	March 11– April 10
Knight of Pentacles	Fixed	♉	20°–29° Aries 0°–19° Taurus	April 11– May 10
King of Swords	Mutable	♊	20°–29° Taurus 0°–19° Gemini	May 11– June 10
Queen of Cups	Cardinal	♋	20°–29° Gemini 0°–19° Cancer	June 11– July 12
Knight of Wands	Fixed	♌	20°–29° Cancer 0°–19° Leo	July 13– August 11
King of Pentacles	Mutable	♍	20°–29° Leo 0°–19° Virgo	August 11– September 11
Queen of Swords	Cardinal	♎	20°–29° Virgo 0°–19° Libra	September 12 – October 12
Knight of Cups	Fixed	♏	20°–29° Libra 0°–19° Scorpio	October 13– November 11
King of Wands	Mutable	♐	20°–29° Scorpio 0°–19° Sagittarius	November 12– December 12
Queen of Pentacles	Cardinal	♑	20°–29° Sagittarius 0°–19° Capricorn	December 13– January 9
Knight of Swords	Fixed	♒	20°–29° Capricorn 0°–19° Aquarius	January 10– February 8
King of Cups	Mutable	♓	20°–29° Aquarius 0°–19° Pisces	February 9– March 10

Notice the patterns: All Queens are cardinal, all Kings are mutable, all Knights are fixed. It's as if the conception energy of the Queen combines with the closure energy of the King to produce a steady, propulsive energy, the Knight.

In a moment, we'll see how these correspond with the decanate minors, numbers 2 through 10. But in the meantime, you're probably wondering: "What have you done with the Pages?" or "What have you done with the Princesses?" if you're a Thoth user. Funny you should ask.

In the Golden Dawn way of looking at things, Pages (and Princesses) aren't just the youngest of the courts. They're special. They anchor the rest of the family and represent its renewal and its strength. They are the receptacles of the power of the King, Queen, and Knight. Whereas the King, Queen, and Knight govern segments of *time*, the Pages or Princesses are said to govern quadrants of space—the four quarters of the celestial zodiac surrounding the earth.

Page of Pentacles	♈♉♊	0°–29° Aries 0°–29° Taurus 0°–29° Gemini	March 21–June 20 [spring]
Page of Wands	♋♌♍	0°–29° Cancer 0°–29° Leo 0°–29° Virgo	June 21–September 22 [summer]
Page of Cups	♎♏♐	0°–29° Libra 0°–29° Scorpio 0°–29° Sagittarius	September 23–December 20 [fall]
Page of Swords	♑♒♓	0°–29° Capricorn 0°–29° Aquarius 0°–29° Pisces	December 21–March 20 [winter]

Even though the Golden Dawn spoke of the Pages as spatial concepts, I still can't help thinking of them as temporal *seasons.* If you look at the zodiacal signs associated with each page or princess, you'll see what I mean.

In the following chart you can see the way the courts and minors align with each other. (If you're anything like me, you'll want to put a sticky note on this chart for future reference.)

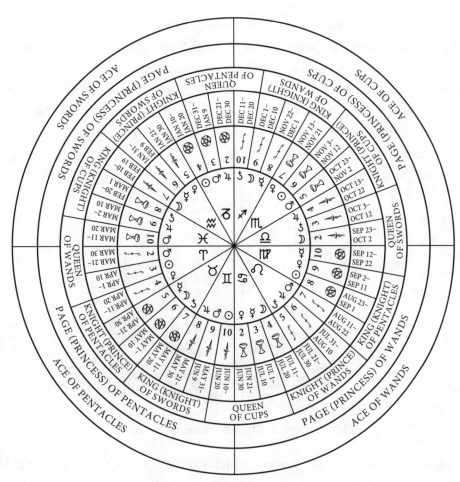

23. Round diagram of decans and minor arcana.

ASTROLOGY AND THE
DECANIC MINORS: HOW IT WORKS

You may be wondering, "What's a decanic minor?" It's a minor card of any number from 2 to 10; i.e., a minor card that is assigned to one of the 36 decans. In the chart on the next page, you'll see the minor cards arranged in sets of three, in chronological order starting from Aries, the beginning of the astrological year. That means that the suits are interwoven: Just as the fire sign of Aries leads to the earth sign of Taurus, the air sign of Gemini, and the water sign of Cancer, the 2-3-4 of Wands leads to the 5-6-7 of Disks, the 8-9-10 of Swords (Gemini) and the 2-3-4 of Cups (Cancer). So it continues—Fire, Earth, Air, Water—until the year's cycle is complete.

As you'd expect, that means all signs of the same element belong to the same suit: Wands are fiery (Aries, Leo, Sagittarius). Cups are watery (Cancer, Scorpio, Pisces). Swords are airy (Libra, Aquarius, Gemini). Pentacles/Disks are earthy (Capricorn, Taurus, Virgo).

The planetary assignments are a bit more complex. If you look at the planet column, you'll see a repeating pattern: **Mars, Sun, Venus, Mercury, Moon, Saturn, Jupiter.**[3] Since 36 ÷ 7 = 5 with one left over, Mars repeats: it shows up at the beginning of the cycle—2 of Wands, Mars in Aries—and at the end, 10 of Cups, Mars in Pisces. Fortunately, Mars has the energy to carry the double load.

24. 10 of Cups, 2 of Wands (Pictorial Key Tarot).

There's a subtle message in the rainbow which I bet you never thought of—fiery Mars in watery Pisces combines like sun and rain to form a shimmering, ephemeral bridge between the opposite elements, as well as the watery dissolution of the old year and the fiery onset of the new year.

Wait, what about Aces? Just like Pages/Princesses, Aces are special. Each covers a quadrant of the sky, centered on the fixed suit of its element. So the Ace of Wands, sometimes called the Root of Fire, has at its heart the fixed fire sign Leo. It extends one sign in each direction: Cancer-Leo-Virgo.

....

3 This has to do with a system used in classical astrology to assign rulership to the decans. The idea is that just as each sign has a ruler (Venus rules Libra, for example), each decan has a sub-ruler or governor of sorts. In this system, the planets are ordered in *descending order of their apparent speed as viewed from the Earth.* It's called "Chaldean" or "descending" order (as opposed to the other system of assigning planetary rulers to decans, which is called "triplicity" order.) It normally starts Saturn first, but that didn't work so well for the Golden Dawn, so they started with Mars.

Now you are astrologically armed with one of the most potent tools imaginable for deepening your understanding of the minor arcana. Congratulations!

	Suit	Planetary glyph	Planet	Zodiacal glyph	Zodiac
02	Wands	♂	Mars	♈	0°–9° Aries
03	Wands	☉	Sun	♈	10°–19° Aries
04	Wands	♀	Venus	♈	20°–29° Aries
05	Disks	☿	Mercury	♉	0°–9° Taurus
06	Disks	☽	Moon	♉	10°–19° Taurus
07	Disks	♄	Saturn	♉	20°–29° Taurus
08	Swords	♃	Jupiter	♊	0°–9° Gemini
09	Swords	♂	Mars	♊	10°–19° Gemini
10	Swords	☉	Sun	♊	20°–29° Gemini
02	Cups	♀	Venus	♋	0°–9° Cancer
03	Cups	☿	Mercury	♋	10°–19° Cancer
04	Cups	☽	Moon	♋	20°–29° Cancer
05	Wands	♄	Saturn	♌	0°–9° Leo
06	Wands	♃	Jupiter	♌	10°–19° Leo
07	Wands	♂	Mars	♌	20°–29° Leo
08	Disks	☉	Sun	♍	0°–9° Virgo
09	Disks	♀	Venus	♍	10°–19° Virgo
10	Disks	☿	Mercury	♍	20°–29° Virgo
02	Swords	☽	Moon	♎	0°–9° Libra
03	Swords	♄	Saturn	♎	10°–19° Libra
04	Swords	♃	Jupiter	♎	20°–29° Libra

	Suit	Planetary glyph	Planet	Zodiacal glyph	Zodiac
05	Cups	♂	Mars	♏	0°–9° Scorpio
06	Cups	☉	Sun	♏	10°–19° Scorpio
07	Cups	♀	Venus	♏	20°–29° Scorpio
08	Wands	☿	Mercury	♐	0°–9° Sagittarius
09	Wands	☽	Moon	♐	10°–19° Sagittarius
10	Wands	♄	Saturn	♐	20°–29° Sagittarius
02	Disks	♃	Jupiter	♑	0°–9° Capricorn
03	Disks	♂	Mars	♑	10°–19° Capricorn
04	Disks	☉	Sun	♑	20°–29° Capricorn
05	Swords	♀	Venus	♒	0°–9° Aquarius
06	Swords	☿	Mercury	♒	10°–19° Aquarius
07	Swords	☽	Moon	♒	20°–29° Aquarius
08	Cups	♄	Saturn	♓	0°–9° Pisces
09	Cups	♃	Jupiter	♓	10°–19° Pisces
10	Cups	♂	Mars	♓	20°–29° Pisces
Ace	Wands			△ / ♋ ♌ ♍	Fire
Ace	Cups			▽ / ♎ ♏ ♐	Water
Ace	Swords			△ / ♑ ♒ ♓	Air
Ace	Disks			▽ / ♈ ♉ ♊	Earth

ASTROLOGICAL VOCABULARY BY PLANET AND SIGN

If you know even a little about astrology, using astrological information instantly adds a rich layer of seasoning to your understanding of the majors. Maybe you've heard that Virgos are typically introverted, sensitive to detail, and devoted to the life of the mind. How do those qualities apply to the Hermit? Maybe you know a thing or two about Mars, the god of warfare, conflict, ambition and physical drives. How does that color your interpretation of the Tower?

Chances are you know more than you think about the planets and the signs. But in case you need a refresher, here's some keywords you can use.

Planet	Areas of Influence
☉ Sun	Health, pride, identity, leadership, self, confidence, fruitfulness, radiance, expressiveness
☽ Moon	Dreams, mothers, intuition, fertility, enchantment, creativity, changefulness, secrets, psychic ability
☿ Mercury	Strategy, writing, divination, magic, messages, travel, communication, deceit
♀ Venus	Love, beauty, attraction, fertility, harmony, the arts, relationship, connections, unity
♂ Mars	Aggression, war, lust, courage, willpower, determination, enmity, power, separation, desire
♃ Jupiter	Generosity, business, responsibility, luck, success, wisdom, wealth, honor
♄ Saturn	Boundaries, longevity, death, justice, limits, authority, time, binding, discipline

Sign	Qualities
♈ Aries	Dynamic, hot-headed, impulsive, assertive, headstrong, pioneering
♉ Taurus	Trustworthy, patient, affectionate, luxury-loving, stubborn, persistent
♊ Gemini	Versatile, chatty, lively, verbal, communicative, mobile, distracted
♋ Cancer	Intuitive, imaginative, protective, domestic, shy, nurturing, emotional
♌ Leo	Expansive, proud, dramatic, fun-loving, creative, generous, bossy
♍ Virgo	Diligent, meticulous, analytical, modest, discerning, self-abnegating
♎ Libra	Diplomatic, sociable, indecisive, easygoing, relationship-oriented
♏ Scorpio	Forceful, magnetic, determined, intense, focused, secretive
♐ Sagittarius	Honest, freedom-loving, tolerant, philosophical, good-humored, expansive
♑ Capricorn	Prudent, ambitious, wry, reserved, hard-working, disciplined, tactical.
♒ Aquarius	Humanitarian, free-thinking, inventive, outgoing, independent, eccentric
♓ Pisces	Unworldly, sensitive, intuitive, imaginative, dreamy, escapist, malleable.

So, we have a correspondence system linking up tarot and astrology. We have a basic astrological vocabulary. Let's start interpreting!

PUTTING IT ALL TOGETHER:
BASIC METHODS FOR TAROT + ASTROLOGY

If I were to present you with the following spread, I bet you'd have an idea what it meant right off the bat. Go ahead, give it a try.

25. 5 of Cups, 9 of Swords, The Tower (Steampunk Tarot).

Fun times, right?

I bet you said something about loss, anxiety, and separation—I know I did. Now go have a look and see what the astrology says about those three cards.

"♂♏. ♂♊. ♂!" says Astrology. And you say, since you now speak fluent Astrologese, "Oh, I see! it's all about ♂." Which sounds like Mars when you say it out loud. That's right, that baleful war god is in every one of these cards. The god of conflict, stress, and so much more. This is Mars on his worst behavior. It's no wonder this spread looks like grim death reheated on a Tuesday, right? (And yes, the Tower can be wonderfully liberating. But don't try to tell me you're going to leap for joy when you see this spread.)

Now, Mars doesn't always wear that face. Suppose you got:

26. 2 of Wands, 3 of Pentacles (Steampunk Tarot).

These are Mars cards too; Mars in Aries and Mars in Capricorn. Here you might experience him as a god of drive and vision—a god whose quest for world domination is constructive rather than destructive. This is a god who *wins*, yes, but also one who can work with others. (Mars is in rulership in Aries and in exaltation in Capricorn. We'll talk more about that later, but for now let's just say that these are places where he can be his best self.)

The two situations may be different, but Mars is still Mars; still the same dude. So if he's acting belligerent and handing out loss and despair like there's no tomorrow, ask yourself if you can't persuade him to channel his more positive side—the confident, sporty, enterprising Mars. Give him some physical activity, some competition, or an afternoon chopping firewood. He'll feel better, and so will you.

INTERPRETATION BY PLANET

Let's try working through an example using the planetary associations of the minors:

Suppose you're interviewing some potential roommates and you'd like to know something about what dynamics to expect from the various candidates. So you choose a card that represents you as a roommate—let's say you see yourself as someone who likes a gracious environment like the 9 of Pentacles, Venus in Virgo. Like Venus, you just want everybody to get along.

27. 9 of Pentacles (Mystical Tarot).

Of the four you interview, they all seem all right. So you draw some cards to help you decide.

28. 7 of Wands, 3 of Pentacles (Mystical Tarot).

Here we have two avatars of Mars: one who's spoiling for a fight (7 of Wands, Mars in Leo) and one who's driven, even possessed by work (3 of Pentacles, Mars in Capricorn). As a creature of Venus, you're probably not looking for someone who feeds on Martial conflict. But of these two, the Mars in Capricorn would perhaps be the less risky fit, and he's earthy (like you!)

29. 9 of Cups, 4 of Wands (Mystical Tarot).

The 9 of Cups is associated with Jupiter in Pisces. Jupiter, the greater benefic, has some affinity for Venus, the lesser benefic. While their expansive nature may not be the perfect match for Venus-in-Virgo's controlled beauty, their good nature can do much to ease relations. As for the 4 of Wands (Venus in Aries)—here's a kindred Venus-spirit, someone who can understand your need to unwind in a safe and peaceful space. She may not be in it for the long-term, but the two of you can happily share a rental for a while.

INTERPRETATION BY SIGN

Sometimes it makes sense to analyze your draws by their associated zodiacal signs. Suppose you're choosing between two jobs, and you draw two cards for each:

30. Queen of Cups, 4 of Cups (top)
The Hermit, 8 of Pentacles (bottom) (Animal Totem Tarot).

Here you have two cards (Queen of Cups and 4 of Cups) associated with the sign of Cancer on the one hand, and two cards associated with Virgo (Hermit and 8 of Cups) on the other. Using what you know about the signs, what can you infer about what the Queen of Cups/4 of Cups job will be like? How about the Hermit/8 of Pentacles job?

What patterns do I need to learn about in my relationships?

31. Lovers, Death (Animal Totem Tarot).

Suppose one of these cards represents Self, and one of them represents the Other. Using what you know about restless Gemini and tenacious Scorpio, what can you conclude about recurring patterns (the kind of person you're drawn to, the qualities you find attractive, the arguments you have, the habits you form) in your close relationships?

INTERPRETATION BY ELEMENT

We covered elements in depth in the previous example, but here's a simple example by way of refresher:

What do I need to know about going to my in-laws' for the holiday?

32. Moon, 5 of Cups, Hanged Man (Animal Totem Tarot).

What do the Moon (Pisces) and the 5 of Cups (Mars in Scorpio) and the Hanged Man (elemental water) have in common? If you answered "Water!" congratulations!—and condolences. You know you're going into an extremely watery situation, where feelings will run just about as high as they can. What can you do to ground yourself (Earth), or maintain a clear head (Air)?

FURTHER METHODS: USING PLANETARY DIGNITY

The planets travel through the signs of the zodiac, each at their own speed. But while they travel eternally, in some signs they are more than travelers—they are rulers, starry kings and queens. And in others, they are nobodies, little known and less respected. In some signs they are powerful and capable, and we call them well-dignified. In others, they are weak and out of sorts, and then we say they're ill-dignified.

Each of the seven classical planets we deal with in astrological tarot rules one or two signs: the Sun rules Leo, the Moon rules the neighboring sign Cancer; together these two serve as a kind of hub of rulership. Mercury rules the two signs before and after, Gemini and Virgo, Venus rules the next two out from there—Taurus and Libra, and so forth.

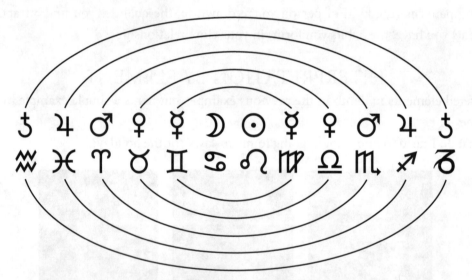

33. Graphic of planetary rulership.

♄	♃	♂	♀	☿	☽	☉	☿	♀	♂	♃	♄
♒	♓	♈	♉	♊	♋	♌	♍	♎	♏	♐	♑

Opposite the houses *of rulership* (their domiciles), the planets are in *detriment*. There they are thought to express themselves weakly or negatively. Besides their signs of rulership and detriment, each also has a sign of exaltation, where it is treated like an honored guest; and an opposite sign of fall, where it is overlooked and diminished.

Here's the basic chart of rulership, exaltation, detriment, and fall.

Planet	Rulership	Rulership	Detriment	Detriment	Exaltation	Fall
Saturn	Capricorn	Aquarius	Cancer	Leo	Libra	Aries
Jupiter	Sagittarius	Pisces	Gemini	Virgo	Cancer	Capricorn
Mars	Aries	Scorpio	Libra	Taurus	Capricorn	Cancer
Sun	Leo	—	Aquarius	—	Aries	Libra
Venus	Taurus	Libra	Scorpio	Aries	Pisces	Virgo
Mercury	Gemini	Virgo	Sagittarius	Pisces	Virgo	Pisces
Moon	Cancer	—	Capricorn	—	Taurus	Scorpio

If we look at each minor card through a planetary lens, we can detect certain themes running through each.

34. 10 of Wands (Pictorial Key Tarot).

Saturn minors—*themes of restriction*
Saturn in Leo: 5 of Wands (in detriment)
Saturn in Sagittarius: 10 of Wands
Saturn in Pisces: 8 of Cups
Saturn in Libra: 3 of Swords (exaltation)
Saturn in Taurus: 7 of Pentacles

35. 9 of Cups
(Pictorial Key Tarot).

Jupiter minors—*themes of expansion*
Jupiter in Leo: 6 of Wands
Jupiter in Pisces: 9 of Cups (rulership)
Jupiter in Libra: 4 of Swords
Jupiter in Gemini: 8 of Swords (detriment)
Jupiter in Capricorn: 2 of Pentacles (fall)

36. 9 of Swords
(Pictorial Key Tarot).

Mars minors—*themes of passion and confrontation*
Mars in Aries: 2 of Wands (rulership)
Mars in Leo: 7 of Wands
Mars in Scorpio: 5 of Cups (rulership)
Mars in Pisces: 10 of Cups
Mars in Gemini: 9 of Swords
Mars in Capricorn: 3 of Pentacles (exaltation)

37. 8 of Pentacles
(Pictorial Key Tarot).

Sun minors—*themes of creating*
Sun in Aries: 3 of Wands (exaltation)
Sun in Scorpio: 6 of Cups
Sun in Gemini: 10 of Swords
Sun in Capricorn: 4 of Pentacles
Sun in Virgo: 8 of Pentacles

38. 4 of Wands
(Pictorial Key Tarot).

Venus minors—*themes of attraction*
Venus in Aries: 4 of Wands (detriment)
Venus in Cancer: 2 of Cups
Venus in Scorpio: 7 of Cups (detriment)
Venus in Aquarius: 5 of Swords
Venus in Virgo: 9 of Pentacles (fall)

39. 6 of Swords
(Pictorial Key Tarot).

Mercury minors—*themes of communication*
Mercury in Sagittarius: 8 of Wands (detriment)
Mercury in Cancer: 3 of Cups
Mercury in Aquarius: 6 of Swords
Mercury in Taurus: 5 of Pentacles
Mercury in Virgo: 10 of Pentacles (exaltation)

40. 6 of Pentacles
(Pictorial Key Tarot).

Moon minors—*themes of flux*
Moon in Sagittarius: 9 of Wands
Moon in Cancer: 4 of Cups (rulership)
Moon in Libra: 2 of Swords
Moon in Aquarius: 7 of Swords
Moon in Taurus: 6 of Pentacles (exaltation)

But how does it help us in a reading to consider a card to be in detriment or rulership, exaltation or fall? Is it better to think of it as *strong vs. weak*, as *positive vs. negative*, as *comfortable vs. uncomfortable*?

41. 4 of Swords, 7 of Cups, Hierophant (Steampunk Tarot).
Afflicted planet (in detriment) surrounded by signs in which it rules.

Here we have Venus, struggling in Scorpio in the 7 of Cups, preoccupied by her addictions, lurching from one craving to the next.[4] Venus is in detriment in both signs ruled by Mars. But what if she's propped up by cards in the signs she rules, Libra and Taurus—here represented by the 4 of Swords (Jupiter in Libra) and the Hierophant (Taurus). Where can she find respite from her delusions? Who can provide structure for her dangerous distraction? Now try this story:

42. Knight of Cups, 6 of Pentacles, Devil (Mystical Tarot).

....

4   This dark vision of the 7 of Cups is not the only framework I use for this card. But it is, however, one legitimate, rather Thoth-influenced interpretation.

Here in the 6 of Pentacles we have the Moon, exalted in Taurus. (Remember she is also in rulership in Cancer, in fall in Capricorn, and in detriment in Scorpio.) How might her policy of generous give-and-take be affected by the surrounding cards? What might the Scorpionic Knight of Cups whisper in her ear? Or for that matter, the lucre-obsessed Capricornian Devil?

FURTHER METHODS: USING MODAL DIGNITY (CARDINAL, FIXED, OR MUTABLE)

Another type of filter used in astrology is *mode*—sometimes known as *quadruplicity* or "group of four." Just as each sign corresponds with one of the four elements, each sign corresponds with a mode: cardinal, fixed, or mutable. Cardinal signs readily initiate new actions and enterprises. Fixed signs prefer a "steady as she goes" approach. And mutable signs easily adapt to changing circumstances. Here's my favorite anecdote differentiating the three.

A cardinal, a fixed, and a mutable person (let's say they're an Aries, a Taurus, and a Gemini for argument's sake) are walking down the road when they encounter a giant boulder blocking their way. Cardinal Aries shouts "Yahoo!," improvises a harness and climbing tackle, throws a rope up to the boulder's summit, and is up and over in no time. Fixed Taurus sighs, hires a contractor and road crew, buys a giant drill, and sets to work tunneling through the rock. Seven years later, he's done. And mutable Gemini? She simply walks around it.

	△ Fire	▽ Water	△ Air	▽ Earth
Cardinal	♈ Aries 2-3-4 Wands	♋ Cancer 2-3-4 Cups	♎ Libra 2-3-4 Swords	♑ Capricorn 2-3-4 Pentacles
Fixed	♌ Leo 5-6-7 Wands	♏ Scorpio 5-6-7 Cups	♒ Aquarius 5-6-7 Swords	♉ Taurus 5-6-7 Pentacles
Mutable	♐ Sagittarius 8-9-10 Wands	♓ Pisces 8-9-10 Cups	♊ Gemini 8-9-10 Swords	♍ Virgo 8-9-10 Pentacles

And as I'm sure you've noticed, this means:

Each 2, 3, and 4 is CARDINAL.

Each 5, 6, and 7 is FIXED.

Each 8, 9, and 10 is MUTABLE.

It also means, if you look back at our astrology + court cards section:

Each Queen is CARDINAL.
Each Knight is FIXED.
Each King is MUTABLE.[5]

Sometimes when you look at cards that appear to have nothing much in common, the answer lies concealed in mode.

Diana has been working on a creative project and is starting to feel discouraged. She does a chronological reading to gain some perspective and confront her thoughts of abandoning it for something new.

"I feel worried I don't have the inspiration to complete my first novel. What should I do?"

43. 2 of Batons (Cardinal), 7 Batons (Fixed), Knight of Cups (Fixed), Pope (Fixed), 6 of Coins (Fixed) (Dame Fortune's Wheel Tarot).

Here we have a spread that is clearly dominated by fixed signs (in particular, Leo, Scorpio, and Taurus). We see Diana's initial enthusiasm and energy in the 2 of Batons, the only cardinal card in the spread.

With the rest of the spread in fixed signs, it's almost as if the cards are shouting "Keep at it!" though each does so in a different way.

How does the 7 of Batons comment on her feelings about persisting in the work?

What does the Knight of Cups say about what she has to offer if she keeps going?

What does the Pope suggest might help her to continue?

And what does the 6 of Coins say about her likely outcome if she perseveres?

....

5 Pages/Princesses are special, as previously noted. They span all three, but if you had to choose, you could assign them a fixed quality, like the Knights/Princes.

READING MAJORS THROUGH MINORS
(OR, INTERPRETING MINOR ARCANA THROUGH THEIR ASSOCIATED PLANET-IN-SIGN MAJORS)

While many readers find they're most inspired by the major arcana, I've always had something of a weakness for the minors—particularly the "decanic," or 2 through 10, minors.

When I first realized that each of those 36 small cards had a planet *and a* sign associated with it, I'd run through them in my head while swimming laps—in order by sign, in order by suit, in order by planet—to take up residence in my memory and trying to understand just what Jupiter in Gemini might have to do with the 8 of Swords. By the time I'd formed some idea about how the freewheeling nature of Jove might chafe against the systemic order of eights, and how that related to the self-imposed constraints suffered by the figure on the card, my laps were done. Down with the tedium of exercise! Up with the mental playground of esoterics!

This was fascinating of course, but I eventually realized that each major also had a planet or a sign associated with it (not counting the three elemental majors). One evening in 2015, as I lay prostrate on a couch with a stomach bug, I thought, *What if there were a connection between those astrological minors and their associated majors? What if something in that 8 of Swords was a comment about the Wheel of Fortune card (Jupiter) and the Lovers (Gemini)?*

Little did I know that not thirty miles away, someone else was doing the same thing. The deck creator M. M. Meleen, who would later become my good friend and podcast co-host, was conceptualizing the cards of her Tabula Mundi deck. And she was using the same strategy of reading the majors into the minors, and illustrating that explicitly in her cards.

44. Wheel of Fortune, 8 of Swords, Lovers (Tabula Mundi).

Here you can see the lunar, watery Scorpio eagle and the solar, fiery Leo lion from the Lovers card (where they are Emperor/Empress figures, human from the waist up). You can see the thread of Fate from the Fortune card; the eight-daggered wheel is another reference to Fortune. The four armed double *dorje* or *vajra*, from both Tibetan Buddhist and Hindu tradition is the thunderbolt of Zeus. Here it's a shuttle holding the thread of fate in both the minor and major card.

For me, these images tied in beautifully with my own thinking about the 8 of Swords. I associate the Lovers with choice, free will, the happy fault or *felix culpa* of the Garden of Eden when Eve decides to sample the apple. And I see the Wheel as the influence of fate, the great pattern we barely perceive but whose twists and turns shape our lives. In the 8 of Swords, Fate and Free Will confront each other. Irresistible force meets immovable object! In the collision of our freedom to act and what fate deals us, we are paralyzed until and unless we can unpick our own threads, remove our own blindfolds and move on.

Here's another one you can try:

THE EMPRESS   FOUR OF WANDS   THE EMPEROR
COMPLETION

45. Empress (Venus), 4 of Wands (Venus in Aries), Emperor (Aries) (Tabula Mundi).

How do the Empress's life-giving powers of attraction interact with the Emperor's impulse to shape and structure his world?

Does it surprise you that so many people connect the 4 of Wands with engagement, weddings, or marriage?

And consider this—Venus is in detriment in Aries, so not at her strongest. Maybe this refers to *just the party,* the good time, the celebration itself, not the lifelong work, joy, ups and downs of the marriage that follows.

And here's a few more to try your hand at. What connections can you see between the minor card and its associated majors?

46. Tower (Mars), 5 of Cups (Mars in Scorpio), Death (Scorpio) (Tabula Mundi).

47. Magus (Mercury), 6 of Swords (Mercury in Aquarius), Star (Aquarius) (Tabula Mundi).

48. Empress (Venus), 9 of Disks (Venus in Virgo), Hermit (Virgo) (Tabula Mundi).

Not every combination will make sense right up front, but I guarantee that the process of trying to work out the connections will deepen and greatly enrich your understanding of the minors.

TIMING USING ASTROLOGICAL CORRESPONDENCES

Timing is one of the trickiest things to do in divination. In a free will universe, how can we know whether you're going to move across the country on June 29 or in fall of next year, or in a decade…or never? Nevertheless, some readers report reasonable successes using tarot to predict timing. And now that you know the zodiacal correspondences of the cards, you can put a date on just about anything! Every card except the Fool, the Hanged Man, and Judgement (the three elemental cards) has a season or a month or a decan (remember, that's ten days or one-third of a month) or a day of the week associated with it.

Obviously, this works best if the event you're trying to time takes place in the next year, as this system makes no provision for "next year," "the year after that," or "some other year."

If you like, you can set aside all your other interpretive filters and give timing a spin like this:

When should I buy a new car?

49. 6 of Swords (Pictorial Key Tarot).

5, 6, and 7 of Swords represent the three decans of Aquarius (January 20 to February 18). The 6 of Swords is the second decan. Buy your new car between January 30 and February 8! Actually, January 30 or 31 would be a particularly good time to try—car dealers try to move their inventory in the last days of each month.

When will I meet the One?

50. The Empress, Death (Pictorial Key Tarot).

Wow! That means sometime in Scorpio (October 23 to November 21) *on a Friday* (Empress = Venus = ruler of Friday). Plan to be out and about for those four Fridays to help give probability a boost!

When's my next opportunity for a trip abroad?

51. Page of Wands (Pictorial Key Tarot).

That's Cancer, Leo, Virgo—in other words, summertime. So you can pack light!

Personally, I've had some success with this method, particularly when the time span is less than a year. The advantage is that it's very specific, and you can do it even if you only have a pack of playing cards handy (Wands are clubs, Cups are hearts, Swords are spades, Pentacles are diamonds). Try it and see if it works for you!

THREE

USING NUMERIC CORRESPONDENCES

A Tale of Ten Great Mysteries

I think the story of Ten is perhaps my favorite story in esotericism. I like the story of Twenty-Two, and the story of Seven, and the story of Sixteen. But it's the story of Ten, or One to Ten, that I return to again and again.

Where do we encounter ten? In our ten fingers, our ten toes, in the decimal system that grew from our ten digits. In the world of correspondences, we find ten at the heart of numerology, we find ten in the degrees of and number of days in each decan (a decan, remember, is one-third of each 30-degree zodiacal sign). Above all, we find ten in the Tree of Life. In its ten sephiroth we find the story of creation, endlessly repeating, growing from the seed of Kether to the fruit of Malkuth. But we'll be talking much, much more about that in the next chapter

NUMBER MEANINGS, 1–10

You can find meanings for numbers 1 through 10 anywhere, but let's start with some basic keywords:

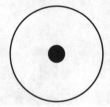

52. Sun (point and circle) glyph.

1:

Themes of unity: wholeness, immortality, potential

Themes of action: beginning, conception, initiative

Themes of self: assertiveness, independence, creativity, will

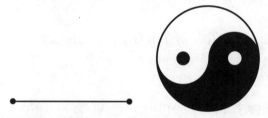

53. Line segment with endpoints, yin-yang symbol.

2:

Themes of balance: equilibrium, adaptability

Themes of opposition: polarity, electrical charge, choice, crossroads, challenges

Themes of the Other: insight, mirroring, romance, the "gaze," self-consciousness

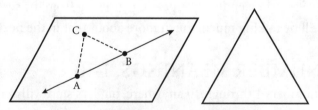

54. Plane with points ABC, triangle.

3:

Themes of birth: manifestation, movement, ambition

Themes of formation: control, realization, boundaries

Themes of community: community, collaboration, friendship, controls

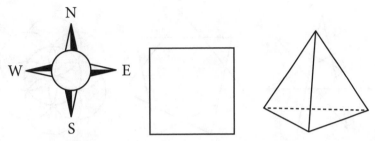

55. Compass, square, triangle-base pyramid (tetrahedron).

4:

Themes of order: the family, discipline, the home, protection

Themes of accomplishment: business, money, respect

Themes of stability: boundaries, the elements of matter, stillness, earth, solidity

56. 5-point star, square-base pyramid.

5:

Themes of Disruption: freedom from the cycle of matter (4), spirituality, risk, change, imbalance

Themes of Creativity: travel, desire, sexuality, energy, attraction

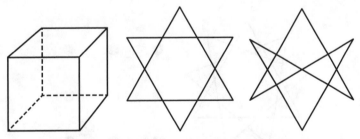

57. Cube, compound hexagram, unicursal hexagram.

6:

Themes of harmony: beauty, love, well-being

Themes of purpose: procreation, sacrifice, responsibility

Themes of wholeness: balance, completion, male & female united

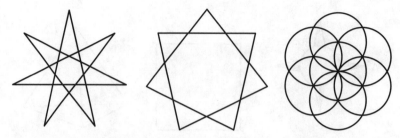

58. Acute heptagram, obtuse heptagram, Seed of Life.

7:

Themes of mystery: Imagination, secrets, enchantment, power, fertility
Themes of heroism: quests, ego, resourcefulness, passion
Themes of skill: intelligence, intuition, knowledge

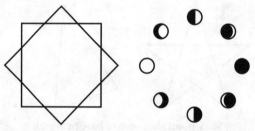

59. 8-point star of Lakshmi, moon phase chart.

8:

Themes of government: discipline, leadership, accomplishment
Themes of rationality: mastery, success, authority

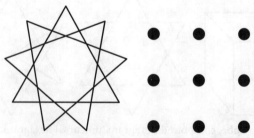

60. Compound nonagram, 9-point matrix.

9:

Themes of magic: psychic ability, insight, healing

Themes of power: idealism, courage, independence

Themes of spirituality: compassion, generosity, inspiration

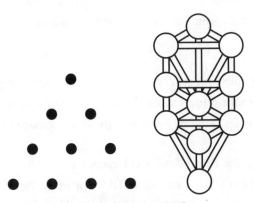

61. Tetractys, Tree of Life.

10:

Themes of renewal: cycles, birth and death, fertility, overripeness, the harvest, completion

INDIVIDUAL NUMBER TECHNIQUES— NUMERIC DIGNITY

Perhaps the most obvious way to deal with numbers in a reading is to simply see if there's a number that predominates.

62. 3 of Pentacles, 3 of Wands, 3 of Cups, 7 of Pentacles, 7 of Wands, 7 of Cups (Tarot of Marseille).

Suppose the threes are person A and the sevens are person B. Which querent is happier in their job? Which one feels claustrophobic and has a need to move on? If it doesn't seem obvious at first glance, consider that threes have to do with collaboration, manifestation, communication. Sevens have to do with quests, secrets, and intuition.

In the cartomantic tradition, pairs, triples and quartets are significant in different ways. Here's an example taken from Jonathan Dee's *Fortune Telling Using Playing Cards* (Charlesbridge, 2004):

Four sevens: "cunning schemes and worrying pitfalls which are likely to arise from envy."
Three sevens: "a sad combination foretelling the loss of friends, regret and possibly also guilt."
Two sevens: "welcome surprises, a happy event and the development of deep, lasting, mutual love."

Fortunetelling systems like these have a coherence and validity of their own, but they do depend on rote memorization—you can't intuit them or infer them. So personally I'd prefer to simply acknowledge that a seven is making its presence felt, a little bit or a lot, and then freely interpret just how "sevenish" the situation is.

Many readers choose to read major arcana by number as well (although that leaves out our favorite Zero, the Fool). Can you see some common threads between the Emperor and the fours?

63. Emperor, 4 of Coins, 4 of Swords (Dame Fortune's Wheel Tarot).

What do these cards have to say to you about order, stillness, solidity? What might they tell you in a reading about buying a new home versus going on a round-the-world adventure?

But wait, there's more! If you use numerological reduction (adding together the digits in a multi-digit number) you can connect the rest of the major arcana, the ones numbered higher than ten.

0	0—The Fool		
01	1—The Magician	10—The Wheel of Fortune	19—The Sun
02	2—The High Priestess	11—Justice (or 11—Strength)	20—Judgement
03	3—The Empress	12—The Hanged Man	21—The World
04	4—The Emperor	13—Death	
05	5—The Hierophant	14—Temperance	
06	6—The Lovers	15—The Devil	
07	7—The Chariot	16—The Tower	
08	8—Strength (or 8—Justice)	17—The Star	
09	9—The Hermit	18—The Moon	

So now, suppose you draw something along these lines:

64. 9 of Swords, Moon, 9 of Cups (Steampunk Tarot).

What do these cards suggest to you about magic and power, nightmares and dreams? What would they say to you in a reading about manifesting your heart's desire?

NUMBER PATTERNS: PROCESSES & CYCLES

So much for individual numbers. What about groups of numbers? Well, we are pattern-making creatures, so when we see a group of different numbers we naturally want to impose a logic, a structure on them.

EVENS VS. ODDS

Perhaps the simplest number pattern of all is the idea of even numbers and odd numbers. This is a method which works really well with Marseille decks, where the minor cards bear no figurative illustrations.

65. 2, 4, 6, and 8 of Coins (Tarot of Marseille).

Here you can see that the even cards show a certain kind of stasis and balance, while the central pip in the odd cards looks set apart, or as if it's trying to burst free.

66. 3, 5, 7, and 9 of Coins (Tarot of Marseille).

In a reading about family dynamics, imagine you saw something like this:

67. Hanged Man, 3 of Swords, 5 of Swords (Tarot of Marseille).

How do feelings of confinement lead to a desire to assert one's independence?

1 THROUGH 10—A LINEAR PROCESS

Simply counting from one to ten or from ten to one is a powerful story of its own. Although each number has its own character, as we've seen above, each also unfolds naturally into the next. Once you've learned the feeling of a three or a six or an eight, it's fascinating to start seeing where they fit in the larger journey or narrative.

If you develop keywords for each station, you'll be able to locate yourself in the sequence easily. Many tarot authors offer keywords, but the best way to derive them is just to do it yourself. Here's how:

Lay out all forty numeric minors in order in rows of four, the Aces at the top and the 10s at the bottom. Study each row and see if you can come up with a single word that applies to all four cards. Then try it out by combining it with suit keywords: For example:

68. 4 of Wands, 4 of Cups, 4 of Swords, 4 of Coins (Dame Fortune's Wheel Tarot).

It took me a long time to come up with a single keyword which described all fours to me, but eventually I settled on the keyword "gathering:" Gathering of drives/will to live. Gathering of emotions. Gathering of thoughts. Gathering of material resources.

Once you've come up with ten keywords, see if you can trace a story when you follow them from one to ten.

Here's mine:

1. Seed

2. Balance (or Reflection)

3. Shaping

4. Gathering

5. Imbalance

6. Purpose

7. Skills and Seeking

8. Realization

9. Peak Power

10. End and begin again; return

Here we see a story unfolding: birth and growth followed by challenge and resolution, leading to maturity and passing on the baton.

Like most universal stories, this may seem pretty abstract when you reduce it to its bones. But one of the most powerful things you can do to bring this narrative to life is to apply it to something you know well. (This is a method Marcus Katz teaches in *Tarosophy: Tarot to Engage Life, Not Escape It*.)

For example, suppose I'm making muffins—something I do pretty often:

1. Seed. I look for a recipe.

2. Balance (or Reflection). I take out the ingredients.

3. Shaping. I measure them out.

4. Gathering. I start mixing them together.

5. Imbalance. Oh no, I'm out of muffin liners! Or my pan's too small! Or the oven won't light! (There's always *something*.)

6. Purpose. I correct the fault and my muffins are now looking all set to go, albeit raw.

7. Skills and Seeking. Final touches. I decide they need some almond extract or pumpkin seeds on top, so they'll really be mine and not just somebody else's recipe.

8. Realization. I bake them.

9. Peak Power. I take them out, let them cool, and devour them.

10. End and begin again. I clean up, run the dishwasher, and whoa! I'm hungry again!

PROCESS EXERCISE

Try breaking down something you know well into ten steps—whether it's mowing the lawn, writing a poem, planning a party, washing your car, painting your nails. Feel free to cross out my keywords and use your own.

1—Seed	
2—Balance (or Reflection)	
3—Shaping	
4—Gathering	
5—Imbalance	
6—Purpose	
7—Skills and Seeking	
8—Realization	
9—Peak Power	
10—End and begin again; Return	

WORD CLOUDS IN THE MINORS

Another way to come up with one to ten keywords is to create a word cloud. It's simple: use a thesaurus. You may wish to add in the Hermetic titles for your number cards for inspiration. For example, threes would be: Virtue, Abundance, Sorrow, Work. Then lay out your four suit cards of that number and see if you can find a keyword in the cloud that works for all four.

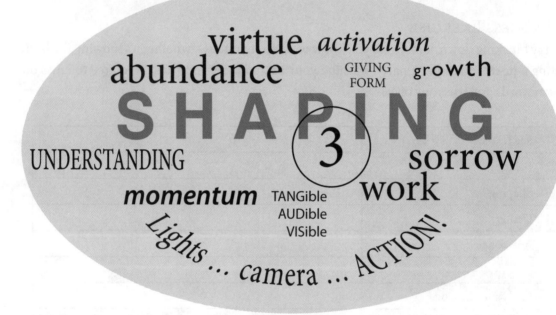

69. Number 3 Word Cloud.

1-10 Cyclical Processes

While this linear narrative works beautifully in any number of settings, it's not the only pattern you can use. The French esotericist Gérard Encausse, better known by his pseudonym, Papus, used a framework based on the philosopher Hegel to break down the tarot in the following arrangement of triple cycles.

1 (Ace)	Commencement	of Commencement
2	Opposition	
3	Equilibrium	
4	Commencement	of Opposition
5	Opposition	
6	Equilibrium	
7	Commencement	of Equilibrium
8	Opposition	
9	Equilibrium	
10	*indeterminate*	

As you can see, Papus's dialectic offers a convincing explanation for why fives ("opposition of opposition") are so rife with conflict.

70. 5 of Wands (Opposition of Opposition) (Pictorial Key Tarot).

Papus's dialectic is also reminiscent of the way the astrological decans work. Just as you can think of signs as *cardinal, fixed,* and *mutable,* decans are classified as *ascendant, succedent,* and *cadent.* Different terms, same basic idea: the ascendant decan expresses the initial energy of the sign, the succedent decan expresses it fully, and in the cadent the energy declines.

1 (Ace)		
2	Ascendant decan	of cardinal sign (♈ ♋ ♎ ♑)
3	Succedent decan	
4	Cadent decan	
5	Ascendant decan	of fixed sign (♉ ♌ ♏ ♒)
6	Succedent decan	
7	Cadent decan	
8	Ascendant decan	of mutable sign (♊ ♍ ♐ ♓)
9	Succedent decan	
10	Cadent decan	

71. 2 of Cups (Ascendant decan of cardinal sign) (Steampunk Tarot).

How does the 2 of Cups express the energy of newness and beginnings?

Although these patterns—the linear, the dialectic, the astrological—may seem hopelessly intellectualized, it's not so convoluted in practice.

Imagine you have a reading where you see lots of eights and nines. Suppose it's someone who's thinking of moving.

72. 8 of Cups, 8 of Swords, 9 of Wands, 9 of Pentacles (Pictorial Key Tarot).

Linear approach: Realization and peak power. According to the linear approach, we're nearing the end of a story. All the systems have been set in motion and are arriving at the climax of their intended purpose.

Dialectic approach: Opposition of Equilibrium, Equilibrium of Equilibrium. According to Papus's dialectic, we see a final destabilization leading to a final balance.

Astrological approach: Ascendant decan of mutable sign, succedent decan of mutable sign. We see all four mutable signs represented here. In the 8 of Cups and Swords, we see issues of emotional (Pisces) and mental (Gemini) transition erupting. In the 9 of Wands and 9 of Pentacles, we see the power of Sagittarius and Virgo to stabilize the journey to one's destination and bring order to one's changing affairs.

No matter which system you use to read this pattern, it will set the move in context for your querent—it will show her that one phase of her life is truly coming to an end. The details of the cards add color, rounding out what that moment feels like: the stories—and the baggage—she leaves behind, the frustration of not having been able to progress in her old world, the determination to make a new start, the establishment of a place of her own.

FOUR

USING KABBALISTIC CORRESPONDENCES

*Climbing the Tree
of Unknowable Fruit*

As tarot readers, why should we care about Kabbalah? What does a centuries-old Jewish mystical tradition have to do with our familiar deck of 78 cards?

Kabbalah means "that which is received." It is a body of received wisdom (i.e., handed down to human understanding from the divine) that offers insights into the nature and structure of the universe as we know it, and a conceptual map of the cosmogony. The image around which Kabbalah teachings center is the Tree of Life. As you can see, the Tree of Life is not a literal, earthly tree. It's a diagram showing ten *sephiroth*, ten spheres, through which the energy of creation spills and condenses into matter. Each *sephira* represents an aspect of creation; a quality of the divine.

As we've been discussing throughout this book, it is the timeless habit of magicians to mash together the traditions of every culture they can, with the idea of making something powerful and new. Algebra, astronomy, astrology, gods from Greece and Rome and Mesopotamia and India, runes, I Ching, alchemy, Platonic geometry, nature worship, numerology—if there is an idea, there is a magician who has tried to connect it to another idea. The Tree of Life is at the center of that, a giant Grand Central of Western esotericism that's been pressed into service as a hub for all that magic. The Golden Dawn took this great matching game as far as anyone did, hanging the most complex imaginable system of attributions on the eternal branches of the Tree. This is what came to be known as Hermetic Qabalah. It is inspired by, but quite different from, the original mystical Kabbalah of Judaism.

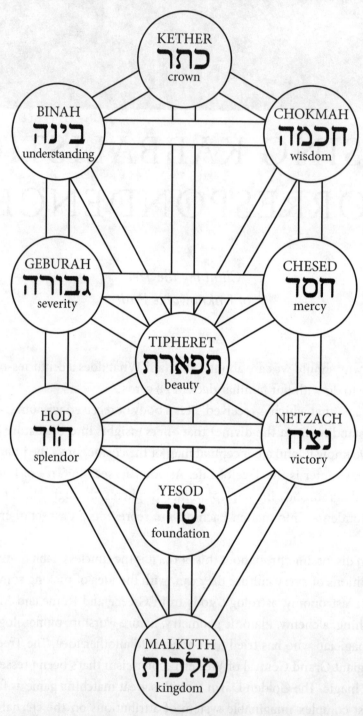

73. The Tree of Life, as adapted and conceptualized by the Golden Dawn. For a Tree diagram more closely tied to Jewish Kabbalah, see Figure 4 in Part 1.

For those with academic inclinations (or those who simply like to learn) the Hermetic version of the Tree of Life is like walking into a massive warehouse of knowledge. Each card has a place in its branches. Open the door marked "9 of Cups" and you enter a room full of star lore, myths, plants, and animals (especially fish), living and dead gods. It's illuminated by moonlight and bathed in water and purple mist. Its four exits are marked Temperance and Star and Sun and World. It's the place where dreams and wishes go to shape reality, and you know all that because of what is in that room. All the answers are there, if only you can find them.

It's like busting into the Federal Reserve of Magic and adding fuel and power and centuries of wisdom to what you know, and adding your bit to it, too. The Tree of Life is the original Room of Requirement, where you can find what you need if you can just wish hard enough as you're passing by.

AUTHENTICITY AND ATTRIBUTIONS

Kabbalah predates tarot by centuries; astrology predates tarot by millennia. Long before anyone shuffled and drew their first Fool, Kabbalists were drawing connections between the stars, planets and elements, and the Hebrew alphabet as arranged on the paths of the Tree. The Jewish Kabbalists were followed by the Christian Cabalists and Hermetic "Qabalists," who coopted the Tree for their own interpretive purposes. (It was the Hermetic Qabalists who would most influence esotericists interested in tarot.) When tarot practitioners began joining tarot to the Tree, they followed the example of their predecessors by assigning Hebrew letters to paths and then adding the major arcana to those letter/path attributions.

But everything from the shape of the Tree to the letters assigned to its paths shifted tremendously from the early days of Jewish Kabbalah to the era of tarot. So if you encounter someone who is learning about the Tree in rabbinical school, there is a good chance they will look askance at your Hermetic Tree and the cards dangling from it. And they'd be justified in doing so.

The Golden Dawn's way of assigning tarot to the Tree (or to astrology, or anything else) isn't the only way, even within the tarot tradition itself. There are different ways of drawing the Tree, different ways of assigning the planets to the Tree, different ways of determining which cards are associated with which paths on the Tree.[6]

Nevertheless, as the chaos magician Peter Carroll once wrote: "Magic works in practice, but not in theory." Wherever your Kabbalah study comes from, and no matter how muddied its origins, you *will* find that it adds depth and power to your readings if you are willing to stick with it.

....

6 I've included a diagram of the second most commonly used variant Tree in tarot in the tables at the front of the book.

NUMBERS ON THE TREE OF LIFE

The sephiroth are said to be fundamentally unknowable, yet we shall make the attempt anyway. The Tree of Life is said to represent the process of Creation, where divine light spills from the topmost sephira, Kether, sequentially through the ten sephiroth until it ends up, made manifest and physical, in the final sephira, Malkuth. Malkuth represents our earth, our plane of existence, the world we know from our five senses.

1. *Kether*—Crown: The source that contains all things, the number which contains all other numbers, energy without form. (Associated with the Primum Mobile, or "first mover," the force that moves the universe.)

2. *Chokmah*—Wisdom: The male principle, expansion, the idea of direction, the impulse to being. (Associated with the celestial band of the zodiac.)

3. *Binah*—Understanding: The female principle, the idea of restriction, the impulse to form. (Associated with Saturn.)

4. *Chesed*—Mercy: The source of the knowable world, structure and increase, growth. (Associated with Jupiter.)

5. *Gevurah* or *Gevurah* or *Geburah*—Severity: Destruction and separation, restraint, the force of division. (Associated Mars.)

6. *Tiphereth* or *Tiferet*—Beauty: The place of harmony, the meeting of above and below, balance, sacrificial gods, the fixing or righting of 5/Geburah. (Associated with the Sun.)

7. *Netzach*—Victory: "Eternity," emotional connection, instinct, the will to endure and to connect, the force of attraction (Associated with Venus.)

8. *Hod*—Splendor/Glory: The intellect , the system, the rational mind, invention, travel between worlds (Associated with Mercury.)

9. *Yesod*—Foundation: Imagination, the backstage of reality, the astral plane, the place of magic. (Associated with the Moon.)

10. *Malkuth*—Kingdom: The physical world, home of the Shekinah or feminine aspect of god, manifest reality, the body. (Associated with the Earth).

From the list above (or from your own understanding of what you've read), choose one word for each sephira that seems to best fix its essential qualities in your mind. Write this Kabbalistic keyword in the middle column of the table below. Then take the numeric keywords you developed in the previous chapter and write them in the final column, too.

Sephira	Meaning	Kabbalah keyword	No.	Numeric keyword
Kether	Crown		1	
Chokmah	Wisdom		2	
Binah	Understanding		3	
Chesed	Mercy		4	
Geburah	Severity		5	
Tiphereth	Beauty		6	
Netzach	Victory		7	
Hod	Glory		8	
Yesod	Foundation		9	
Malkuth	Kingdom		10	

So know you have another powerful way of conceptualizing the sequence from one to ten. You've recreated the cosmogony of the earth in miniature! simply by relating it to the ten-part process you already know of cooking a recipe, writing a poem, or mowing your lawn. How unlikely! (and yet how elegant as well).

Now that you've got a solid understanding of what the numbers one through ten mean to you, it's time to look at them on the Tree of Life. At the same time, we can add the court cards into the equation as well.

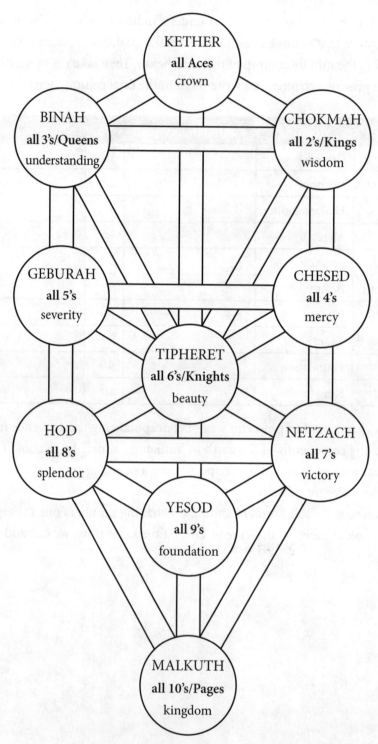

74. 1-10 Sephiroth, Minors only. The Minor Arcana on the Tree of Life.

THE SEPHIROTH AND THE MINOR ARCANA

Pick a number, any number—say 2, 3, 6, or 10. Let's start with three. Take out all the minor cards that are threes—3 of Wands, 3 of Cups, 3 of Swords, 3 of Pentacles. Take out one Queen, say the Queen of Pentacles. We'll work with the three-ish keyword verb of "shaping," but you can substitute any three-ish keyword verb you like.

75. **Queen of Pentacles (top), 3 of Wands, 3 of Cups, 3 of Swords, 3 of Pentacles (bottom) (Steampunk Tarot).**

Set the Queen of Pentacles next to the 3 of Wands and complete the following sentence:
"With my will, I shape my ambitions into _____."

Next, set her next to the 3 of Cups and complete the following sentence:
"With my heart, I shape my feelings into _____."

Then do the same with the 3 of Swords:
"With my mind, I shape my thoughts into _____."

And the 3 of Pentacles:

"With my hands, I shape the world around me into _____."

PATHWORKING WITH THE MAJOR ARCANA

Tarot readers who use the Kabbalistic Tree of Life rely on one technique more than all the others, and that is pathworking. Recall that there are twenty-two paths between the sephiroth, each assigned to a Hebrew letter—and each assigned to one of the trumps by the Golden Dawn. Pathworking is a form of meditation where you travel, in your mind, along the path of a card and between the sephiroth at each terminus, beginning with what you know but allowing your imagination to fill in the blanks.

Pathworking probably originated as an initiatory technique of the Golden Dawn. Members of that society invested tremendous effort and belief into their rituals. While they were partly theatrical affairs, with roles to play, costumes, and props, they also relied heavily on the visualization abilities of the participants. Following the paths was part of their heavily structured ritualistic approach to self-knowledge, but pathworking can be much more personal, flexible, and individual.

Israel Regardie's *A Garden of Pomegranates* is an excellent guide to meditative pathworking based in Hermetic Kabbalah. And Edwin Steinbrecher's *Inner Guide Meditation* goes even further, setting out the method as a self-guided meditation into tarot that anyone can undertake with a little time and patience.

A similar practice is that of shamanic journeying, a practice where you use an external driver (like a drumming track) to carry you forward into non-ordinary reality, meet with helping spirits, and explore the true nature of tangible and intangible concepts in your world. This is my currently my primary method of pathworking, and I have used it successfully to visit tarot entities on a number of occasions.

A STRUCTURE FOR PATHWORKING

- Physically clear a space. Using the correspondences, introduce any objects that might stimulate your senses to keep the relevant card in mind. Prop the card up so that you can see it.

- Mentally clear the space. If you know the lesser banishing ritual of the Pentagram, or a Wiccan or other cleansing ritual, or an angel invocation, you can do it now. Most invoke the four elements or four directions. Or you can simply imagine your space as simply being filled with white light and all negative influences leaving, not to return.

- Sit comfortably and empty your mind. If you wish, call on a guide or helping spirit to help you.

- Imagine a door or threshold with the image of the card imprinted on it. Pass through the door (if you wish, you can use a key in the form of the Hebrew letter, the Hermetic title of the card, or another correspondence). You can also imagine the sephiroth that the path connects. For example, if you are traveling the path of the Hermit, you might imagine yourself entering the path from the expansive, blue-lit world of Chesed, and later emerging into warm golden light of Tiphereth.

- Start imagining the scene depicted on the card, with as much concentration as you can muster. Allow the rest of the world to fade away. Try to observe not only what you see in the scene, but what you hear, smell, taste, and touch. Turn in all directions, travel any paths you find, interact with anyone you encounter. When you encounter the figure or archetype representing the card, you can ask: (1) what you can do to honor and acknowledge their presence in your ordinary reality; and (2) if they have a gift to share with you.

- When you are done, return to your door, pass through it, return to ordinary consciousness.

- Don't forget to put away any ritual trappings you may have used so they maintain their suggestive power.

COMBINING NUMBERS AND PATHS

There's one final, rather advanced technique you can use which is based on the Tree of Life,

Remember that the numeric minors correspond to the ten sephiroth of the Tree? And remember that each path between sephiroth is the path of a major? Well, you can use the numbers and the paths to work with major and minor arcana.

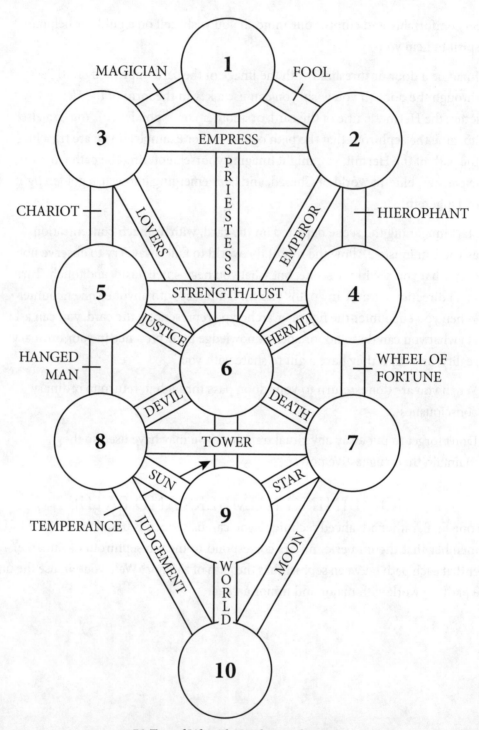

76. Tree of Life with Numbers and Majors.

In Marcus Katz and Tali Goodwin's *Secrets of the Waite-Smith Tarot*, I've seen this method used to connect opposite sephiroth. For example, you can travel between:

All twos (Chokmah) and all threes (Binah) via the Empress.
All fours (Chesed) and fives (Geburah) via Strength
All sevens (Netzach) and eights (Hod) via the Tower

77. 8 of Cups, the Tower (XVI), 9 of Cups (Animal Totem Tarot).

Here we see the upending of everything you know, the dark night of the soul, the burning rupture. What dreams does that clear the way for? How do you shape a life from a blank slate?

This method, which I first saw in Marcus Katz's *Secrets of the Waite Smith Tarot* can lead to profound insights about the polarities represented by the Pillar of Force and the Pillar of Form.

But why not extend that model? What if all threes and all sixes are connected through the Lovers card? What if all sevens and tens are connected through the Moon?

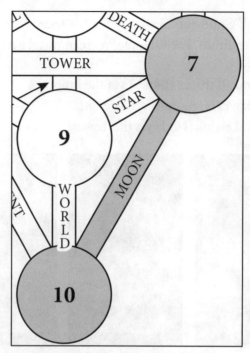

78. Path from 7 to 10 via Moon graphic.

79. 7 of Swords, The Moon, 10 of Wands (Mystical Tarot).

Looks like once again the seven has bitten off more than he can chew, thanks to an overactive imagination.

Now it's your turn:

80. 7 of Wands, Death, 6 of Swords (Mystical Tarot).

The 7 of Wands has been fighting an uphill battle for so long. What remedy might the path of Death suggest, in moving from the quests of a seven to the resolutions of a six?

Some card pairings have no direct path on the Tree. For example, if you want to connect a five to a nine, you have two choices: you can take the path of Justice and then the path of Temperance. Or you can take the path of the Hanged Man and then the path of the Sun.

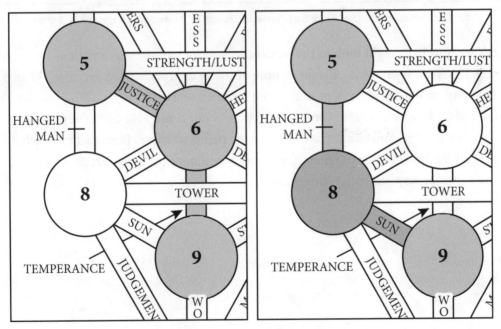

81. Paths from 5 to 9 graphic. There's more than one way to get from Geburah (5) to Yesod (9).

82. 5 of Pentacles, Justice, 6 of Pentacles, Temperance, 9 of Pentacles (Pictorial Key Tarot).

83. 5 of Pentacles, Hanged Man, 8 of Pentacles, Sun, 9 of Pentacles (Pictorial Key Tarot).

Let's see how that might look in the actual cards. Which of these is a path of tweaking and refinement? Which is one that calls for a more absolute approach, even sacrifice? Which path depends more on the help of others, and which more on oneself?

You *could* take an even more roundabout route—you could visit *all* the sephiroth on your way from five to nine. You could travel eight, nine paths, or more. Perhaps that is what we all are doing all the time, in a way—searching for our destinations along circuitous routes, never realizing a shorter way was within our grasp.

FIVE

PUTTING IT ALL TOGETHER

Interpretation, Creation, Magic

If you've gotten this far, you've become familiar with a lot of different single methods. You've learned to harness the power of the four elements—flame and wind, water and earth! You've turned your gaze to the stars and learned to discern the patterns strewn across the sky. You've closed your eyes and counted to ten, up and down and back again. And you've started climbing the grandest Tree of all, exploring its celestial branches for fruits of insight. Like filters in front of a camera lens, these individual methods each highlight different aspects of your cards, and by switching them out you can learn something new every time you look.

The correspondences are the study of a lifetime, to be sure. But it's one thing to study them in the peace of your home or library or office, and another to use them in an actual reading. Pity the client who comes in with her broken heart, looking for guidance, and here's you going on about some succedent decan in a mutable sign … along the path from Binah to Tiphereth … the septenary of fire and the Earth of Water! Recall that correspondences are left-brain work … analytical and systems-based. I believe much of what we do in divination originates in the province of the right brain, where the creative and intuitive spirit has its home. So: how are you going to use correspondences without shutting down your intuition and getting a busy signal from the world of spirit?

I think of the correspondences as something like practicing your scales, if you're a musician, or maybe your chord progressions. Scales serve a lot of purposes—they strengthen your fingers, they improve your speed, but most importantly they strengthen the neural pathways in your brain. (You can even gain some benefit just from practicing them in your head.) When the time comes to perform, you forget about the scales completely, but the paths you've strengthened activate effortlessly. Like magic, the music comes to life and you lose yourself in its flow.

At its best, a reading is like that. You may have had the experience of not even really knowing where the words you're saying are coming from, or not remembering what you said afterward. That's a good sign—it tells you that your ego wasn't involved in the reading, and you probably weren't projecting anything onto your client.

But there are things you can do to encourage those scales to embed themselves more deeply and build stronger, deeper connections—that's what this section is about. I don't believe there's a true divide between intuitive readers and esoteric readers; if you're an intuitive reader, learning some systematic information will not diminish your gift of insight. Likewise if you're an esoteric reader, you can indeed find your way through all the trees and see the forest again from the other side, becoming a more powerful intuitive reader in the process.

In this part of the book, we'll talk about interpretive techniques, like deriving themes from the correspondences. We'll talk about "working backward" with your cards from real life (chapter 5). We'll talk about creative techniques like meditation, memory palaces, and poetry (chapter 6). And we'll talk about talismans and planetary magic (chapter 7). All of this is just a stepping-off point, however; when it comes to tarot and the correspondences, the sky is truly the limit.

INTERPRETIVE TECHNIQUES: DRAWING OUT OVERALL THEMES IN EACH CARD

When you work with correspondences, it's as though you have a huge pile of little threads, each connected to another. The puzzle is to figure out how to weave them all together into an image that makes sense.

Suppose you're thinking about the High Priestess, everyone's favorite tarot divinity. Maybe you'll start with a table that looks something like this:

Title	**The High Priestess**, The Priestess, the Popess, Pope Joan, The Priestess of the Silver Star La Papesse, La Papessa, Junon/Juno, La Pances
Astrology	☽ **Moon** Rulership: Cancer, Exaltation: Taurus Detriment: Capricorn, Fall: Scorpio
Element	▽ Water
Hebrew letter, type, meaning, and associated number	ג Gimel (double letter) Sound : hard *G* Meaning: camel, foot, pride Associated number: 3
Tree of Life path	Kether (Crown) to Tiphereth (Beauty)
Attributes	Wisdom, folly
Body part	Right ear
Colors in the Four worlds (Golden Dawn)	Blue [Atziluth/King scale] Cold pale blue [Briah/Queen scale] Silver [Yetzirah/Prince scale] Rayed sky blue [Assiah/Princess scale]
Related musical note	G♯ (by color of path in Atziluth, blue) A♯/Bb (by colors of sephira, purple/Yesod)
Magical weapon	Bow and Arrow
Associated deities	Artemis, Hecate, Chomse, Chandra, Isis, Hathorn, Nut, Demeter, Persephone, Hekate
Associated animals	Deer, camel, dog, boar, cow, bear
Associated plants	Hazel, pomegranate, moonwort, cypress, cabbage, camellia, coconut, cotton, cucumber, gardenia, jasmine, lily, lotus, mushrooms, poppy, potato, turnip, willow
Associated perfumes	Camphor, aloe, myrrh, jasmine, "all sweet and virginal odors"
Associated gemstones and metals	Moonstone, pearl, crystal, chalcedony, silver

I love lists, but lists can only get you so far when it comes to reading tarot. Somehow your brain has to take all those raw materials, those attributes and correspondences, and digest them into something that gives meaning to your understanding of the card in the same way that food gives nourishment to your body.

In *Llewellyn's Complete Book of Correspondences*, I saw the following word cloud connecting correspondences relating to love: the color red, roses, Aphrodite, etc.

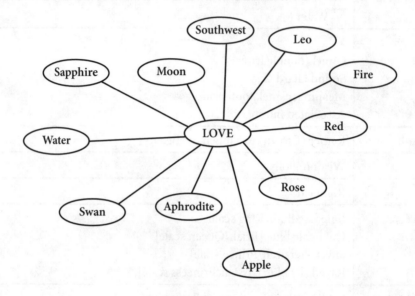

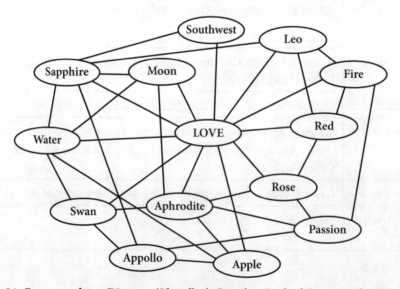

84. Correspondence Diagram (*Llewellyn's Complete Book of Correspondences*).

"What if you were to take that idea," I thought, "and place all the correspondences in the middle?" You could sort them into ideas that had something to do with each other and try to figure out what that something was.

For example, what could "crystal," "Artemis," "lily," "cold pale blue," and the "Maiden" form of the moon all have in common? They set me thinking of *purity* and *virginity*. (It might be something different for you.)

Lotus, camphor, moonstones, myrrh, the color blue, the concept of madness, and the element of water make me think of *wateriness* (obvious, maybe), *changefulness*, and *adaptability*.

If I keep going along these lines, I come up with a manageable handful of related keyword-concepts:

wateriness—changefulness—adaptability
purity—virginity—the sacred feminine
travel between realms
magic—mystery—secrets

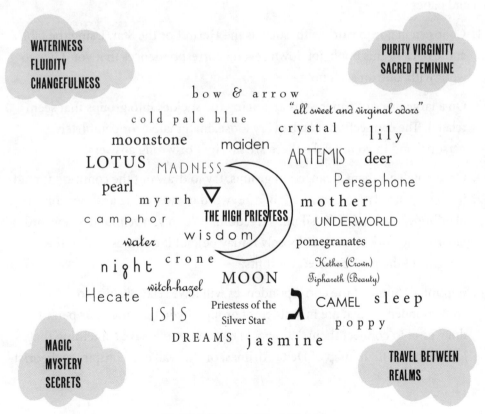

85. High Priestess Word Cloud.

Those concepts now live with me, awakening every time I see the High Priestess, animating the dozens of correspondences I've studied. If the Priestess is suggesting that my client be adaptable and open to her intuition, I can point to the lunar and water references in the card and talk about fluidity and the changing face of the moon. If the Priestess is suggesting my client take a quiet "wait and see" approach, I can point out references to night, sleep, secrets, the oyster closed around its pearl.

This is, of course, a really subjective process. You might look at the same correspondences I do and come up with very different concepts or keywords. That's a good thing. What is tarot if not a way of connecting to the magic of a language and worldview that is uniquely your own? There are no right answers in tarot, but bit by bit, you can uncover the sublime architecture of your own mind and its connection to everything around you.

Major Arcana Word Cloud exercise
You'll need:
Small Post-its (or large Post-its cut up into strips) each with a sticky end.
Pen and paper

1. Choose a major to work with, such as the Hermit or the Star. Using the tables at the back of this book, jot down several correspondences that you'd like to work with, one on each note.

2. On a large piece of paper, start arranging the stickies into groups that seem related. The connections can be very loose, imaginative, or completely personal and in your head—there are no right or wrong answers.

3. Once you have them arranged in groups, try to draw out the common thread in each group. Try to describe it in a keyword or two, using abstract concepts like "hope," "solitude," "wisdom," "freedom." When you've found a keyword or two that works (however loosely it may be), jot it down as well in the margins of the page or wherever it fits.

4. (Optional) Some of the correspondences will have relationships to correspondences that are in a different group. If you like, use your pen to draw lines to connect them. When you're done, you'll have something that looks like the flight map of Delta Airlines, or the wall of a conspiracy theorist.

5. Now's the fun part. Take your final handful of keywords. Take out the relevant card from your deck—or if you have multiple decks, pull the same card out of all of them so you can compare them. Now test drive your keywords. Can you see "solitude" in every version of the Hermit? Can you see "mystery" in the Priestess? "Hope" in every Star?

6. Jot your personal keywords for that card down in your tarot journal. You do have a tarot journal, don't you? (If not, go get one; you need it!) If you're the artistic type, you could doodle a picture that captures the feeling of the keyword or paste in a copy of the card image. Now those keywords are a part of you.

INTERPRETIVE TECHNIQUES: RETHINKING THE CARD OF THE DAY

Do you draw a card of the day? I do—in fact I draw two, so they can talk to each other while I go about my business all day.[7] A lot of people wonder what they should do with their card of the day. Sometimes it seems like it doesn't relate to anything at all. Or when you try to relate it to something you've scheduled, it becomes so vague it doesn't seem to have much point in the first place.

One practice I've found very helpful is simply stopping in the middle of whatever I'm doing several times a day and checking in with the card to see if its message—any of its messages—is starting to resonate. I'll think about my card of the day when I catch myself procrastinating, or when I'm transitioning from one task to the next. Sometimes it's when I'm discouraged about something or brooding over a conversation I've had. It could also be when I start to yawn at three in the afternoon, or at the end of the day when all is said and done. Chances are there will be a moment when something in life will echo something you see in the cards.

For example, today I drew the Page of Cups. I associate the Page of Cups with my daughter. And you know how the Page of Cups is holding a cup in the air and kind of looking at it in a very preoccupied way? Well, just an hour or so ago, my daughter strolled through my office holding a measuring cup with some water in it. She held it in the air and took a ruler to it to see if she had two centimeters' worth of water. Guess who she looked just like? Sometimes a COTD whose messages seems really vague at the outset is turns out to be very literal.

Fleeting moments like in my example happen all the time, often so quickly that you'd miss them if your card of the day didn't give you a reason to notice them. When you do notice them and they begin to add up, you start to feel as if you are living in a world of secret meaning, a

....

7 I owe this two-card practice to Peter Stuart, who in 2015 persuaded me to try it.

work of art, or a poem. Your card of the day may point to the theme of that poem, making the rhythm of your day is its meter, and the moments of convergence its rhyme.

Sometimes the rhyme will be visual, looking just like the picture on the card. Often it will be something more subtle, something from your correspondence-based web of meaning. How can you use correspondences to catch and hold those moments or "rhymes" within your day? Here's some examples, all of which have to do with the 4 of Pentacles. You can go to the individual card tables at the back of this book to look up these and other correspondences:

86. 4 of Pentacles (left to right)
(Pictorial Key Tarot, Animal Totem Tarot, Tarot de Marseille, Steampunk Tarot).

4 of Pentacles [visual interpretation]
You see a table set for a meal with four plates.

Sun in Capricorn [astrological interpretation]
You eat some goat cheese, in a shaft of sunlight on your porch

Lord of Power / Earthly Power [Hermetic title]
You plug your laptop into an outlet with four sockets.

Sun / Devil [Associated Majors]
You overhear a conversation on the street. "The devil made me do it!" she says.

Pisces australis [Constellation located in the astrological decan]
You go for a swim, a few miles to the south.

January 11—January 20 [Dates associated with the astrological decan]
You book a trip for a mid-winter vacation.

Any Sets of **four**: Elements, seasons, directions, Apostles, Archangels [Numerological]
 You see a weathervane, a calendar, a GPS compass, etc.

Chesed—Mercy [Kabbalistic]
 Your son apologizes for leaving the car windows open in the rain, and you say it's okay.

Ruler gods—Zeus, Thor, Jupiter, etc. [Mythological]
 You hear a clap of thunder.

You might see something from the image for this decan, the third decan of Capricorn, from the *Picatrix*: "A man **opening and closing a book**, with the **tail of a fish** before him. It indicates intensity, desire, monopoly, accumulation, and greed."

From Agrippa: "A **woman**, chaste in body and **wise** in her work, and **a banker** gathering **money on a table**. This is the significator for prudent government, and for ambitious and greedy substances."

In isolation, each instance of synchronicity you observe may not seem like much. But as in a mosaic or a collage, the picture comes into focus as you step back to observe it. You find yourself in the middle of a world defined by the 4 of Pentacles. It's a story of order, stability, natural design, the family, the kind of freedom that money buys and knowing your place in the world. Perhaps you struggle against confinement, beating your fists against its four solid walls. Perhaps you revel in the comfort and safety of its solid structures. You can fight it or you can savor it, but the point is that you are aware that this story—the story of the 4 of Pentacles—is happening all around you.

SIX

CREATIVE TECHNIQUES

The Power of the Pen

To read tarot is to forge a connection—perpetually changing, perpetually growing—with your cards and yourself. You can do it by interpretation, by reading for yourself and others, by research, by memorization, and by observation (see "reading backward from life").

As diviners, we hunt for meaning in signs and symbols. Some look there for insight, some for prediction. But what all these approaches have in common is that they describe the way things are or the way they are going to be.

In recent years, I've come to recognize another side to tarot—not the way things are or will be, but the way they *could* or *might* be. Call it the way of the magician. A card doesn't need to be simply a window to look through. It can also be a door that leads you to places of your choosing. Until the moment you step through, the nature of that place is undetermined. You don't just choose to read, you choose to act. By acting, you enter into a pact with the living tarot, and you can change the nature of your fate.

When you draw your card of the day (and I hope you do draw a card of the day!), do you ever have an uncontrollable reaction? Maybe after drawing the 10 of Swords you think, "Oh no, my day is shot!" Or maybe you have a feeling of jubilation: "I've drawn the 3 of Cups! What could possibly go wrong?" only to find yourself bereft at nightfall, when the day's promise seems to have evaporated without a trace?

I've certainly experienced these reactions; we all have. The great danger of divination is the creeping fatalism that tempts to you to throw up your hands and say *Why even bother?* A palm reader told me I'm destined to meet my soul mate, so why haven't they shown up? I have Sun in Libra, and that's why I can't decide on anything. I've drawn the 5 of Pentacles so I'll be poor forever! Cancel the party, I'm going back to bed. In the game of uncertainty and certainty, a little knowledge is a dangerous thing indeed.

It's easy to forget that every card is both a warning and a reassurance. Every card holds something to avoid and something to embrace. Still, at the moment when your eyes fall on that guy playing pincushion with the ten swords in your back, it's hard to rock a grin and say, "Groovy!" What's the alternative? How do you break out of the predictive headlock? One way is to just draw your cards at the end of the day and see how they describe what's already happened. An even better alternative is to work with your cards, not just read them. In magic, a ritual is called a "working"; it is an active process, not a passive one. You don't just receive, you transmit.

"BACKSTAGE"

	THE READING	THE WORKING	
THE DIVINER'S WAY	PERCEPTION	INTENTION	**THE MAGICIAN'S WAY**
	ACCEPTANCE & PERSPECTIVE	ACTION	

ORDINARY REALITY

87. Graphic model of reality, magic, and divination.

When we do magic, we go to a place beyond what our ordinary senses can perceive. I call this place "the backstage" because in the moment of the reading, it's like you're backstage at the theatre. The diviner sees how things really work, and accepts that the nature of the reality in front of the curtain is not as it appears. The magician seizes a roll of gaffer's tape and a ladder and gets to work changing reality.

Which is better: magic or divination? To be honest, each has its downsides. In divination, we sometimes run the risk of suffering from fatalism. If we know what is likely to happen, what's the point in taking action? It's a good question. But fate affects whether we act or don't act. Like passengers who suffers motion sickness until they switch places with the driver, we do better as humans when we take action. As diviners, we could use a bit of the magician's certainty and sense of free will.

Conversely, the magical mindset can lead you to believe that it's a good idea to do something simply because you can. If you can clear every obstacle to your heart's desire, why not do it? (Because it might not actually be the best thing for everyone concerned, that's why, and you might be sorry you got what you wished for.) It's not a bad idea for magicians to take a page from the diviner's book and look before leaping. It never hurts to ask: "What is the likely outcome if I do X?"

WRITING YOUR WAY INTO THE FUTURE

How do you get started using tarot to magically connect with your future (or at least the day ahead)? Well, the most powerful tool I've found is writing. There's a reason that gods of divination and magic are almost always also gods of writing. You're drawing a card or cards of the day, right? That practice represents a perfect opportunity to start writing. You could write in your journal, post, or even tweet—whatever's more your style. I've discovered that condensing thoughts and intentions into just a couple of lines you can remember throughout the day is a really effective way to carry your cards with you in your mind. Correspondences give you the wherewithal to construct powerful mental images that can offer up insight for the length of the day.

HAIKUS—TINY SNAPSHOTS

Here's one I wrote last year, on a winter morning when I drew the Fool and 2 of Cups.

88. Fool, 2 of Cups (Dame Fortune's Wheel Tarot).

Frozen dove of glass
Shining in the rosy air
Heartbeats in the cold.

Nearly every word in here draws on a correspondence. 2 of Cups = Venus in Cancer, a water sign. The Fool = elemental Air, on the Tree of Life path from Kether to Chokmah.

Dove, rosy, heartbeats—all are Venus references. *Glass* refers to the magic mirror of Venus, as well as the icy effect you get when water meets cold air; air is associated with the Fool. *Shining* has to do with the radiance of Kether, the crown sephira at the top of the Tree.

I doubt the words stayed with me long, but that vision of the lovely glass dove floating in a haze of pink colored my sight. It turned out to be a delightful day, full of affectionate gift exchanges and surprises, a brace of client readings, an emphasis on one-on-one interactions and the pleasantly unexpected. Although I had a headache, the haiku put me in a frame of mind to profoundly appreciate what the day had to offer.

Sometimes you can end up giving yourself warnings you'd do well to heed. A year ago, I drew the 5 of Pentacles (Mercury in Taurus, Lord of Worry) and the 7 of Pentacles (Saturn in Taurus, Lord of Failure) and wrote myself a little haiku about my travel plans for the day.

The Slow Messenger
Riding on a Leaden Bull
Waits on Fallow Earth

If I'd examined that picture closely, if I'd paid attention to what Saturn (*leaden, waits),* Mercury *(messenger)*, and Taurus (*slow, bull, earth*) were trying to tell me, I might have recognized how slow I was moving. I might not have missed my bus and had to scramble six ways from Sunday to catch a very expensive train ride to my destination. Nowadays when I get the 7 of Pentacles, I have a keen awareness of Murphy's Law; I check anything that could possibly go wrong.[8]

....

8   Just this morning, the Lord of Failure's "Check it twice!" message saved me from eating a breakfast sandwich full of cheddar cheese, which I loathe. I'd ordered it without cheese, but the cook made it that way anyway. Epic fail! Well, not so epic. But that's typical card-of-the-day manifestation for you— big drama in very small packages.

89. 5 of Pentacles, 7 of Pentacles (Animal Totem Tarot).

If you'd like to try your hand at a tarot haiku, the steps are simple:

1. Arrange some keywords

2. In five-, seven-, five-beat lines.

3. (See what I did there!)

More seriously:

1. Look up the correspondences for your card and choose a few words that resonate with you—words you might want to invite into your life for the day. I find that concrete nouns and vivid adjectives work best partly because they make good mental pictures, and they're *short*. It's easier to build a haiku about the Emperor around the words *ram, armor, fire, sight, king, Mars,* and *rule* than it is to build one around the words *decisiveness, authority,* and *military intervention.*

2. Find a way to join them up using the standard haiku format of three lines. You can also weave in themes you expect to encounter during the day, like work, travel, someone you expect to see, or the weather outside. What you're doing is creating a bond between the backstage (your cards) and the stage itself (your life). That bond will come alive again every time you think about your haiku or the image it conjures, as well as times when you don't think you're thinking about it at all. Choose an image you'll be happy living with for your waking hours.

For example, here's the correspondences for the 3 of Wands, if you'd like to give it a try.

3 of Wands	
Hermetic title (Thoth/*Golden Dawn*)	Virtue/*Established Strength*
Planet ruling decan*	Sun
Zodiac	10°–19° Aries
Planetary glyph	☉
Zodiacal glyph	♈
Associated planetary major	The Sun
Associated zodiacal major	The Emperor
Dates	March 31–April 10
Decan image from the Picatrix	A woman dressed in green clothes, lacking one leg
Decan signification from the Picatrix	High rank, nobility, wealth, rulership
Number	3
Geometric forms of number	Triad, Triangle, Plane
Number correspondences	Father/Son/Holy Spirit; Mother/Maiden/Crone, Trinities
Tree of Life sephira	Binah
Traditional meaning	Understanding
Color associated with Number on the Tree of Life	Crimson
Type of deities associated with number	Mother and chthonic goddesses; time
Papus's dialectic	Equilibrium of Commencement
Number significations	Collaboration, community Manifestation, action, movement

90. 3 of Wands (Steampunk Tarot).

Your haiku:

_____

_____

_____

COUPLETS—TWO-LINE SORCERY

Writing fundamentally changes the structure of reality. If you don't believe me, just think back to the last time you listened to a song and it radically altered your mood. That's why so many spells come with incantations, like the witches in *Macbeth*:

> Fillet of a fenny snake,
> In the cauldron boil and bake.
> Eye of newt and toe of frog,
> Wool of bat and tongue of dog
>   —(*Macbeth* IV, i, 14–15)

I've found rhyming couplets particularly effective and easy to remember, so they're currently my main way of working with my two cards of the day. They're a good way to fuse your intentions for the day with your cards—it's like writing a very small spell for yourself. And when you encounter those half-dozen or more moments during the day when you're stuck, or confused, or worried, you can think back to your cards, remember your spell, and ask how it can help you through that moment.

The correspondences can help suggest themes or subject matter. Here's an elemental one:

The vision beckons, but be wise:
Bubbles burst when vast in size. (King of Swords, 10 of Cups)

91. 10 of Cups, King of Swords (Pictorial Key Tarot).

Bubbles are a combination of water (Cups) and air (Swords). The King is the "greatest" of the courts, and the 10 is the greatest of the numbered cards, hence the reference to size. I think of 10 of Cups as a vision of happiness. On the one hand, the King of Swords's sharp, penetrating grasp of reality could puncture that bubble. On the other, his discernment could provide a firm footing for a card that often gets lost chasing rainbows.

The messenger god's passing flight
Disperses fleeting heat and light.

92. 8 of Wands, Ace of Wands (Animal Totem Tarot).

That's a reference to Mercury in Sagittarius, the astrological correspondence to 8 of Wands. I don't always use correspondences, though. Sometimes I just work off the image:

In stillness, thoughts can be aligned
When suffering a restless mind.

93. 4 of Swords, Knight of Swords (Mystical Tarot).

You can see how drafting just a few words can be a way of crystallizing advice, comfort, or encouragement into a digestible form to take when you need it the rest of the day.

How do you get started writing your own couplet? There's hardly anything to it, but here's a quick guide:

Start with feelings and keywords.
(Take extra care to find good verbs.)
Rhyme your lines at the end;
Try to make the meanings blend.
Remember or keep near at hand.
For extra strength, Phrase as Command!

Why not give it a try with the Mr. Perpetual Motion himself, the 2 of Pentacles? Keywords and concepts, if you need some inspiration, on page 355.

94. 2 of Pentacles (Mystical Tarot).

_____

_____

_____

PROVERBS—ARROWS OF INSIGHT

If you want to be even pithier, you can condense your card to a proverb. Wisdom for the day in just one line!

What does a proverb sound like? Well—as a game—you could start with a few well-known proverbs and see if you can assign a card to them.

95. 6 of Wands "Fortune favors the bold" (Pictorial Key Tarot).

96. Knight of Swords "Better late than never" (Pictorial Key Tarot).

97. Tower "Where there's smoke, there's fire" (Pictorial Key Tarot).

Now, see if you can do it in reverse: can you come up with a proverb for the 7 of Cups?

98. 7 of Cups (Pictorial Key Tarot). [9]

_____

_____

_____

"WHAT IF I GET A 'BAD' CARD?"

Obligatory truism: There are no bad cards. OK, now that that's out of the way, what do you do when you get one?

Writing something about it is an ideal way to broker a truce with the card and keep yourself focused on what you want to do with it. Even if you get the Porcupine of Doom, the dreaded 10 of Swords, you can probably think of a way to work with it.

Try it yourself! (Some themes to consider: sun, twins, ruins, air, kingdom, sunrise, sunset, last words, thoughts, etc.)

....

9   I'm instantly reminded of "All that glitters is not gold." However, nothing's stopping me from coming up with my own proverb. Maybe I don't want a warning about the dangers of a tempting exterior; maybe I want one that emphasizes the card's creative fertility. "Dreamers live and die by dreams." Or "Artists go where lawyers fear to tread." Or "Imagination is the wellspring of the soul."

99. 10 of Swords (Dame Fortune's Wheel Tarot).

Proverb:

_____

_____

_____

Couplet:

_____

_____

_____

Haiku:

_____

_____

_____

SEVEN

MAGICAL TECHNIQUES

So Mote It Be!

In the previous chapter, I've written about ways you can use writing and tarot to enter into a magical frame of mind. There are also many more magical approaches you can take that go well beyond the written word.

I should make clear that I'm not a longtime magical practitioner myself, but ritual and magical workings have become an increasingly important part of my tarot practice. I can point you in a few of the right directions.

What exactly are we talking about when we say "magic"? Here are a few definitions:

- "The Science and Art of causing Change to occur in conformity with Will." (Aleister Crowley, *Magick in Theory and Practice*).

- "To cause active and potent change in the world in conformity with your will." (Donald Tyson, *Portable Magic*—an essential primer on using tarot for magical purposes)

- "The ability to make desired changes in your life controlled by your will … usually by means not commonly understood by Western science." (Donald Michael Kraig, *Tarot and Magic*)

- "… magic can either bind the human mind and spirit by its own subtle power, or the magician can make the appearance of something wonderful and use that appearance to catch and guide the mind. Magic is difficult to understand because it uses connections hidden from our senses and sight." (The *Picatrix*, tr. John Michael Greer and Christopher Warnock).

- "Magic is a culture specific way of using or interacting with the natural consciousness capacities of a particular human." (Gordon White, *Rune Soup* podcast)

In reality, what does this kind of magic look like? Do you wave a wand and exclaim *"Alohomora!"* and the door before you magically unlocks? Do you rub a dodgy-looking lamp and assign tasks to whatever comes out of it? With all due respect to the creators of these and other fictions—magicians in their own right—that's not what we're talking about.

Magic of the sort we're talking about is sometimes called "probability enhancement." It is likely to manifest in the form of coincidences, synchronicities, and plausible strokes of luck. You're trying to get home late at night, you're out of cash, and you find a $10 bill that's just enough for cab fare on the sidewalk. You're job-hunting and you happen to run into an old friend who knows someone who knows someone who's hiring. You're madly searching the house for your keys and you shout, out loud, to no one in particular, "Where are my damn keys?!" and there they are, right in front of you, in a spot you searched five times before. Real magic is fate masquerading as chance, and it's happening all around you all the time.

Let me bring back that little graphic I introduced in the previous chapter:

"BACKSTAGE"

THE DIVINER'S WAY	THE READING	THE WORKING	THE MAGICIAN'S WAY
	PERCEPTION	INTENTION	
	ACCEPTANCE & PERSPECTIVE	ACTION	

ORDINARY REALITY

100. Divination/Magic graphic.

For a fairly detailed, fairly ceremonial form of tarot magic, good sources are Books Six and Seven of Israel Regardie's *The Golden Dawn* (affectionately known as "the black brick"), as well as Donald Michael Kraig's *Tarot & Magic* and Donald Tyson's *Portable Tarot*.

MEDITATIVE TECHNIQUES

The gloriously diverse worlds of magic have one thing in common: the cultivation of an active imagination—yes, the very thing you were told was "overactive" when you were young; that very faculty which you learned to stifle so you'd someday fit in with the world of normalcy and adulthood. Magic asks you to invite that force back into your life; to welcome it as a friend while learning to respect its power; to actively shape it rather than either suppressing or surrendering to it. Needless to say, that's the challenge of a lifetime.

When we think of meditation, we usually think of the kind of practice where you work to silence or empty the mind. Learning to do that is so valuable you might think of it as a prerequisite for another form of meditation: one which uses the imaginative technique of *visualization*. Here's a really simple way to practice visualization:

1. Select a card you'd like to meditate on.

2. Find a comfortable seated position and set the card upright before you, where you can see it easily. Study it for a moment, and then close your eyes.

3. Try to recreate the card in your mind, in as much detail as possible. If you need to refresh your visual memory, open your eyes and then close them again.

4. Continue doing this for five to ten minutes, allowing the image to grow clearer and clearer in your mind.

When you feel comfortable with this technique, add in the correspondences. For example, you might smell the roses and hear the doves of Venus in your 2 of Cups meditation, or you might imagine the taste of honey.

For a more elaborate version of this technique, an excellent resource is Edwin Steinbrecher's *Inner Guide Meditation*, which charts a detailed route into the unconscious for the seeker and helps you discover your own archetypal inner guides to take you on the journey. For a more Kabbalistic/Golden Dawn approach, Israel Regardie's *A Garden of Pomegranates* is a detailed guide used by many.

Pathworking uses the imaginative technique of astral projection—the act of creating a spirit-double of yourself to do your traveling for you. In this technique, the card becomes a little world of its own. In an open-ended fashion, you explore that world, allowing it to populate itself with whatever arises.

A related practice is shamanic journeying, in which the practitioner visits non-ordinary reality in spirit to perform healing, gain insight, or work transformations. (In this area, Sandra Ingerman's *Walking in Light : The Everyday Empowerment of a Shamanic Life* is a foundational text.) Whichever meditative modality you choose, the basic structure can be described as follows:

- Find a comfortable seated or recumbent position where you will not be disturbed. You can use props to shift your atmosphere (candles, a special garment, scent, and so on) if that is helpful; shamanic practitioners often use a "sonic driver" (i.e., shamanic drumming track, widely available on music streaming services) to help them onto their journey.

- Create a portal in your mind. It could be a curtain with the image of the relevant tarot card on it, or a simple natural opening like a cave mouth or hollow tree trunk. Enter the portal.

- Look for a guide to lead you to your destination (it could be human, animal, or a figure from the card).

- Enter further into the world, interact with the figures you encounter, ask what you can learn, ask what you can offer. It is good to both give and receive. If in doubt as to the trustworthiness of anyone or anything you meet, ask your guide for help.

- Give thanks; exit by the same portal you came in. Return to ordinary reality and ground yourself by stretching your limbs or eating and drinking a little.

TAROT TALISMANS/AMULETS

Another simple one-card technique is to charge a talisman or amulet. What's the difference between a talisman and an amulet? An amulet wards off something you want to avoid. A talisman brings you something you want to attract. Lots of people carry around lucky rabbit's feet, or four-leaf clovers, or lucky pennies, or they maybe tack a horseshoe over their door. Belief and symbolism give them their power. As a tarot reader, you have access to seventy-eight symbol-packed images, easy to carry on your person, deeply meaningful to you in a way some poor animal's foot likely isn't—and reproducible with a copier or scanner if you don't want to expose your original cards to the rigors of your carry bag.

What makes an ordinary tarot card different from a magical tarot talisman or amulet? The actively magical card needs to be charged with intent. That means thinking about the purpose while you prepare it for use.

Step 1: Determine your intent (talisman: bring love, success, confidence, great bargains; amulet: ward off enemies, accidents, illness). It helps to also determine a set time period in which the talisman is to discharge its duties.

Step 2: Charge the talisman by any one of several correspondence-based methods:

- if using a paper copy, color it in while thinking of your intent;

- anoint it with an appropriate perfume while thinking of your intent;

- pass it through appropriate incense smoke while thinking of your intent;

- write an appropriate couplet or brief statement of intent and recite it while focusing on the image

Step 3: Put the talisman in a safe place and *forget about it.*

Step 4: When the time period has elapsed, destroy the talisman or discharge it using moonlight, salt, or visualizing a cleansing in white light.

CRAFTING A SIMPLE TAROT SPELL

By now it won't surprise you to learn that you can create your own tarot spell using the same general guidelines of design, intent, and execution.

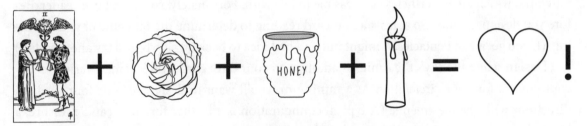

101. Graphic of simple 2 of Cups spell.

Design: Although the rich visual imagery of the card is enough, the correspondences can help you bring in ingredients appropriate to its energy. If you visualized roses and doves and the taste of honey in your 2 of Cups meditation, now you can use actual roses, or rose quartz, and actual honey. You could even download an MP3 of doves cooing to accompany your ritual! You could light a pink candle! You could dress in green from head to toe!

Intent. Determine your intention and find a way to phrase it in the present tense. "I love and am loved by another." (Or: "I have a satisfying job." "I am confident and beautiful." "My children are happy." "My friendships are strong." "My book is successful!")

Execution: Arrange your magical items in a pleasing arrangement with the card at its center. State your goal, in the present tense, meanwhile imagining the desired outcome as clearly as if it were already real. Feel it with all the intensity you can—and then let it go completely. Snuff the candle, toss the rose petals, shuffle the card back into the deck. If you like, "banish with laughter."

DESIGNING A TAROT CEREMONY OR RITUAL

Simple tarot spells, as above, are techniques borrowed from some very basic witchcraft. They're simple, direct, and pretty unfussy. But if you are a follower of "ceremonial magic" or "ritual magic," you can incorporate tarot into your practice as well. Ceremonial magic is theatrical, verbal, and immersive. It takes effort and advance planning, and it plunges your sensorium into a complete magical landscape. In short, it's a way of seriously 'getting in the mood'.

The best guide I know to doing so is Donald Michael Kraig, whose 2002 *Tarot and Magic* discusses a number of different ways to combine magical and tarot practice (including more detailed talisman/amulet instructions than those I've given above). But magic is a creative practice, and you do not need to follow a strict recipe to create an effective ritual.

Decide what to do. As with all other magical practices, it starts with intent, although a ceremonial magician is more likely to talk about 'Will'. It could be as pragmatic as "Manifest a better place to live" or as spiritually-minded as "Connect with my Higher Self."

Divine. Magic can be unpredictable. It can play tricks on you and render technically correct outcomes which are nevertheless impossible to live with. Fortunately, you are a tarot reader. Before you design, divine! Do at least a one-card reading to determine the outcome of your working. (If you get a 5 of Pentacles, it might not be a bad idea to back off slowly and try another day.)

Design. Here the sky's the limit. In addition to your tarot card, you'll want a variety of accoutrements for your circle/altar. At a minimum, you'll want to designate your four cardinal directions with the 4 elements. (A typical configuration is a feather for air, a candle for fire, a bowl of water, and a dish of salt for earth.) Then, you can address the other senses: You can dress in appropriate colors or use colored candles or not dress at all. You can use appropriate-smelling incense or perfume. You can select appropriate music. Anything and everything you consider for spellwork is fair game.

Banish. This means "Clean." But in both the physical and astral sense. So you clear away everything *not* related to your magic if you possibly can, sweep or vacuum, start arranging your items. For the astral portion, you can smudge with sage or another cleansing herb. You can declaim "*Hekas hekas este bebeloi!*" which is Greek for "Begone, evil spirits!" If you really like your rituals, you can do the Lesser Banishing Ritual of the Pentagram, which is easy to Google and takes about 3 minutes. I do mine in Latin because I find it less embarrassing.

Invoke. A lot of magicians call on a spirit, deity, or angel to help at this point. You can call on whoever's your personal guardian, or you can call on someone who's specifically helpful for the task at hand. I like Orphic Hymns. The Planetary Invocations from the *Picatrix* are good.

Declare. Use your props and verbalize your intentions with as much conviction as you can master.

Charge. As in give a charge to your card, like charging your phone's battery. There are different ways to do this. "Excitatory" methods include spinning, drumming, dancing, pain, and, yes, orgasm. "Inhibitory" methods include meditation, "death posture," self-hypnosis or trance. You probably already know which one of these you prefer. The important thing is that each of these methods has a clear endpoint when you have definitely, positively, removed yourself from a mundane state of mind and entered an "other" mentality.

Banish. See above.

TAROT-ONLY MAGIC

If powerful, elaborate rituals appeal to you, but you can't be bothered with candles, oils, incense, plants, etc., then Don Tyson's *Portable Magic* technique may be perfect for you. All you need is a deck and a table, and a working knowledge of the astrological correspondences. (A smaller deck works well, since you'll be pulling out a lot of cards.) The book is incredibly informative and thoughtful on both theory and practice, and you should buy it. But here's a very brief rundown of the method so you know whether it sounds right for you.

1. **Preliminaries**: Pull out the 12 zodiacal majors, the 4 Aces, and the 3 elemental majors (Fool, Hanged Man, Judgement). Select a court card to be your significator. Select a card from the numeric minors (say, the 6 of Pentacles for a job offer) to represent your desired goal and place it atop the elemental triangle.

2. **Build the "altar"**: Place the 4 Aces in a cross at the center. Lay your significator on top. Touch the significator, visualizing it as yourself and naming it with a powerful title ("the heart of the four," is Tyson's phrase, but any equivalent will do: "the union of the world," "the center of the universe"). Visualize the suit symbols charged with power and name them, touching each card as you do. Visualize and name yourself once again.

3. **Build the 'circle'**: Arrange the zodiacal cards in a clockwise circle with the Emperor/Aries at the east. Touch and name your significator. Visualize the 12 cards charged with power, with glowing portals above them. Touch and name them by their card names, starting and ending with the Emperor ("The Circle is complete"). Touch and name the significator once again.

4. **Build the 'triangle'**: Arrange the three elemental majors (Fool, Hanged Man, Judgement) in an overlapping triangle outside the circle, across from whichever Ace is most appropriate (for your job quest, for example, perhaps the Ace of Pentacles). Place whichever numeric minor you chose to represent your desired goal atop the elemental triangle. Touch and name the three elemental cards by their card names, starting and ending with the Fool (and then "The Triangle is complete"). Visualize a glowing triangle (drawn counterclockwise from the apex) charged with power rising above it.

5. Finally, **visualize** a clockwise vortex of energy swirling into a funnel focused on you/the significator in the center. Touch the significator ("The purpose is willed") and then the goal card ("The purpose is fulfilled"). Visualize yourself casting the light through the triangle with your right hand.

When you are done, empty your mind, collect the cards back into the deck in reverse order, and shuffle them back in.[10]

---

10 It is also possible to use the planetary cards (the Empress, the High Priestess, etc.) to enhance the ritual, but for that it is best to consult the original text for a thoughtful explanation.

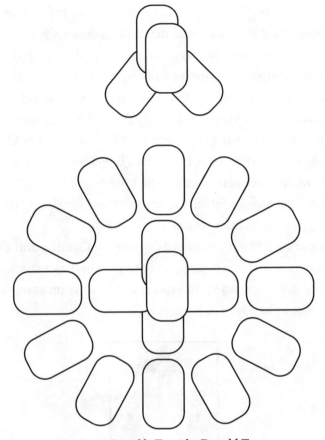

102. From *Portable Tarot*, by Donald Tyson.

SYMPATHETIC AND APOTROPAIC TAROT MAGIC

"Sympathetic" and "apotropaic" are Sunday-go-to-meeting words for the simplest tarot spells imaginable. "Sympathetic" magic is simply a form of ritualizing "like attracts like," and "apotropaic" magic is a type of sympathetic magic that's specifically geared toward averting harm. As I approach them, these are opportunistic, ritual-free, everyday kinds of magic that can be very compatible with your Card of the Day draw.

When you draw your card of the day, chances are you expect it to do predictive work for you. But remember that divination and magic are two sides of the same coin—you can take an active role in bringing its meaning to pass! Cards of the Day often surface in the most literal, minor things. It's up to you to make as much or as little of those manifestations as you wish.

For example, I used to draw the 8 of Pentacles routinely on the weekends. So I'd make pancakes—our griddle can make 8 at a time—and direct the industrious, focused energy of the card into the pancakes with the hope that whoever ate them would share in that energy. You could mix a cocktail when you draw Temperance. Got the 3 of Cups? Carry 3 mugs in one hand while you're emptying the dishwasher and then call 3 friends to see if they want to get together for drinks.

As for apotropaic actions: the idea is to deflect a difficult energy into a harmless action. My most common apotropaic action has to do with the 10 of Swords. I'm like anybody else—I'm not crazy about getting it. But when I do, I will often buy a pack of 10 sewing needles. "OK," I will announce to no one in particular, "I've satisfied the requirements!" Because wouldn't you rather experience your 10 of Swords by buying needles than, say, falling flat on your face? (Also good would be having an acupuncture session.)

9 of Swords? Try pork kabobs! (9 of Swords = Mars in Gemini, and the boar is associated with Mars.) The idea here is that you're going to have to experience the nature of that card one way or another, so why not encourage it to express itself in the most innocuous way possible? (A sense of humor comes in handy here.)

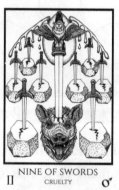

103. 9 of Swords (Tabula Mundi).

PLANETARY MAGIC USING TAROT

Nearly every card in tarot has an astrological association, and from that association you can figure out which planet it has an affinity for. In the Golden Dawn system, only the Aces, the Pages or Princesses, and the Fool, Hanged Man, and Judgement cards are unassociated with a planet. The remaining 67 all do.

For example, the Hierophant is associated with Taurus, which is ruled by **Venus**.

The Wheel of Fortune is associated with **Jupiter.**

The Knight of Cups is associated with Scorpio, which is ruled by **Mars.**

The 7 of Swords is associated with the **Moon** and Aquarius, which is ruled by **Saturn.**

At the end of this chapter you'll find a collection of seven charts—one for each classical planet—listing the cards associated with each planet and suggesting specific aspects of the god or goddess that's associated with each planet and each card. Suppose you're a writer and you'd like to be on better terms with Mercury, god of writing, magic, commerce, etc. You'd like his help landing on the right word at the right time.

1. Choose one of the Mercury cards.

104. Magician, Lovers, Hermit, 5 of Pentacles (top)
3 of Cups, 10 of Pentacles, 8 of Wands, 6 of Swords (bottom) (Pictorial Key Tarot).

Since each addresses a different aspect of Mercury, so you can target quite specifically which mercurial skill you'd like to address. For a writer trying to choose the most effective language possible, you might try the Lovers (for persuasiveness) or the Hermit (for thoroughness):

Magician	Mercury	all-around resourcefulness, wily strategy, deceptiveness as a skill, magical efficacy, salesmanship
Lovers	Mercury as ruler of Gemini	gift of the gab, charm, unlocking of multiple choices, eloquence, doubleness, the spoken word
Hermit	Mercury as ruler of Virgo	grasp of detail, focus and concentration, linguistic skill, divination, uncovering secrets, economy of expression, the written word
5 of Pentacles	Mercury ruling Taurus I decan	advance planning, anticipation and prevention of obstacles
3 of Cups	Mercury ruling Cancer II decan	easy communication between friends and family, bridge building
10 of Pentacles	Mercury ruling Virgo III decan	great money and resource management; wise investments, general prosperity, skill in trade
8 of Wands	Mercury ruling Sagittarius I decan	removing obstacles and offering protection in travel, greater processing speed, carrying messages
6 of Swords	Mercury ruling Aquarius II decan	psychopomp functions; communication with the dead; escaping a sticky situation; problem-solving

2. On a Wednesday, at the hour of Mercury (the 1st or 8th planetary hour of the day [11]), call upon Mercury. You can use an Orphic or Homeric hymn, or the invocations from the Picatrix, or you can make up your own.

3. Take out the card and consecrate it. You can do this by passing it back and forth in mercurial incense (sandalwood, for example) or over a diffuser holding mercurial oil (lavender, for example). If you've made a copy of

....

11 The first planetary hour always starts at sunrise. Planetary hours are calculated by dividing the hours of daylight and the hours of darkness into twelve sections each. So on the equinoxes, each planetary hour will be 60 minutes. But on the summer solstice, the daylight planet hours will be 76 minutes long and the nocturnal planetary hours will be 44 minutes long at my latitude; and vice versa at the winter solstice. Though tedious, it's not terribly difficult to calculate planetary hours if you know the sunrise and sunset times at your location. But there are lots of planetary hours apps that will do it for you; I have the "Planetary Times" app installed on my own phone.

the card, you can color it in. You can write a two-line spell (see Creative Techniques chapter) and recite it while playing mercurial music. You can burn mercurial colored (orange or multicolored) candles. Spend a few moments visualizing the success of your goal, or the attainment of the skill desired.

In terms of designing planetary ritual, I owe a debt to Christopher Warnock, the leading astrological magician of our time. His *Secrets of Planetary Magic* is a good companion for those who wish to incorporate this kind of planetary attunement into their daily practice. *The Celestial Art*, a collection of essays edited by Austin Coppock, offers some extended context for planetary magic.

MAINTAINING MAGICAL INTENT

Magic is like a joke—it's funny until you try to explain it. So don't try to explain it.

No matter which technique you use, you don't want to dwell on the problem you are trying to solve either in a positive or, especially, in a negative way. Apart from any practical steps you may need to take to advance towards your goal, it's best to trust the magic to do its work. (And by "work," we are talking about "probability manipulation.")

If you catch yourself trying to mentally "push" your intent along, stop and remind yourself: "That's all taken care of already!" If you catch yourself fretting that it won't work, *stop* and do something else—hum a tune, think about your favorite baseball team, do ten push-ups, knit a scarf. Don't sap the power of your intent by focusing conscious energy on it. Support your intention with appropriate actions (e.g., go out to that party on Friday, if you're looking to meet someone! Update your LinkedIn profile if you're looking for a job!), but leave the emotional energy out of it—the emotional energy belongs to the magic, and there it should stay.

Needless to say, one indisputable side benefit of magic is the great reduction in anxiety levels. You can outsource all that to the talisman, sigil, amulet, ritual, spell, or whatever it is—and then avail yourself of the most magical word of all—*fuggedaboutit*.

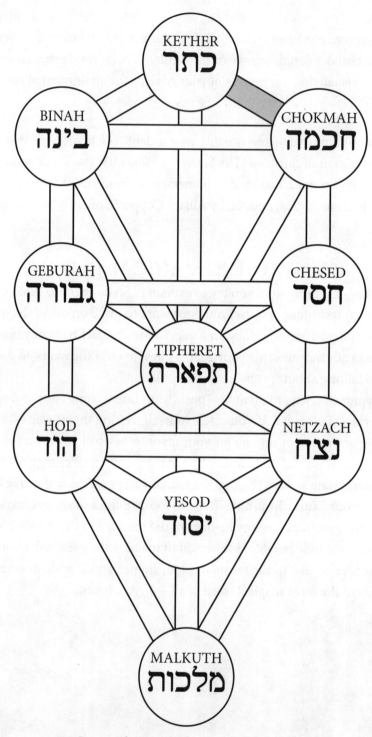

105. Large scale Tree of Life to be used in Part Three.

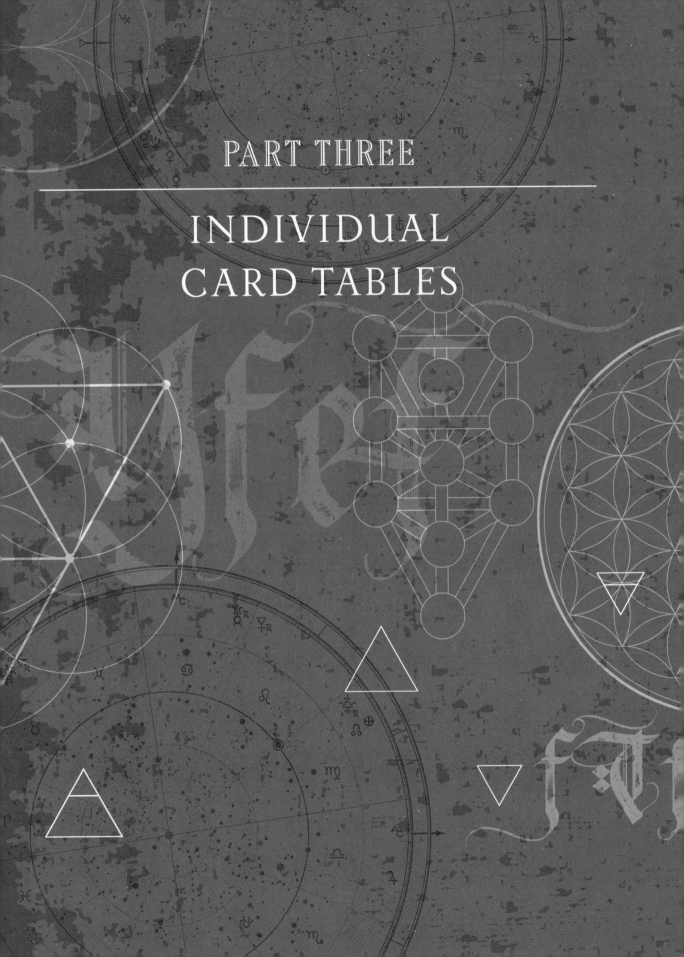

PART THREE

INDIVIDUAL
CARD TABLES

Conventional card numbering	**0**
Conventional card title	**The Fool**
Alternate English titles	The Foolish Man, "the Unnumbered Card," the Crocodile
Romance language titles	Le Mat, Le Fou, Il Matto, Mattello, Il Pazzo, Le Fol, Velim fundam dari mihi! [Rouen]
Hermetic Titles	The Spirit of Ether
Zodiacal glyph	△ ♅ ♅
Planet, sign, or element	Air or Uranus
Hebrew alphabet letter	א
Hebrew transliteration/pronunciation	Aleph (AH-lef)
Type of letter	Mother
English letter equivalent	A
Hebrew letter meanings	Ox Strength Teach
Number equivalent	1
Gifts and attributes	Air—Temperate
Gateways	Chest

Conventional card numbering	**0**
Conventional card title	**The Fool**
Sephirothic Path	Kether to Chokmah ("Crown" to "Wisdom")
King Scale	Bright pale yellow
Queen Scale	Sky blue
Prince Scale	Blue emerald green
Princess Scale	Emerald, flecked gold
Animal	Eagle, crocodile, birds, butterflies, insects
Plant	Aspen, bamboo, linden, almond, pine, papyrus, fern, dill, peppermint, lavender
Perfume/Incense	Galbanum, grass, pines/firs, synthetic aldehydes
Gemstone/metal	Topaz, chalcedony, aluminum, tin, pumice, clear quartz, all oxides
Mythic figures	Hoor-paar-Kraat/Harpocrates, Zeus, Jupiter as air, Vayu, Valkyries
Magical weapon	The Dagger or Fan
Musical note	E
Color correspondence for musical note	Yellow

106. (0) The Fool
Tree of Life.

Conventional card numbering	**I (1)**
Conventional card title	**The Magician / The Magus**
Alternate English titles	The Juggler, the Mountebank, the Thimble-Rigger, the Quarter-penny
Romance language titles	Le Jongleur, Il Bagat, Le Pagad, Le Bateleur, Il Bagatino, Il Bagatto, Il Bagattel, Il Ciabattino
Hermetic Titles	The Magus of Power
Zodiacal glyph	☿
Planet, sign, or element	Mercury
Hebrew alphabet letter	ב
Hebrew transliteration/pronunciation	Beth (BET/VET)
Type of letter	Double
English letter equivalent	B
Hebrew letter meanings	House Household "In"
Number equivalent	2
Gifts and attributes	Life and Death
Gateways	Right eye
Sephirothic Path	Kether to Binah ("Crown" to "Understanding")
King Scale	Yellow
Queen Scale	Purple
Prince Scale	Grey
Princess Scale	Indigo, rayed violet

Conventional card numbering	I (1)
Conventional card title	**The Magician / The Magus**
Animal	Baboon, monkey, ibis, coyote, fox, greyhound, hare, weasel, ape, nightingale, thrush, lark, parrot, mullet, jackal
Plant	Marjoram, vervain, almond, aspen, bamboo, caraway, clover, coriander, dill, fennel, lily of the valley, laurel, cinquefoil, horehound, lavender, mint, papyrus, parsley, wildflowers
Perfume/Incense	Cinnamon, mace, citrus peel, bayberries, all odoriferous seeds, mastic, white sandalwood, mace, storax, nutmeg, "all fleeting odors"
Gemstone/metal	Quicksilver, marcasite, agate, opal, quartz, coral, emerald, glass/imitation gems, all metals struck as coins, all metals of mixed color
Mythic figures	Mercury, Hermes, Hermes Trismegistus, Odin, Thoth, Hanuman, Loki
Magical weapon	The Wand or Caduceus
Musical note	E
Color correspondence for musical note	Yellow

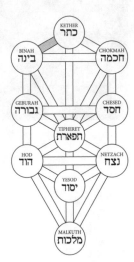

107. I (1) The Magician
Tree of Life.

Conventional card numbering	**II (2)**
Conventional card title	**The High Priestess (The Priestess)**
Alternate English titles	The Popess, Pope Joan, the Door of the Occult Sanctuary
Romance language titles	La Papesse, La Papessa, Junon, La Pances
Hermetic Titles	The Priestess of the Silver Star
Zodiacal glyph	☽
Planet, sign, or element	Moon
Hebrew alphabet letter	ג
Hebrew transliteration/pronunciation	Gimel (GEE-mel)
Type of letter	Double
English letter equivalent	G
Hebrew letter meanings	Camel Prize/reward Lift up
Number equivalent	3
Gifts and attributes	Wisdom and Folly
Gateways	Right ear
Sephirothic Path	Kether to Tiphereth ("Crown" to "Beauty")
King Scale	Blue
Queen Scale	Silver
Prince Scale	Cold pale blue

Conventional card numbering	**II (2)**
Conventional card title	**The High Priestess (The Priestess)**
Princess Scale	Silver, rayed sky blue
Animal	Deer, camel, dog, boar, cow, bear, cats, watery fowl, dung beetle, herons, owls, shellfish, egg whites, eels, all aquatic creatures
Plant	Hazel, pomegranate, moonwort, cypress, cabbage, camellia, coconut, cotton, cucumber, gardenia, jasmine, lettuce, lily, lotus, melons, vines, mushrooms, poppy, potato, turnip, willow, melons
Perfume/Incense	Myrtle, bay, hyssop, olives all leaves, camphor, aloe, myrrh, jasmine, "all sweet and virginal odors"
Gemstone/metal	Silver, moonstone, pearl, crystal, chalcedony, selenites
Mythic figures	Artemis, Hecate, Chomse, Chandra, Isis, Hathor, Nut, Demeter, Persephone, Hekate
Magical weapon	Bow and arrow
Musical note	G#
Color correspondence for musical note	Blue

108. II (2) The High
Priestess Tree of Life.

Conventional card numbering	III (3)
Conventional card title	**The Empress**
Alternate English titles	The Queen, Isis-Urania
Romance language titles	L'Imperatrice
Hermetic Titles	Daughter of the Mighty Ones
Zodiacal glyph	♀
Planet, sign, or element	Venus
Hebrew alphabet letter	ד
Hebrew transliteration/pronunciation	Daleth (DAHL-it)
Type of letter	Double
English letter equivalent	D
Hebrew letter meanings	Door Path, weakness To move in or out
Number equivalent	4
Gifts and attributes	Peace & War
Gateways	Right nostril
Sephirothic Path	Chokmah to Binah ("Wisdom" to "Understanding")
King Scale	Emerald green
Queen Scale	Sky blue

Conventional card numbering	III (3)
Conventional card title	**The Empress**
Prince Scale	Early spring green
Princess Scale	Bright rose or cerise, rayed pale green
Animal	Bee, dove, pigeon, gazelle, rabbit, calf, nightingale, swan, swallow
Plant	Clover, rose, cypress, myrtle, apple, blackberry, buckwheat, cardamom, cherry, corn, daffodil, elder, figs, foxglove, hyacinth, lilac, passion flower, peach, pear, quince, strawberry, thyme, tomato, tulip, valerian, vervain, vanilla
Perfume/Incense	Rose, violet, saffron, all flowers, labdanum, ambergris, musk, sandalwoods, coriander, patchouli, oakmoss, "all soft voluptuous odors"
Gemstone/metal	Copper, emerald, turquoise, brass, all green stones
Mythic figures	Venus, Aphrodite, Demeter, Gaia, Nephthys, Lalita, Hathor, Freya
Magical weapon	The Girdle
Musical note	F#
Color correspondence for musical note	Green

**109. III (3) The Empress
Tree of Life.**

Conventional card numbering	**IV (4)**
Conventional card title	**The Emperor**
Alternate English titles	The King, the Cubic Stone*
Romance language titles	L'Empéreur, L'Imperatore, L'Imperadore
Hermetic Titles	Son of the Morning, Chief Among the Mighty
Zodiacal glyph	♈
Planet, sign, or element	Aries
Hebrew alphabet letter	ה
Hebrew transliteration/pronunciation	He (HEY)
Type of letter	Single
English letter equivalent	H
Hebrew letter meanings	Window To show, reveal
Number equivalent	5
Gifts and attributes	Sight
Gateways	Right foot
Sephirothic Path	Chokmah to Tiphereth ("Wisdom" to "Beauty")

* in Crowley's Thoth deck and Thoth-derived decks.

Conventional card numbering	IV (4)
Conventional card title	**The Emperor**
Alternate Hebrew letter	צ / Tzaddi / Tz ("fish hook")*
Alternate Sephirothic Path	Netzach to Yesod ("Victory" to "Foundation")
King Scale	Scarlet
Queen Scale	Red
Prince Scale	Brilliant flame
Princess Scale	Glowing red
Animal	Ram, eagle, hawk, owl
Plant	Geranium, oak, thorn, bloodroot
Perfume/Incense	Myrrh, dragon's blood, basil
Gemstone/metal	Bloodstone, topaz, ruby, diamond
Mythic figures	Athena, Shiva, Mars, Minerva, Mentu, Tyr
Magical weapon	The Horns, the Energy
Musical note	C
Color correspondence for musical note	Red

* in Crowley's Thoth deck and Thoth-derived decks.

110. IV (4) The Emperor
Tree of Life.

Conventional card numbering	V (5)
Conventional card title	**The Hierophant**
Alternate English titles	The Pope, the High Priest, Master of the Arcanum, Master of the Sacred Mysteries
Romance language titles	Jupiter, Le Pape, Il Papa, Pontifex Pontificum (Priest of Priests, Rouen)
Hermetic Titles	Magus of the Eternal Gods
Zodiacal glyph	♉
Planet, sign, or element	Taurus
Hebrew alphabet letter	ו
Hebrew transliteration/pronunciation	Vav (VAV)
Type of letter	Single
English letter equivalent	V/W
Hebrew letter meanings	Nail or hook joining together making fast
Number equivalent	6
Gifts and attributes	Hearing
Gateways	Right kidney

Conventional card numbering	V (5)
Conventional card title	**The Hierophant**
Sephirothic Path	Chokmah to Chesed ("Wisdom" to "Mercy")
King Scale	Red orange
Queen Scale	Deep indigo
Prince Scale	Deep warm olive
Princess Scale	Rich brown
Animal	Beaver, bull, tiger
Plant	Mallow, sage, hawthorn, linden, dandelion, lily of the valley, "straight vervain"
Perfume/Incense	Costus, storax, mastic
Gemstone/metal	Sapphire, garnet, carnelian, jade, topaz
Mythic figures	Shiva, Osiris, Apis, Hera, Hymen, Bacchus, Parsifal, the Trinity
Magical weapon	The Labor of Preparation (The Throne and Altar)
Musical note	C#
Color correspondence for musical note	Red-orange

111. V (5) The Hierophant
Tree of Life.

Conventional card numbering	**VI (6)**
Conventional card title	**The Lovers**
Alternate English titles	The Lover, Love, The Two Roads, the Ordeal
Romance language titles	L'Amoureux, L'Amore, Gli Amanti, Gli Inamorati
Hermetic Titles	Children of the Voice Divine, the Oracles of the Mighty Gods
Zodiacal glyph	♊
Planet, sign, or element	Gemini
Hebrew alphabet letter	ז
Hebrew transliteration/pronunciation	Zayin (ZAH-een)
Type of letter	Single
English letter equivalent	Z
Hebrew letter meanings	Sword or weapon axe to cut
Number equivalent	7
Gifts and attributes	Smell
Gateways	Left foot

Conventional card numbering	VI (6)
Conventional card title	**The Lovers**
Sephirothic Path	Binah to Tiphereth ("Understanding" to "Beauty")
King Scale	Orange
Queen Scale	Pale mauve
Prince Scale	New yellow leather
Princess Scale	Reddish grey, inclined to mauve
Animal	Magpie, all hybrids
Plant	Nut trees, orchids, "bending vervain"
Perfume/Incense	Mastic, wormwood, lavender, bergamot
Gemstone/metal	Agate, emerald, topaz, tourmaline, calcite, rose quartz, Alexandrite
Mythic figures	Aphrodite, Inanna, Venus, Eros, Amor, Cupid All twin gods (Rekht/Merti, Castor/Pollux, Apollo as soothsayer, Janus, Hoor-paar-Kratt as Horus + Harpocrates)
Magical weapon	The Tripod
Musical note	D
Color correspondence for musical note	Orange

112. VI (6) The Lovers
Tree of Life.

Conventional card numbering	**VII (7)**
Conventional card title	**The Chariot**
Alternate English titles	The Triumphal Car, The Chariot of War, Chariot of Osiris, the Cubic Chariot
Romance language titles	Victoriae Premium ("Reward of Victory"), Il Carro, Le Chariot, La Carrozza
Hermetic Titles	Child of the Power of the Waters, Lord of the Triumph of Light
Zodiacal glyph	♋
Planet, sign, or element	Cancer
Hebrew alphabet letter	ח
Hebrew transliteration/pronunciation	Cheth (KHET)
Type of letter	Single
English letter equivalent	Ch
Hebrew letter meanings	Fence Inner Chamber to separate or protect
Number equivalent	8
Gifts and attributes	Speech

Conventional card numbering	**VII (7)**
Conventional card title	**The Chariot**
Gateways	Right hand
Sephirothic Path	Binah to Geburah ("Understanding" to "Severity")
King Scale	Amber
Queen Scale	Maroon
Prince Scale	Rich bright russet
Princess Scale	Dark greenish brown
Animal	Crab, sphinx, turtle, dog, horse, rabbit, beetle
Plant	Lotus, cypress, olive, comfrey
Perfume/Incense	Camphor, onycha, labdanum
Gemstone/metal	Amber, emerald, sapphire, chalcedony, antique silver
Mythic figures	Khephra, Nermod, Mercury and Apollo as messengers, Shiva, Ezekiel, Elijah, Osiris
Magical weapon	The Furnace [the Cup or Grail]
Musical note	D#
Color correspondence for musical note	Yellow-orange

113. VII (7) The Chariot
Tree of Life.

Conventional card numbering	**VIII (8)**
Conventional card title	**Strength (Lust)**
Alternate card numbering	XI (11) **
Alternate English titles	Fortitude, Force, the Tamed Lion
Romance language titles	La Force, La Fortezza, La Forza
Hermetic Titles	Daughter of the Flaming Sword, Leader of the Lion
Zodiacal glyph	♌
Planet, sign, or element	Leo
Hebrew alphabet letter	ט
Hebrew transliteration/pronunciation	Teth
Type of letter	Single
English letter equivalent	T
Hebrew letter meanings	Snake knot to twist or coil
Number equivalent	9
Gifts and attributes	Taste
Gateways	Left kidney
Sephirothic Path	Chesed to Geburah ("Mercy" to "Severity")
King Scale	Yellow (greenish)

**in all early decks (including all Tarot de Marseille decks), Crowley's Thoth deck, and Thoth-derived decks.

Conventional card numbering	**VIII (8)**
Conventional card title	**Strength (Lust)**
Queen Scale	Deep purple
Prince Scale	Grey
Princess Scale	Reddish amber
Animal	Lion, serpent
Plant	Sunflower, citrus, bay, palm, cyclamen
Perfume/Incense	Frankincense
Gemstone/metal	Onyx, diamond, jasper, cat's eye
Mythic figures	Pasht, Sekhmet, Mau, Ra-Hoor-Khuit, Demeer, Venus, Anuket, Hebe
Magical weapon	The Discipline [the Phoenix wand]
Musical note	E
Color correspondence for musical note	Yellow

**in all early decks (including all Tarot de Marseille decks), Crowley's Thoth deck, and Thoth-derived decks.

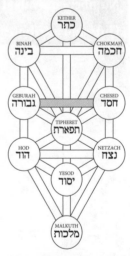

114. VIII (8) Strength
(Lust) Tree of Life.

Conventional card numbering	IX (9)
Conventional card title	**The Hermit**
Alternate English titles	The Old Man, the Veiled Lamp
Romance language titles	Rerum Edax ("Devourer of Things"), L'Eremite, Le Vieillard, Capuchin, Le Prêtre, L'Eremita, Il Gobbo, L'Ermita, Il Vecchio
Hermetic Titles	The Magus of the Voice of Light, the Prophet of the Gods
Zodiacal glyph	♍
Planet, sign, or element	Virgo
Hebrew alphabet letter	י
Hebrew transliteration/pronunciation	Yod (YUD)
Type of letter	Single
English letter equivalent	I/Y
Hebrew letter meanings	Closed hand power to share
Number equivalent	10
Gifts and attributes	Sex

Conventional card numbering	IX (9)
Conventional card title	**The Hermit**
Gateways	Left hand
Sephirothic Path	Chesed to Tiphereth ("Mercy" to "Beauty")
King Scale	Green (yellowish)
Queen Scale	Slate grey
Prince Scale	Green grey
Princess Scale	Plum color
Animal	Bear, cat, pig, squirrel
Plant	Beech, chestnut, mimosa, walnut, aster, hyacinth, violet, snowdrop, narcissus, calamint
Perfume/Incense	Sandalwood, narcissus
Gemstone/metal	Carnelian, zircon, peridot, bloodstone, sardonyx, aluminum, mercury
Mythic figures	Cronos, Hermes, Mercury, Isis, Nephthys, Narcissus, Adonis, Baldur
Magical weapon	The Lamp and Wand; the Bread
Musical note	F

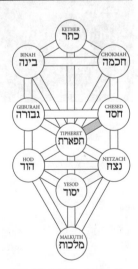

115. IX (9) The Hermit
Tree of Life.

Conventional card numbering	X (10)
Conventional card title	**The Wheel of Fortune**
Alternate English titles	The Wheel, The Sphinx
Romance language titles	Omnium Dominatrix (Mistress of Everything), La Roue de Fortune, La Ruota, Rota di Fortuna, Ruota della Fortuna, Fortuna
Hermetic Titles	The Lord of the Forces of Life
Zodiacal glyph	♃
Planet, sign, or element	Jupiter
Hebrew alphabet letter	כ/ך
Hebrew transliteration/pronunciation	Kaph (KAF/KHAF)
Type of letter	Double
English letter equivalent	K
Hebrew letter meanings	Palm of hand/the hand bent to open the hand to receive
Number equivalent	20; 500
Gifts and attributes	Riches and Poverty
Gateways	Left eye
Sephirothic Path	Chesed to Netzach ("Mercy" to "Victory")
King Scale	Violet
Queen Scale	Blue

Conventional card numbering	X (10)
Conventional card title	**The Wheel of Fortune**
Prince Scale	Rich purple
Princess Scale	Bright blue, rayed yellow
Animal	Eagle, owl, deer, hens, cuckoo, pheasant, dolphin, whale, elephant, sheep, all domestic animals
Plant	oak, anise, elm, beech clove, alkanet, pistachio, ash, pineapples, rhubarb, cinnamon, fruit trees, leeks, dandelion, fig, hyssop, maple, nutmeg, grains. wines, mastic, mints
Perfume/Incense	Nutmeg, cloves, storax, all odoriferous fruits saffron, mace, ash, balm of Gilead, nutmeg, cinnamon, cloves, oud, "all expansive odors"
Gemstone/metal	Tin, sapphire, amethyst, lapis lazuli, silver, marble, gold, zinc
Mythic figures	Fortuna, Jupiter, Zeus, Brahma, Indra, Njord
Magical weapon	The Scepter
Musical note	G#
Color correspondence for musical note	Blue

116. X (10) The Wheel of
Fortune Tree of Life.

Conventional card numbering	**XI (11)**
Conventional card title	**Justice (Adjustment)**
Alternate card numbering	VIII (8) **
Alternate English titles	Themis
Romance language titles	La Justice, La Giustizia
Hermetic Titles	Daughter of the Lord of Truth, The Holder of the Balances
Zodiacal glyph	<u>Ω</u>
Planet, sign, or element	Libra
Hebrew alphabet letter	ל
Hebrew transliteration/pronunciation	Lamed
Type of letter	Single
English letter equivalent	L (LAH-mid)
Hebrew letter meanings	Ox-goad To urge forward or teach To Learn
Number equivalent	30
Gifts and attributes	Work

***in all early decks (including all Tarot de Marseille decks), Crowley's Thoth deck, and Thoth-derived decks.

Conventional card numbering	**XI (11)**
Conventional card title	**Justice (Adjustment)**
Gateways	Gall bladder
Sephirothic Path	Geburah to Tiphereth ("Severity" to "Beauty")
King Scale	Emerald green
Queen Scale	Blue
Prince Scale	Deep blue-green
Princess Scale	Plum color
Animal	Hare, elephant, spider
Plant	Ash, aloe, mugwort
Perfume/Incense	Galbanum
Gemstone/metal	Sapphire, peridot, agate, carnelian, cat's eye
Mythic figures	Themis, Pallas Athena, Maat, Dike, Nemesis
Magical weapon	The Cross of Equilibrium
Musical note	F#
Color correspondence for musical note	Green

***in all early decks (including all Tarot de Marseille decks), Crowley's Thoth deck, and Thoth-derived decks.

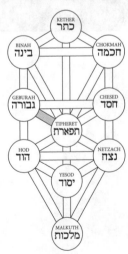

117. XI (11) Justice
(Adjustment) Tree of Life.

Conventional card numbering	**XII (12)**
Conventional card title	**The Hanged Man**
Alternate English titles	The Hanging Man, The Traitor, Prudence, The Sacrifice
Romance language titles	Le Pendu, Il Penduto, L'Appeso, Il Traditore, L'Impiccato
Hermetic Titles	The Spirit of the Mighty Waters
Zodiacal glyph	▽ Ψ
Planet, sign, or element	Water or Neptune
Hebrew alphabet letter	מ/ם
Hebrew transliteration/pronunciation	Mem (MEM)
Type of letter	Mother
English letter equivalent	M
Hebrew letter meanings	Water Nations People
Number equivalent	40, 600
Gifts and attributes	The Earth—cold
Gateways	Belly/Abdomen

Conventional card numbering	**XII (12)**
Conventional card title	**The Hanged Man**
Sephirothic Path	Geburah to Hod ("Severity" to "Glory")
King Scale	Deep blue
Queen Scale	Sea-green
Prince Scale	Deep olive-green
Princess Scale	White, flecked purple
Animal	Eagle, snake, scorpion, fish, water fowl, dolphin
Plant	Lotus, ash, all water plants, willow, comfrey
Perfume/Incense	Myrrh, iris (orris root), gardenia, jasmine, vanilla
Gemstone/metal	Silver, pearl, moonstone, crystal, beryl, aquamarine, sulfates
Mythic figures	Tum Ptah Auromoth, Poseidon, Neptune, Prometheus, Odin, Attis, Schemchasai
Magical weapon	The Cup and Cross of Suffering; sacramental wine
Musical note	G#
Color correspondence for musical note	Blue

118. XII (12)
The Hanged Man
Tree of Life.

Conventional card numbering	**XIII (13)**
Conventional card title	**Death**
Alternate English titles	The Scythe, "the Unnamed Card"
Romance language titles	La Mort, Il Morte, La Morte
Hermetic Titles	The Child of the Great Transformers, Lord of the Gates of Death
Zodiacal glyph	♏
Planet, sign, or element	Scorpio
Hebrew alphabet letter	נ/ן
Hebrew transliteration/pronunciation	Nun (NOON)
Type of letter	Single
English letter equivalent	N
Hebrew letter meanings	Fish descendants to propagate
Number equivalent	50; 700
Gifts and attributes	Movement
Gateways	Intestines

Conventional card numbering	**XIII (13)**
Conventional card title	**Death**
Sephirothic Path	Tiphereth to Netzach ("Beauty" to "Victory")
King Scale	Green blue
Queen Scale	Dull brown
Prince Scale	Very dark brown
Princess Scale	Livid indigo brown
Animal	Scorpion, eagle, phoenix, bat, panther, wolf, vulture, scarab beetle
Plant	Aspen, myrtle, elder, yew, blackthorn, cactus, scorpion grass
Perfume/Incense	Opoponax (sweet myrrh), benzoin
Gemstone/metal	Aquamarine, beryl, amethyst, snakestone, amber, bloodstone
Mythic figures	Mars, Ares, Apep, Khephri, Hades, Pluto, Thanatos, Hypnos
Magical weapon	The Pain of the Obligation; The Oath
Musical note	G
Color correspondence for musical note	Blue-green

119. XIII (13) Death
Tree of Life.

Conventional card numbering	**XIV (14)**
Conventional card title	**Temperance (Art)**
Alternate English titles	Time, the Solar Spirit
Romance language titles	Atrempance, La Temperance, La Temperanza
Hermetic Titles	Daughter of the Reconcilers, the Bringer Forth of Life
Zodiacal glyph	♐
Planet, sign, or element	Sagittarius
Hebrew alphabet letter	ס
Hebrew transliteration/pronunciation	Samekh (SAH-mekh)
Type of letter	Single
English letter equivalent	S
Hebrew letter meanings	Prop or support Training (as a plant) To trust
Number equivalent	60
Gifts and attributes	Anger

Conventional card numbering	XIV (14)
Conventional card title	Temperance (Art)
Gateways	Lower bowels
Sephirothic Path	Tiphereth to Yesod ("Beauty" to "Foundation")
King Scale	Blue
Queen Scale	Yellow
Prince Scale	Green grey
Princess Scale	Dark vivid blue
Animal	Elk, horse, centaur, dog
Plant	Lime, mulberry, oak, birch, rush, pimpernel
Perfume/Incense	lign-aloe (agarwood), oud
Gemstone/metal	Jacinth, topaz, beryl, amethyst
Mythic figures	Diana, Artemis/Apollo, Iris, Nemesis, Ares
Magical weapon	The Arrow
Musical note	G#
Color correspondence for musical note	Blue

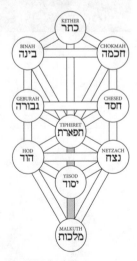

120. XIV (14) Temperance
(Art) Tree of Life.

Conventional card numbering	XV (15)
Conventional card title	**The Devil**
Alternate English titles	Pan, Typhon, Baphomet
Romance language titles	Perditorum Raptor ("Captor of the Lost"), Il Diavolo, Le Diable
Hermetic Titles	Lord of the Gates of Matter, Child of the Forces of Time
Zodiacal glyph	♑
Planet, sign, or element	Capricorn
Hebrew alphabet letter	ע
Hebrew transliteration/pronunciation	Ayin (AH-in)
Type of letter	Single
English letter equivalent	O
Hebrew letter meanings	Eye Expression To see
Number equivalent	70
Gifts and attributes	Mirth
Gateways	Liver

Conventional card numbering	XV (15)
Conventional card title	**The Devil**
Sephirothic Path	Tiphereth to Hod ("Beauty" to "Glory")
King Scale	Indigo
Queen Scale	Black
Prince Scale	Blue-black
Princess Scale	Cold dark grey nearing black
Animal	Elephant, mountain goat, dog, dolphin, ass
Plant	Birch, willow, elm, thistle, poppy, sweet woodruff, thyme, hemp, dock
Perfume/Incense	Benzoin Musk, civet, benzoin
Gemstone/metal	Ruby, onyx, chrysoprase, turquoise, black diamond
Mythic figures	Lucifer, Seth, Beelzebub, Agni, Pan, Dionysus, Khem, Priapus, Bacchus
Magical weapon	The Secret Force, the Lamp
Musical note	A
Color correspondence for musical note	Blue-violet

121. XV (15) The Devil
Tree of Life.

Conventional card numbering	**XVI (16)**
Conventional card title	**The Tower**
Alternate English titles	The House of God, the Blasted Tower, the Lightning-Struck Tower, the Hospital, the Arrow, the Thunderbolt, the Fire, the Lightning-Struck Temple, the Ruined Tower
Romance language titles	La Maison Dieu, Le Foudre, La Torre, Il Fuoco, La Saetta, La Sagitta
Hermetic Titles	Lord of the Hosts of the Mighty
Zodiacal glyph	♂
Planet, sign, or element	Mars
Hebrew alphabet letter	פ/ף
Hebrew transliteration/pronunciation	Pe (PAY/FAY)
Type of letter	Double
English letter equivalent	P
Hebrew letter meanings	Mouth Entrance To speak
Number equivalent	80; 800
Gifts and attributes	Grace and Indignation
Gateways	Left ear
Sephirothic Path	Netzach to Hod ("Victory" to "Glory")
King Scale	Scarlet
Queen Scale	Red
Prince Scale	Venetian red

Conventional card numbering	XVI (16)
Conventional card title	**The Tower**
Princess Scale	Bright red, rayed azure or emerald
Animal	Wolf, bear, crow, screech owl, vulture, scorpion, kestrels, pike, sturgeon, wasps, all stinging insects
Plant	Rue, wormwood, pepper, cumin, chili, ginger, asafoetida, capers, hoseradish, garlic, leek, onion, mustard, radish, hops, pennyroyal, tobacco, hellebore, thistle, radish, nettle, chestnut, all thorny and lacrimatory plants
Perfume/Incense	Sandalwood, cypress, agarwood, all odoriferous wood, pepper, dragon's blood, benzoin, "all hot and pungent odors"
Gemstone/metal	Iron, garnet, diamond, ruby, lodestone, bloodstone, jasper
Mythic figures	Horus, Krishna, Odin, war gods, Shiva, Zeus, Thor, Mars, Ares
Magical weapon	The Sword
Musical note	C
Color correspondence for musical note	Red

122. XVI (16) The Tower
Tree of Life.

Conventional card numbering	XVII (17)
Conventional card title	**The Star**
Alternate English titles	The Stars, the Blazing Star, Star of the Magi
Romance language titles	Inclitum Sydus (Renowned Star, Star of Wonder, Rouen), L'Etoile, La Stelle, Le Stelle
Hermetic Titles	Daughter of the Firmament, Dweller Between the Waters
Zodiacal glyph	♒
Planet, sign, or element	Aquarius
Hebrew alphabet letter	צ/ץ
Hebrew transliteration/pronunciation	Tzaddi (TZAH-dee)
Type of letter	Single
English letter equivalent	Tz
Hebrew letter meanings	Fish hook righteous to pull toward
Number equivalent	90; 900
Gifts and attributes	Imagination
Gateways	Stomach
Sephirothic Path	Netzach to Yesod ("Victory" to "Foundation")
Alternate Hebrew letter	ה/Heh/H ("window")*
Alternate Sephirothic Path	Chokmah to Tiphereth ("Wisdom" to "Beauty")

****in Crowley's Thoth deck and Thoth-derived decks.

Conventional card numbering	**XVII (17)**
Conventional card title	**The Star**
King Scale	Violet
Queen Scale	Sky blue
Prince Scale	Bluish mauve
Princess Scale	White, tinged purple
Animal	Otter, eagle, peacock
Plant	Olive, fir, skullcap, moss, fruit trees, dracunculus plants
Perfume/Incense	Euphorbium Galbanum
Gemstone/metal	Chalcedony, amethyst, garnet, jasper, crystal, quartz, turquoise
Mythic figures	Juno, Athena as artisan, Ganymede, Ishtar, Astarte, Isis
Magical weapon	The Censer or Aspergillus
Musical note	A#
Color correspondence for musical note	Violet

****in Crowley's Thoth deck and Thoth-derived decks.

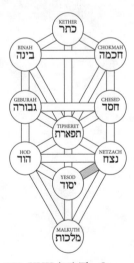

123. XVII (17) The Star
Tree of Life.

Conventional card numbering	XVIII (18)
Conventional card title	**The Moon**
Alternate English titles	Twilight
Romance language titles	La Lune, La Luna
Hermetic Titles	Ruler of Flux and Reflux, Child of the Sons of the Mighty
Zodiacal glyph	♓
Planet, sign, or element	Pisces
Hebrew alphabet letter	ק
Hebrew transliteration/pronunciation	Qoph (KOOF)
Type of letter	Single
English letter equivalent	Q
Hebrew letter meanings	Back of the head final or last to circle
Number equivalent	100
Gifts and attributes	Sleep
Gateways	Genitals/Sleep

Conventional card numbering	**XVIII (18)**
Conventional card title	**The Moon**
Sephirothic Path	Netzach to Malkuth ("Victory" to "Kingdom")
King Scale	Crimson (ultra violet)
Queen Scale	Buff, flecked silver white
Prince Scale	Light translucent pinkish brown
Princess Scale	Stone color
Animal	Crab, dog, jackal, crayfish, horse, rabbit, fish, dolphin
Plant	Hazel, fig, willow, heartwort
Perfume/Incense	Red storax Ambergris
Gemstone/metal	Amethyst, ruby, pearl, coral, moonstone
Mythic figures	Anubis, Hecate, Vishnu as fish, Neptune, Poseidon, Khephra, Christ, Oannes
Magical weapon	The Twilight of the Place, the Magic Mirror
Musical note	B
Color correspondence for musical note	Red-violet

124. XVIII (18) The Moon
Tree of Life.

Conventional card numbering	**XIX (19)**
Conventional card title	**The Sun**
Alternate English titles	The Blazing Light
Romance language titles	Le Soleil, il Sole
Hermetic Titles	Lord of the Fire of the World
Zodiacal glyph	☉
Planet, sign, or element	Sun
Hebrew alphabet letter	ר
Hebrew transliteration/pronunciation	Resh (RESH)
Type of letter	Double
English letter equivalent	R
Hebrew letter meanings	Head Chief Poverty
Number equivalent	200
Gifts and attributes	Fertility and Barrenness
Gateways	Left nostril
Sephirothic Path	Hod to Yesod ("Glory" to "Foundation")
King Scale	Orange
Queen Scale	Gold yellow
Prince Scale	Rich amber

Conventional card numbering	**XIX (19)**
Conventional card title	**The Sun**
Princess Scale	Amber, rayed red
Animal	Deer, lion, crocodile, horse, snake, dolphin, swan, ox/bull, rooster, peacock, sparrowhawk, salamanders, hummingbird
Plant	Sunflower, cypress, angelica, bay laurel, carnation, chamomile, chrysanthemum, date, eucalyptus, ginseng, hazel, heliotrope, juniper, lemon, lime, marigold, oak, olive, peony, oranges. pineapple, sesame, sugarcane, tea, walnut, witchhazel, all yellow flowers
Perfume/Incense	Frankincense, mastic, benzoin, storax, labdanum, ambergris, musk, pepper, sandalwood, cinnamon, amber, saffron, cloves, "all brilliant odors"
Gemstone/metal	Gold, diamond, tiger's eye, chrysolite, sunstone, rubies,
Mythic figures	Apollo, Helios, Hyperion, Ra, Krishna, Legba, Vishnu
Magical weapon	The Lamen, the Bow and Arrow
Musical note	D
Color correspondence for musical note	Orange

125. XIX (19) The Sun
Tree of Life.

Conventional card numbering	**XX (20)**
Conventional card title	**Judgement (The Aeon)**
Alternate English titles	The Last Judgement, the Angel, Creation, the Awakening of the Dead
Romance language titles	Le jugement, L'Ange, L'Angelo, Il Giudizio, La Trompete
Hermetic Titles	The Spirit of the Primal Fire
Zodiacal glyph	△♀
Planet, sign, or element	Fire /Spirit or Pluto
Hebrew alphabet letter	ש
Hebrew transliteration/pronunciation	Shin (SHEEN/SEEN)
Type of letter	Mother
English letter equivalent	Sh
Hebrew letter meanings	Tooth ivory to sharpen, devour
Number equivalent	300
Gifts and attributes	The Heavens—Hot
Gateways	Head
Sephirothic Path	Hod to Malkuth ("Glory" to "Kingdom")

Conventional card numbering	**XX (20)**
Conventional card title	**Judgement (The Aeon)**
King Scale	Glowing orange scarlet
Queen Scale	Vermilion
Prince Scale	Scarlet, flecked gold
Princess Scale	Vermilion, flecked crimson and emerald
Animal	Lion, tiger, horse, hedgehog, porcupine
Plant	Red poppy, hibiscus, nettles, pepper, garlic, mustard, warm spices, marigold, sunflower
Perfume/Incense	Frankincense, citruses, cedar, warming spices, "all fiery odors"
Gemstone/metal	Fire opal, malachite, gold, iron, brass, all nitrates
Mythic figures	Agni, Hades, Vulcan, Pluto, Harpocrates, Horus
Magical weapon	The Wand or Lamp, the Pyramid of Fire, the Thurible
Musical note	C
Color correspondence for musical note	Red

126. XX (20) Judgement
(The Aeon) Tree of Life.

Conventional card numbering	**XXI (21)**
Conventional card title	**The World (The Universe)**
Alternate English titles	Time, Crown of the Magi
Romance language titles	Le Monde, Il Mondo
Hermetic Titles	The Great One of the Night of Time
Zodiacal glyph	♄
Planet, sign, or element	Saturn/Earth
Hebrew alphabet letter	ת
Hebrew transliteration/pronunciation	Tav (TAHV)
Type of letter	Double
English letter equivalent	Th
Hebrew letter meanings	Mark or cross seal of ownership to join or bind
Number equivalent	400
Gifts and attributes	Power & Servitude
Gateways	Mouth
Sephirothic Path	Yesod to Malkuth ("Foundation" to "Kingdom")
King Scale	Indigo
Queen Scale	Black
Prince Scale	Blue-black

Conventional card numbering	**XXI (21)**
Conventional card title	**The World (The Universe)**
Princess Scale	Black, rayed blue
Animal	Basilisk, toad, snake, flies, carrion birds, all black creatures, all nocturnal creatures, all creatures living in holes.
Plant	Aconite, cypress, yew, beet, beech, belladonna, comfrey, fern, hemlock, ivy, lobelia, morning glory, mosses, oleander, patchouli, poplar, tamarind, wolfsbane, rye, nightshade, rue, narcotic plants
Perfume/Incense	Pepperwort, all odoriferous roots asafoetida, sulfur, civet, musk, "all dark or unpleasant odors"
Gemstone/metal	Lead, onyx, jet, marble, hematite, lapis lazuli, black opal, golden marcasite
Mythic figures	Brahma, Pan, Gaea, Vidar, Saturn. Sobek, Tamogunam
Magical weapon	The Sickle
Musical note	A
Color correspondence for musical note	Blue

127. XXI (21) The World
(The Universe)
Tree of Life.

Ace of Wands	
Hermetic title (Thoth/*Golden Dawn*)	The Root of the Powers of Fire
Element	Fire
Zodiacal glyph	△/♋ ♌ ♍
Associated zodiacal majors	The Chariot Strength/Lust The Hermit
Dates	June 21–Sept. 22
Number	1
Geometric forms of number	Monad, the point
Number correspondences	Everything and Nothing
Tree of Life sephira	Kether
Traditional meaning	Crown
Tree of Life world	Atziluth
Color associated with Number and World on the Tree of Life	Brilliance
Type of deities associated with number	Creator gods
Papus's dialectic	Commencement of Commencement
Number significations	Wholeness, immortality, unity Potential, conception, initiative Independence, creativity, will

2 of Wands	
Hermetic title (Thoth/*Golden Dawn*)	Dominion
Planet ruling decan	Mars
Zodiac	0°–9° Aries
Planetary glyph	♂
Zodiacal glyph	♈
Associated planetary major	The Tower
Associated zodiacal major	The Emperor
Dates	March 21–March 30
Decan image from the Picatrix	A black man with a large and restless body, having red eyes and with an axe in his hand, girded in white cloth.
Decan signification from the Picatrix	Strength, high rank, wealth without shame
Decan image from Agrippa	A black man, standing and clothed in a white garment, girdled about, of a great body, with reddish eyes, and great strength, and like one that is angry.
Decan signification from Agrippa	Boldness, fortitude, loftiness, and shamelesness
Number	2
Geometric forms of number	Duad or dyad, the line
Number correspondences	Yin/Yang, Heaven/Earth
Tree of Life sephira	Chokmah
Traditional meaning	Wisdom
Tree of Life world	Atziluth
Color associated with Number and World on the Tree of Life	Pure soft blue
Type of deities associated with number	Father and Sky gods
Papus's dialectic	Opposition of Commencement
Number significations	Electrical charge, balance, mirror, equilibrium, opposition, the Other, the "gaze," self-consciousness, Choice, crossroads

3 of Wands	
Hermetic title (Thoth/*Golden Dawn*)	Virtue / *Established Strength*
Planet ruling decan	Sun
Zodiac	10°–19° Aries
Planetary glyph	☉
Zodiacal glyph	♈
Associated planetary major	The Sun
Associated zodiacal major	The Emperor
Dates	March 31–April 10
Decan image from the Picatrix	A woman dressed in green clothes, lacking one leg.
Decan signification from the Picatrix	High rank, nobility, wealth, rulership
Decan image from Agrippa	A woman, outwardly clothed with a red garment, and under it a white, spreading abroad over her feet.
Decan signification from Agrippa	Nobleness, height of a kingdom, and greatness of dominion
Number	3
Geometric forms of number	Triad, Triangle, Plane
Number correspondences	Father/Son/Holy Spirit; Mother/Maiden/Crone, Trinities
Tree of Life sephira	Binah
Traditional meaning	Understanding
Tree of Life world	Atziluth
Color associated with Number and World on the Tree of Life	Crimson
Type of deities associated with number	Mother and chthonic goddesses; time
Papus's dialectic	Equilibrium of Commencement
Number significations	Collaboration, community manifestation, action, movement

4 of Wands	
Hermetic title (Thoth/*Golden Dawn*)	Completion/Perfected Work
Planet ruling decan	Venus
Zodiac	20°–29° Aries
Planetary glyph	♀
Zodiacal glyph	♈
Associated planetary major	The Empress
Associated zodiacal major	The Emperor
Dates	April 11–April 20
Decan image from the Picatrix	A restless man, holding in his hands a gold bracelet, wearing red clothing, who wishes to do good, but is not able to do it.
Decan signification from the Picatrix	Subtlety, subtle mastery, new things, instruments
Decan image from Agrippa	A white man, pale, with reddish hair, and clothed with a red garment, who carrying on the one hand a golden bracelet, and holding forth a wooden staff, is restless, and like one in wrath, because he cannot perform that good he would.
Decan signification from Agrippa	Wit, meekness, joy, and beauty
Number	4
Geometric forms of number	Tetrad, Square, Pyramid, Solid
Number correspondences	Elements, seasons, directions, the world of matter, Apostles, Archangels, Humors, Tetragrammaton, Tetramorph
Tree of Life sephira	Chesed
Tree of Life world	Atziluth
Traditional meaning	Mercy
Color associated with Number and World on the Tree of Life	Deep violet
Type of deities associated with number	Ruler gods
Papus's dialectic	Commencement of Opposition
Number significations	Order, solidity, stability, the family, accomplishment, stillness

5 of Wands	
Hermetic title (Thoth/*Golden Dawn*)	Strife
Planet ruling decan	Saturn
Zodiac	0°–9° Leo
Planetary glyph	♄
Zodiacal glyph	♌
Associated planetary major	The World
Associated zodiacal major	Strength
Dates	July 21–August 1
Decan image from the Picatrix	A man wearing dirty clothes, and … the image of a rider looking to the north, and his body looks like the body of a bear and the body of a dog.
Decan signification from the Picatrix	Strength, generosity, and victory
Decan image from Agrippa	A man riding on a Lion.
Decan signification from Agrippa	Boldness, violence, cruelty, wickedness, lust and labors to be sustained
Number	5
Geometric forms of number	Pentad, pentagram, square pyramid
Number correspondences	Spirit + Matter, tattwas, Chinese elements
Tree of Life sephira	Geburah
Tree of Life world	Atziluth
Traditional meaning	Severity
Color associated with Number and World on the Tree of Life	Orange
Type of deities associated with number	War gods
Papus's dialectic	Opposition of Opposition
Number significations	Disruption—freedom from cycle of matter, creativity, risk

6 of Wands	
Hermetic title (Thoth/*Golden Dawn*)	Victory
Planet ruling decan	Jupiter
Zodiac	10°–19° Leo
Planetary glyph	♃
Zodiacal glyph	♌
Associated planetary major	The Wheel of Fortune
Associated zodiacal major	Strength
Dates	August 2–August 10
Decan image from the Picatrix	A man who wears a crown of white myrtle on his head, and he has a bow in his hand, the ascension of a man who is ignorant and base.
Decan signification from the Picatrix	Beauty, riding, the ascension of a man who is ignorant and base, war and naked swords
Decan image from Agrippa	An image with hands lifted up, and a man on whose head is a crown; he hath the appearance of an angry man, and one that threateneth, having in his right hand a sword drawn out of the scabbard, and in his left a buckler.
Decan signification from Agrippa	Hidden contentions, and unknown victories, & upon base men, and upon the occasions of quarrels and battles
Number	6
Geometric forms of number	Hexad, hexagram Octahedron (6 points, 8 faces), cube (6 faces)
Number correspondences	As above, so below, union of male and female
Tree of Life sephira	Tiphereth
Traditional meaning	Beauty
Tree of Life world	Atziluth
Color associated with Number and World on the Tree of Life	Clear pink rose
Type of deities associated with number	Solar and sacrificial gods
Papus's dialectic	Equilibrium of Opposition
Number significations	Harmony, beauty, love, reconciliation of opposites, well-being, responsibility, purpose

7 of Wands	
Hermetic title (Thoth/*Golden Dawn*)	Valor
Planet ruling decan	Mars
Zodiac	20°–29° Leo
Planetary glyph	♂
Zodiacal glyph	♌
Associated planetary major	The Tower
Associated zodiacal major	Strength
Dates	August 11–August 22
Decan image from the Picatrix	A man who is old and black and ugly, with fruit and meat in his mouth and holding a copper jug in his hand.
Decan signification from the Picatrix	Love and delight and food trays and health
Decan image from Agrippa	A young man in whose hand is a whip, and a man very sad, and of an ill aspect.
Decan signification from Agrippa	Love and society, and the loss of one's right for avoiding strife
Number	7
Geometric forms of number	Heptad, heptagram
Number correspondences	Planets, days of the week, chakras, musical whole notes
Tree of Life sephira	Netzach
Tree of Life world	Atziluth
Traditional meaning	Victory
Color associated with Number and World on the Tree of Life	Amber
Type of deities associated with number	Love and beauty goddesses
Papus's dialectic	Commencement of Equilibrium
Number significations	Imagination, secrets, quests, enchantment, mystery, ego

8 of Wands	
Hermetic title (Thoth/*Golden Dawn*)	Swiftness
Planet ruling decan	Mercury
Zodiac	0°–9° Sagittarius
Planetary glyph	☿
Zodiacal glyph	♐
Associated planetary major	The Magician
Associated zodiacal major	Temperance
Dates	November 23–December 2
Decan image from the Picatrix	The bodies of three men and one body is yellow, another white and the third is red.
Decan signification from the Picatrix	Heat, heaviness, growth in plains and fields, sustenance and division
Decan image from Agrippa	A man armed with a coat of mail, and holding a naked sword in his hand.
Decan signification from Agrippa	Boldness, malice, and liberty
Number	8
Geometric forms of number	Octad, octahedron (8 faces)
Number correspondences	*ba gua*, eight-spoked wheel of Wicca, eight-channel model of consciousness
Tree of Life sephira	Hod
Traditional meaning	Glory
Tree of Life world	Atziluth
Color associated with Number and World on the Tree of Life	Violet-purple
Type of deities associated with number	Knowledge gods
Papus's dialectic	Opposition of Equilibrium
Number significations	Order, discipline, accomplishment, leadership, success, mastery

9 of Wands	
Hermetic title (Thoth/*Golden Dawn*)	Strength / *Great Strength*
Planet ruling decan	Moon
Zodiac	10°–19° Sagittarius
Planetary glyph	☽
Zodiacal glyph	♐
Associated planetary major	The High Priestess
Associated zodiacal major	Temperance
Dates	December 3–December 12
Decan image from the Picatrix	A man leading cows and in front of him he has an ape and a bear.
Decan signification from the Picatrix	Fear, lamentations, grief, sadness, misery and troubles
Decan image from Agrippa	A woman weeping, and covered with clothes.
Decan signification from Agrippa	Sadness and fear of his own body
Number	9
Geometric forms of number	Nonad, Enneagram
Number correspondences	3 x 3, number of magic
Tree of Life sephira	Yesod
Traditional meaning	Foundation
Tree of Life world	Atziluth
Color associated with Number and World on the Tree of Life	Indigo
Type of deities associated with number	Lunar goddesses
Papus's dialectic	Equilibrium of Equilibrium
Number significations	Magic, psychic ability, power, completion, idealism

10 of Wands	
Hermetic title (Thoth/*Golden Dawn)*	Oppression
Planet ruling decan	Saturn
Zodiac	20°–29° Sagittarius
Planetary glyph	♄
Zodiacal glyph	♐
Associated planetary major	The World
Associated zodiacal major	Temperance
Dates	December 13–December 22
Decan image from the Picatrix	A man with a cap on his head, who is murdering another man.
Decan signification from the Picatrix	Evil desires, adverse and evil effects, and fickleness in these and evil wishes, hatred, dispersion, and evil conduct
Decan image from Agrippa	A man like in colour to gold, or an idle man playing with a staff.
Decan signification from Agrippa	Following our own wills, and obstinacy in them, and activeness for evil things, contentions, and horrible matters
Number	10
Geometric forms of number	Decad, decagram
Number correspondences	Digits, decans, sephiroth
Tree of Life sephira	Malkuth
Traditional meaning	Kingdom
Tree of Life world	Atziluth
Color associated with Number and World on the Tree of Life	Yellow
Type of deities associated with number	Harvest goddesses
Papus's dialectic	Uncertainty
Number significations	Renewal

Page/Princess of Wands	
Hermetic title (Thoth/*Golden Dawn*)	Princess of the Shining Flame The Rose of the Palace of Fire Princess and Empress of the Salamanders Throne of the Ace of Wands
Elemental glyph	▽△
Elemental title	Earth of Fire
Zodiacal glyph	♋♌♍
Zodiacal decans	0°–29° Cancer 0°–29° Leo 0°–29° Virgo
Corresponding Majors	The Chariot Strength/Lust The Hermit
Dates	June 21–September 22
Corresponding Minors	2 of Cups 3 of Cups 4 of Cups 5 of Wands 6 of Wands 7 of Wands 8 of Disks 9 of Disks 10 of Disks
Corresponding Minors Hermetic Titles	Love Abundance Luxury/Blended pleasure Strife Victory Valor Prudence Gain/Material gain Wealth
Tree of Life sephira	10: Malkuth
Tree of Life world	Atziluth

Knight of Wands (Rider Waite Smith) Prince of Wands (Thoth)	
Hermetic title (Thoth/*Golden Dawn)*	Prince of the Chariot of Fire Prince and Emperor of Salamanders
Elemental glyph	△△
Elemental title	Air of Fire
Zodiacal modality	Fixed
Zodiacal glyph	♌
Zodiacal decans	20°–29° Cancer III 0°–19° Leo I, II
Corresponding Majors	[The Chariot] Strength
Dates	July 13–August 11
Corresponding Minors	4 of Cups 5 of Wands 6 of Wands
Corresponding Minors Hermetic Titles	Luxury/Blended pleasure Strife Victory
Tree of Life sephira	6: Tiphereth
Tree of Life world	Atziluth

Queen of Wands	
Hermetic title (Thoth/*Golden Dawn*)	Queen of the Thrones of Flame Queen of the Salamanders
Elemental glyph	▽△
Elemental title	Water of Fire
Zodiacal modality	Cardinal
Zodiacal glyph	♈
Zodiacal decans	20°–29° Pisces III 0°–19° Aries I & II
Corresponding Majors	[The Moon] The Emperor
Dates	March 11–April 10
Corresponding Minors	10 of Cups 2 of Wands 3 of Wands
Corresponding Minors Hermetic Titles	Satiety/Perpetual Success Dominion Virtue/Established Strength
Tree of Life sephira	3: Binah
Tree of Life world	Atziluth

King of Wands (Rider Waite Smith) Knight of Wands (Thoth)	
Hermetic title (Thoth/*Golden Dawn*)	Lord of the Flame and the Lightning King of the Spirits of Fire King of the Salamanders
Elemental glyph	△△
Elemental title	Fire of Fire
Zodiacal modality	Mutable
Zodiacal glyph	♐
Zodiacal decans	20°–29° Scorpio III 0°–19° Sagittarius I & II
Corresponding Majors	[Death] Temperance/Art
Dates	November 12–December 12
Corresponding Minors	7 of Cups 8 of Wands 9 of Wands
Corresponding Minors Hermetic Titles	Debauch/Illusionary success Swiftness Strength/Great Strength
Tree of Life sephira	2: Chokmah
Tree of Life world	Atziluth

Ace of Cups	
Hermetic title (Thoth/*Golden Dawn*)	The Root of the Powers of the Waters
Element	Water
Zodiacal glyph	$\nabla/\Omega \,$ ♏ ♐
Associated zodiacal majors	Justice Death Temperance
Dates	October 10–December 20
Number	1
Geometric forms of number	Monad, the point
Number correspondences	Everything & Nothing
Tree of Life sephira	Kether
Traditional meaning	Crown
Tree of Life world	Briah
Color associated with Number and World on the Tree of Life	White brilliance
Type of deities associated with number	Creator gods
Papus's dialectic	Commencement of Commencement
Number significations	Wholeness, immortality, unity Potential, conception, initiative, independence, creativity, will

2 of Cups	
Hermetic title (Thoth/*Golden Dawn*)	Love
Planet ruling decan	Venus
Zodiac	0°–9° Cancer
Planetary glyph	♀
Zodiacal glyph	♋
Associated planetary major	The Empress
Associated zodiacal major	The Chariot
Dates	June 21–July 1
Decan image from the Picatrix	A man whose fingers and head are distorted and slanted, and his body is similar to a horse's body; his feet are white, and he has fig leaves on his body.
Decan signification from the Picatrix	Instruction, knowledge, love, subtlety and mastery
Decan image from Agrippa	A young virgin, adorned with fine clothes, and having a crown on her head.
Decan signification from Agrippa	Acuteness of senses, subtlety of wit, and the love of men
Number	2
Geometric forms of number	Duad or dyad, the line
Number correspondences	Yin/Yang, Heaven/Earth
Tree of Life sephira	Chokmah
Traditional meaning	Wisdom
Tree of Life world	Briah
Color associated with Number and World on the Tree of Life	Grey
Type of deities associated with number	Father and Sky gods
Papus's dialectic	Opposition of Commencement
Number significations	Electrical charge, balance, mirror, equilibrium, opposition, the Other, the "gaze," self-consciousness, Choice, crossroads

3 of Cups	
Hermetic title (Thoth/*Golden Dawn*)	Abundance
Planet ruling decan	Mercury
Zodiac	10°–19° Cancer
Planetary glyph	☿
Zodiacal glyph	♋
Associated planetary major	The Magician
Associated zodiacal major	The Chariot
Dates	July 2–July 12
Decan image from the Picatrix	A woman with a beautiful face, and on her head she has a crown of green myrtle, and in her hand is a stem of the water lily, and she is singing songs of love and joy.
Decan signification from the Picatrix	Games, wealth, joy, and abundance
Decan image from Agrippa	A man clothed in comely apparel, or a man and woman sitting at the table and playing.
Decan signification from Agrippa	Riches, mirth, gladness, and the love of women
Number	3
Geometric forms of number	Triad, triangle, plane
Number correspondences	Father/Son/Holy Spirit; Mother/Maiden/Crone, trinities
Tree of Life sephira	Binah
Traditional meaning	Understanding
Tree of Life world	Briah
Color associated with Number and World on the Tree of Life	Black
Type of deities associated with number	Mother and chthonic goddesses; time
Papus's dialectic	Equilibrium of Commencement
Number significations	Collaboration, community Manifestation, action, movement

4 of Cups	
Hermetic title (Thoth/*Golden Dawn*)	Luxury/Blended pleasure
Planet ruling decan	Moon
Zodiac	20°–29° Cancer
Planetary glyph	☽
Zodiacal glyph	♋
Associated planetary major	The High Priestess
Associated zodiacal major	The Chariot
Dates	July 13–July 20
Decan image from the Picatrix	A celhafe* with a snake in his hand, who has golden chains before him. *Probably a turtle
Decan signification from the Picatrix	Running, riding, and acquisition by means of war, lawsuits, and conflict
Decan image from Agrippa	A man, a hunter with his lance and horn, bringing out dogs for to hunt.
Decan signification from Agrippa	The contention of men, the pursuing of those who fly, the hunting and possessing of things by arms and brawlings
Number	4
Geometric forms of number	Tetrad, square, triangular pyramid, solid
Number correspondences	Elements, seasons, directions, the world of matter, Apostles, Archangels, Humors, Tetragrammaton, Tetramorph
Tree of Life sephira	Chesed
Traditional meaning	Mercy
Tree of Life world	Briah
Color associated with Number and World on the Tree of Life	Blue
Type of deities associated with number	Ruler gods
Papus's dialectic	Commencement of Opposition
Number significations	Order, solidity, stability, the family, accomplishment, stillness

5 of Cups	
Hermetic title (Thoth/*Golden Dawn*)	Disappointment / *Loss in Pleasure*
Planet ruling decan	Mars
Zodiac	0°–9° Scorpio
Planetary glyph	♂
Zodiacal glyph	♏
Associated planetary major	The Tower
Associated zodiacal major	Death
Dates	October 23–November 1
Decan image from the Picatrix	A man with a lance in his right hand and in his left hand he holds the head of a man.
Decan signification from the Picatrix	Settlement, sadness, ill will, and hatred
Decan image from Agrippa	A woman of good face and habit, and two men striking her.
Decan signification from Agrippa	Comeliness, beauty, and strifes, treacheries, deceits, detractations, and perditions
Number	5
Geometric forms of number	Pentad, pentagram, square pyramid
Number correspondences	Spirit + Matter, Tattwas, Chinese elements
Tree of Life sephira	Geburah
Traditional meaning	Severity
Tree of Life world	Briah
Color associated with Number and World on the Tree of Life	Red
Type of deities associated with number	War gods
Papus's dialectic	Opposition of Opposition
Number significations	Disruption–freedom from cycle of matter, creativity, risk

6 of Cups	
Hermetic title (Thoth/*Golden Dawn*)	Pleasure
Planet ruling decan	Sun
Zodiac	10°–19° Scorpio
Planetary glyph	☉
Zodiacal glyph	♏
Associated planetary major	The Sun
Associated zodiacal major	Death
Dates	November 2–November 11
Decan image from the Picatrix	A man riding a camel, holding a scorpion in his hand.
Decan signification from the Picatrix	Knowledge, modesty, settlement, and of speaking evil of one another
Decan image from Agrippa	A man naked, and a woman naked, and a man sitting on the earth, and before him two dogs biting one another.
Decan signification from Agrippa	Impudence, deceit, and false dealing, and for to lend mischief and strife amongst men
Number	6
Geometric forms of number	Hexad, hexagram Octahedron (6 points, 8 faces), cube (6 faces)
Number correspondences	As above, so below, union of male and female
Tree of Life sephira	Tiphereth
Traditional meaning	Beauty
Tree of Life world	Briah
Color associated with Number and World on the Tree of Life	Yellow
Type of deities associated with number	Solar and sacrificial gods
Papus's dialectic	Equilibrium of Opposition
Number significations	Harmony, beauty, love, reconciliation of opposites, well-being, responsibility, purpose

7 of Cups	
Hermetic title (Thoth/*Golden Dawn)*	Debauch/*Illusionary Success*
Planet ruling decan	Venus
Zodiac	20°–29° Scorpio
Planetary glyph	♀
Zodiacal glyph	♏
Associated planetary major	The Empress
Associated zodiacal major	Death
Dates	November 12–November 22
Decan image from the Picatrix	A horse and a rabbit.
Decan signification from the Picatrix	Evil works and flavors, and forcing sex upon unwilling women
Decan image from Agrippa	A man bowed downward upon his knees, and a woman striking him with a staff.
Decan signification from Agrippa	Drunkenness, fornication, wrath, violence, and strife
Number	7
Geometric forms of number	Heptad, heptagram
Number correspondences	Planets, days of the week, chakras, musical whole notes
Tree of Life sephira	Netzach
Traditional meaning	Victory
Tree of Life world	Briah
Color associated with Number and World on the Tree of Life	Emerald
Type of deities associated with number	Love and beauty goddesses
Papus's dialectic	Commencement of Equilibrium
Number significations	Imagination, secrets, quests, enchantment, mystery, ego

8 of Cups	
Hermetic title (Thoth/*Golden Dawn*)	Indolence/*Abandoned Success*
Planet ruling decan	Saturn
Zodiac	0°–9° Pisces
Planetary glyph	♄
Zodiacal glyph	♓
Associated planetary major	World
Associated zodiacal major	The Moon
Dates	February 19–February 28
Decan image from the Picatrix	A man with two bodies, who looks as though he is giving a gesture of greeting with his hands.
Decan signification from the Picatrix	Peace and humility, debility, many journeys, misery, seeking wealth, miserable life.
Decan image from Agrippa	A man carrying burdens on his shoulder, and well clothed.
Decan signification from Agrippa	Journeys, change of place, and in carefulness of getting wealth and clothes
Number	8
Geometric forms of number	Octad, octahedron (8 faces)
Number correspondences	Ba gua, 8-spoked wheel of Wicca, 8-channel model of consciousness
Tree of Life sephira	Hod
Traditional meaning	Glory
Tree of Life world	Briah
Color associated with Number and World on the Tree of Life	Orange
Type of deities associated with number	Knowledge gods
Papus's dialectic	Opposition of Equilibrium
Number significations	Order, discipline, accomplishment, leadership, success, mastery

9 of Cups	
Hermetic title (Thoth/*Golden Dawn*)	Happiness / *Material Happiness*
Planet ruling decan	Jupiter
Zodiac	10°–19° Pisces
Planetary glyph	♃
Zodiacal glyph	♓
Associated planetary major	Wheel of Fortune
Associated zodiacal major	The Moon
Dates	March 1–March 10
Decan image from the Picatrix	A man upside down with his head below and his feet raised up, and in his hand is a tray from which the food has been eaten.
Decan signification from the Picatrix	Great reward, and strong will in things that are high, serious and thoughtful
Decan image from Agrippa	A woman of a good countenance, and well adorned.
Decan signification from Agrippa	To desire and put oneself on about high and great matters
Number	Nonad, enneagram
Geometric forms of number	9
Number correspondences	3 x 3, number of magic
Tree of Life sephira	Yesod
Traditional meaning	Foundation
Tree of Life world	Briah
Color associated with Number and World on the Tree of Life	Violet
Type of deities associated with number	Lunar goddesses
Papus's dialectic	Equilibrium of Equilibrium
Number significations	Magic, psychic ability, power, completion, idealism

10 of Cups	
Hermetic title (Thoth/*Golden Dawn*)	Satiety / *Perpetual Success*
Planet ruling decan	Mars
Zodiac	20°–29° Pisces
Planetary glyph	♂
Zodiacal glyph	♓
Associated planetary major	Tower
Associated zodiacal major	The Moon
Dates	March 11–March 20
Decan image from the Picatrix	A sad man full of evil thoughts, thinking of deception and treachery, and before him is a woman with a donkey climbing atop her, and in her hand is a bird.
Decan signification from the Picatrix	Advancement and lying with women with a great appetite, and of quiet and seeking rest
Decan image from Agrippa	A man naked, or a youth, and nigh him a beautiful maid, whose head is adorned with flowers.
Decan signification from Agrippa	Rest, idleness, delight, fornication, and embracings of women
Number	10
Geometric forms of number	Decad, decagram
Number correspondences	Digits, Decans, Sephiroth
Tree of Life sephira	Malkuth
Traditional meaning	Kingdom
Tree of Life world	Briah
Color associated with Number and World on the Tree of Life	Citrine-Olive-Russet-Black
Type of deities associated with number	Harvest goddesses
Papus's dialectic	Uncertainty
Number significations	Renewal

Page/Princess of Cups	
Hermetic title (Thoth/*Golden Dawn*)	Princess of the Waters Lotus of the Palace of Floods Princess and Empress of Nymphs and Undines Throne of the Ace of Cups
Elemental glyph	▽ ▽
Elemental title	Earth of Water
Zodiacal glyph	♎ ♏ ♐
Zodiacal decans	0°–29° Libra 0°–29° Scorpio 0°–29° Sagittarius
Corresponding Majors	Justice/Adjustment Death Temperance/Art
Dates	September 23–December 20
Corresponding Minors	2 of Swords 3 of Swords 4 of Swords 5 of Cups 6 of Cups 7 of Cups 8 of Wands 9 of Wands 10 of Wands
Corresponding Minors Hermetic Titles	Peace / Peace Restored Sorrow Truce/Rest from Strife Disappointment/Loss in Pleasure Pleasure Debauch/Illusionary Success Swiftness Strength/Great Strength Oppression
Tree of Life sephira	10: Malkuth
Tree of Life world	Briah

Knight of Cups (Rider Waite Smith) **Prince of Cups (Thoth)**	
Hermetic title (Thoth/*Golden Dawn*)	Prince of the Chariot of the Waters Prince and Emperor of Nymphs and Undines
Elemental glyph	△▽
Elemental title	Air of Water
Zodiacal modality	Fixed
Zodiacal glyph	♏
Zodiacal decans	20°–29° Libra III 0°–19° Scorpio I & II
Corresponding Majors	[Justice/Adjustment] Death
Dates	October 13–November 11
Corresponding Minors	4 of Swords 5 of Cups 6 of Cups
Corresponding Minors **Hermetic Titles**	Truce/Rest from Strife Disappointment/Loss in Pleasure Pleasure
Tree of Life sephira	6: Tiphereth
Tree of Life world	Briah

Queen of Cups	
Hermetic title (Thoth/*Golden Dawn*)	Queen of the Thrones of the Waters Queen of Nymphs and Undines
Elemental glyph	▽▽
Elemental title	Water of Water
Zodiacal modality	Cardinal
Zodiacal glyph	♋
Zodiacal decans	20°–29° Gemini III 0°–19° Cancer I & II
Corresponding Majors	[The Lovers] The Chariot
Dates	June 11–July 12
Corresponding Minors	10 of Swords 2 of Cups 3 of Cups
Corresponding Minors Hermetic Titles	Ruin Love Abundance
Tree of Life sephira	3: Binah
Tree of Life world	Briah

King of Cups (Rider Waite Smith) **Knight of Cups (Thoth)**	
Hermetic title (Thoth/*Golden Dawn*)	Lord of the Waves and the Waters King of the Hosts of the Sea King of Undines and of Nymphs
Elemental glyph	△▽
Elemental title	Fire of Water
Zodiacal modality	Mutable
Zodiacal glyph	♓
Zodiacal decans	20°–29° Aquarius III 0°–19° Pisces I & II
Corresponding Majors	[The Star] The Moon
Dates	February 9–March 10
Corresponding Minors	7 of Swords 8 of Cups 9 of Cups
Corresponding Minors **Hermetic Titles**	Futility Indolence/Abandoned Success Happiness/Material Happiness
Tree of Life sephira	2: Chokmah
Tree of Life world	Briah

Ace of Swords	
Hermetic title (Thoth/*Golden Dawn*)	The Root of the Powers of the Air
Planet ruling decan	
Element	Air
Zodiacal glyph	♎/♑ ♒ ♓
Associated zodiacal majors	The Devil The Star The Moon
Dates	December 20–March 20
Number	1
Geometric forms of number	Monad, the point
Number correspondences	Everything and Nothing
Tree of Life sephira	Kether
Traditional meaning	Crown
Color associated with Number and World on the Tree of Life	White brilliance
Type of deities associated with number	Creator gods
Papus's dialectic	Commencement of Commencement
Number significations	Wholeness, immortality, unity Potential, conception, initiative Independence, creativity, will

2 of Swords	
Hermetic title (Thoth/*Golden Dawn*)	Peace / *Peace Restored*
Planet ruling decan	Moon
Zodiac	0°–9° Libra
Planetary glyph	☽
Zodiacal glyph	♎
Associated planetary major	The High Priestess
Associated zodiacal major	Justice
Dates	September 23–October 2
Decan image from the Picatrix	A man with a lance in his right hand, and in his left hand he holds a bird hanging by its feet.
Decan signification from the Picatrix	Justice, truth, good judgment, complete justice for the people and weak persons, and doing good for beggars
Decan image from Agrippa	An angry man, in whose hand is a pipe, and the form of a man reading in a book.
Decan signification from Agrippa	Justifying and helping the miserable and weak against the powerful and wicked
Number	2
Geometric forms of number	Duad or dyad, the line
Number correspondences	Yin/Yang, Heaven/Earth
Tree of Life sephira	Chokmah
Traditional meaning	Wisdom
Tree of Life world	Yetzirah
Color associated with Number and World on the Tree of Life	Blue pearl grey, like mother of pearl
Type of deities associated with number	Father and sky gods
Papus's dialectic	Opposition of Commencement
Number significations	Electrical charge, balance, mirror, equilibrium, opposition, the Other, the "gaze," self-consciousness, Choice, crossroads

3 of Swords	
Hermetic title (Thoth/*Golden Dawn*)	Sorrow
Planet ruling decan	Saturn
Zodiac	10°–19° Libra
Planetary glyph	♄
Zodiacal glyph	Ω
Associated planetary major	The World
Associated zodiacal major	Justice
Dates	October 3–October 12
Decan image from the Picatrix	A black man, a bridegroom having a joyous journey.
Decan signification from the Picatrix	Tranquility, joy, abundance and good living
Decan image from Agrippa	Two men furious and wrathful and a man in a comely garment, sitting in a chair.
Decan signification from Agrippa	Indignation against the evil, and quietness and security of life with plenty of good things
Number	3
Geometric forms of number	Triad, triangle, plane
Number correspondences	Father/Son/Holy Spirit; Mother/Maiden/Crone, Trinities
Tree of Life sephira	Binah
Traditional meaning	Understanding
Tree of Life world	Yetzirah
Color associated with Number and World on the Tree of Life	Dark brown
Type of deities associated with number	Mother and chthonic goddesses; time
Papus's dialectic	Equilibrium of Commencement
Number significations	Collaboration, community Manifestation, action, movement

4 of Swords	
Hermetic title (Thoth/*Golden Dawn*)	Truce/*Rest from Strife*
Planet ruling decan	Jupiter
Zodiac	20°–29° Libra
Planetary glyph	♃
Zodiacal glyph	♎
Associated planetary major	The Wheel of Fortune
Associated zodiacal major	Justice
Dates	October 13–October 22
Decan image from the Picatrix	A man riding a donkey with a wolf in front of him.
Decan signification from the Picatrix	Evil works, sodomy, adultery, singing, joy and flavors
Decan image from Agrippa	A violent man holding a bow, and before him a naked man, and also another man holding bread in one hand, and a cup of wine in the other.
Decan signification from Agrippa	Wicked lusts, singings, sports and gluttony
Number	4
Geometric forms of number	Tetrad, square, triangular pyramid, solid
Number correspondences	Elements, seasons, directions, the world of matter, Apostles, Archangels, Humors, Tetragrammaton, Tetramorph
Tree of Life sephira	Chesed
Traditional meaning	Mercy
Tree of Life world	Yetzirah
Color associated with Number and World on the Tree of Life	Deep purple
Type of deities associated with number	Ruler gods
Papus's dialectic	Commencement of Opposition
Number significations	Order, solidity, stability, the family, accomplishment, stillness

5 of Swords	
Hermetic title (Thoth/*Golden Dawn*)	Defeat
Planet ruling decan	Venus
Zodiac	0°–9° Aquarius
Planetary glyph	♀
Zodiacal glyph	♒
Associated planetary major	The Empress
Associated zodiacal major	The Star
Dates	January 20–January 29
Decan image from the Picatrix	A man whose head is mutilated and he holds a peacock in his hand.
Decan signification from the Picatrix	Misery, poverty, and slavery
Decan image from Agrippa	A prudent man, and of a woman spinning.
Decan signification from Agrippa	The thought and labor for gain, in poverty and baseness
Number	5
Geometric forms of number	Pentad, pentagram, square pyramid
Number correspondences	Spirit + Matter, Tattwas, Chinese elements
Tree of Life sephira	Geburah
Traditional meaning	Severity
Tree of Life world	Yetzirah
Color associated with Number and World on the Tree of Life	Bright scarlet
Type of deities associated with number	War gods
Papus's dialectic	Opposition of Opposition
Number significations	Disruption—freedom from cycle of matter, creativity, risk

6 of Swords	
Hermetic title (Thoth/*Golden Dawn*)	Science, *Earned Success*
Planet ruling decan	Mercury
Zodiac	10°–19° Aquarius
Planetary glyph	☿
Zodiacal glyph	♒
Associated planetary major	The Magician
Associated zodiacal major	The Star
Dates	January 30–February 8
Decan image from the Picatrix	A man who looks like a king, who permits much to himself and abhors what he sees.
Decan signification from the Picatrix	Beauty and position, having what is desired, completion, detriment and debility
Decan image from Agrippa	A man with a long beard.
Decan signification from Agrippa	Understanding, meekness, modesty, liberty and good manners
Number	6
Geometric forms of number	Hexad, hexagram Octahedron (6 points, 8 faces), cube (6 faces)
Number correspondences	As above, so below, union of male and female
Tree of Life sephira	Tiphereth
Traditional meaning	Beauty
Tree of Life world	Yetzirah
Color associated with Number and World on the Tree of Life	Rich salmon
Type of deities associated with number	Solar and sacrificial gods
Papus's dialectic	Equilibrium of Opposition
Number significations	Harmony, beauty, love, reconciliation of opposites, well-being, responsibility, purpose

7 of Swords	
Hermetic title (Thoth/*Golden Dawn*)	Futility/*Unstable Effort*
Planet ruling decan	Moon
Zodiac	20°–29° Aquarius
Planetary glyph	☽
Zodiacal glyph	♒
Associated planetary major	The High Priestess
Associated zodiacal major	The Star
Dates	February 9–February 18
Decan image from the Picatrix	A man having a mutilated head, and an old woman is with him.
Decan signification from the Picatrix	Abundance, accomplishing of will, giving offense
Decan image from Agrippa	A black and angry man.
Decan signification from Agrippa	Insolence and impudence
Number	7
Geometric forms of number	Heptad, heptagram
Number correspondences	Planets, days of the week, chakras, musical whole notes
Tree of Life sephira	Netzach
Traditional meaning	Victory
Tree of Life world	Yetzirah
Color associated with Number and World on the Tree of Life	Bright yellow-green
Type of deities associated with number	Love and beauty goddesses
Papus's dialectic	Commencement of Equilibrium
Number significations	Imagination, secrets, quests, enchantment, mystery, ego

8 of Swords	
Hermetic title (Thoth/*Golden Dawn*)	Interference / *Shortened Force*
Planet ruling decan	Jupiter
Zodiac	0°–9° Gemini
Planetary glyph	♃
Zodiacal glyph	Ⅱ
Associated planetary major	The Wheel of Fortune
Associated zodiacal major	The Lovers
Dates	May 21–May 30
Decan image from the Picatrix	A beautiful woman, a mistress of stitching, two calves and two horses.
Decan signification from the Picatrix	Writing, computation and number, giving and taking, the sciences
Decan image from Agrippa	A man in whose hand is a rod, and he is, as it were, serving another.
Decan signification from Agrippa	Wisdom, and the knowledge of numbers and arts in which there is no profit
Number	8
Geometric forms of number	Octad, octahedron (8 faces)
Number correspondences	*Ba gua*, 8-spoked wheel of Wicca, 8-channel model of consciousness
Tree of Life sephira	Hod
Traditional meaning	Glory
Tree of Life world	Yetzirah
Color associated with Number and World on the Tree of Life	Red-russet
Type of deities associated with number	Knowledge gods
Papus's dialectic	Opposition of Equilibrium
Number significations	Order, discipline, accomplishment, leadership, success, mastery

9 of Swords	
Hermetic title (Thoth/*Golden Dawn*)	Cruelty/*Despair and Cruelty*
Planet ruling decan	Mars
Zodiac	10°–19° Gemini
Planetary glyph	♂
Zodiacal glyph	II
Associated planetary major	The Tower
Associated zodiacal major	The Lovers
Dates	June 1–June 10
Decan image from the Picatrix	A man whose face is like an eagle and his head is covered by linen cloth; clothed and protected by a coat of leaden mail, and on his head is an iron helmet about which is a silk crown, and in his hand he has a bow and arrows.
Decan signification from the Picatrix	Oppression, evils and subtelty
Decan image from Agrippa	A man in whose hand is a pipe, and another being bowed down, digging the earth
Decan signification from Agrippa	Infamous and dishonest agility, as that of jesters and jugglers; it also signifies labors and painful searching.
Number	9
Geometric forms of number	Nonad, enneagram
Number correspondences	3 x 3, number of magic
Tree of Life sephira	Yesod
Traditional meaning	Foundation
Tree of Life world	Yetzirah
Color associated with Number and World on the Tree of Life	Very dark purple
Type of deities associated with number	Lunar goddesses
Papus's dialectic	Equilibrium of Equilibrium
Number significations	Magic, psychic ability, power, completion, idealism

10 of Swords	
Hermetic title (Thoth/*Golden Dawn*)	Ruin
Planet ruling decan	Sun
Zodiac	20°–29° Gemini
Planetary glyph	☉
Zodiacal glyph	Ⅱ
Associated planetary major	The Sun
Associated zodiacal major	The Lovers
Dates	June 11–June 20
Decan image from the Picatrix	A man clothed in mail, with a bow, arrows, and quiver.
Decan signification from the Picatrix	Audacity, honesty, division of labor, and consolation
Decan image from Agrippa	A man seeking for arms, and a fool holding in the right hand a bird, and in his left a pipe.
Decan signification from Agrippa	Forgetfulness, wrath, boldness, jests, scurrilities, and unprofitable words
Number	10
Geometric forms of number	Decad, decagram
Number correspondences	Digits, decans, sephiroth
Tree of Life sephira	Malkuth
Traditional meaning	Kingdom
Tree of Life world	Yetzirah
Color associated with Number and World on the Tree of Life	Citrine-Olive-Russet-Black, but flecked with gold
Type of deities associated with number	Harvest goddesses
Papus's dialectic	Uncertainty
Number significations	Renewal

Page/Princess of Swords	
Hermetic title (Thoth/*Golden Dawn*)	Princess of the Rushing Winds Lotus of the Palace of Air Princess and Empress of the Sylphs and Sylphides Throne of the Ace of Swords
Elemental glyph	▽△
Elemental title	Earth of Air
Zodiacal glyph	♑ ♒ ♓
Zodiacal decans	0°–29° Capricorn 0°–29° Aquarius 0°–29° Pisces
Corresponding Majors	The Devil The Star The Moon
Dates	December 21–March 20
Corresponding Minors	2 of Disks 3 of Disks 4 of Disks 5 of Swords 6 of Swords 7 of Swords 8 of Cups 9 of Cups 10 of Cups
Corresponding Minors Hermetic Titles	Change/Harmonious Change Work/Material Works Power/Earthly Power Defeat Science, Earned Success Futility/Unstable Effort Indolence/Abandoned Success Happiness/Material Happiness Satiety/Perpetual Success
Tree of Life sephira	10: Malkuth
Tree of Life world	Yetzirah

Knight of Swords (Rider Waite Smith) Prince of Swords (Thoth)	
Hermetic title (Thoth/*Golden Dawn)*	Prince of the Chariots of the Winds Prince and Emperor of Sylphs and Sylphides
Elemental glyph	⧍ ⧍
Elemental title	Air of Air
Zodiacal modality	Fixed
Zodiacal glyph	♒
Zodiacal decans	20°–29° Capricorn III 0°–19° Aquarius I & II
Corresponding Majors	[The Devil] The Star
Dates	January 10–February 8
Corresponding Minors	4 of Disks 5 of Swords 6 of Swords
Corresponding Minors Hermetic Titles	Power/Earthly Power Defeat Science/Earned Success
Tree of Life sephira	6: Tiphereth
Tree of Life world	Yetzirah

Queen of Swords	
Hermetic title (Thoth/*Golden Dawn*)	Queen of the Thrones of Air Queen of the Sylphs and Sylphides
Elemental glyph	▽△
Elemental title	Water of Air
Zodiacal modality	Cardinal
Zodiacal glyph	Ω
Zodiacal decans	20°–29° Virgo III 0°–19° Libra I & II
Corresponding Majors	[The Hermit] Justice/Adjustment
Dates	September 12–October 12
Corresponding Minors	10 of Disks 2 of Swords 3 of Swords
Corresponding Minors Hermetic Titles	Wealth Peace/Peace Restored Sorrow
Tree of Life sephira	3: Binah
Tree of Life world	Yetzirah

King of Swords (Rider Waite Smith) Knight of Swords (Thoth)	
Hermetic title (Thoth/*Golden Dawn*)	Lord of the Winds and the Breezes King of the Spirit of Air King of Sylphs and Sylphides
Elemental glyph	△ △
Elemental title	Fire of Air
Zodiacal modality	Mutable
Zodiacal glyph	Ⅱ
Zodiacal decans	20°–29° Taurus III 0°–19° Gemini I & II
Corresponding Majors	[The Hierophant] The Lovers
Dates	May 11–June 10
Corresponding Minors	7 of Disks 8 of Swords 9 of Swords
Corresponding Minors Hermetic Titles	Failure/Success Unfulfilled Interference/Shortened Force Cruelty/Despair and Cruelty
Tree of Life sephira	2: Chokmah
Tree of Life world	Yetzirah

Ace of Pentacles	
Hermetic title (Thoth/*Golden Dawn*)	The Root of the Powers of the Earth
Element	Earth
Zodiacal glyph	▽/♈♉♊
Associated zodiacal majors	The Emperor The Hierophant The Lovers
Dates	March 21–June 20
Number	1
Geometric forms of number	Monad, the point
Number correspondences	Everything & Nothing
Tree of Life sephira	Kether
Traditional meaning	Crown
Tree of Life world	Assiah
Color associated with Number and World on the Tree of Life	White flecked gold
Type of deities associated with number	Creator gods
Papus's dialectic	Commencement of Commencement
Number significations	Wholeness, immortality, unity Potential, conception, initiative Independence, creativity, will

2 of Pentacles	
Hermetic title (Thoth/*Golden Dawn*)	Change/*Harmonious Change*
Planet ruling decan	Jupiter
Zodiac	0°–9° Capricorn
Planetary glyph	♃
Zodiacal glyph	♑
Associated planetary major	The Wheel of Fortune
Associated zodiacal major	The Devil
Dates	December 21–December 30
Decan image from the Picatrix	A man with a reed in his right hand and a hoopoe bird in his left.
Decan signification from the Picatrix	Happiness, joy, and bringing things to an end that are sluggish, weak, and proceeding poorly
Decan image from Agrippa	A woman, and a man carrying full bags.
Decan signification from Agrippa	To go forth and to rejoice, to gain and to lose with weakness and baseness
Number	2
Geometric forms of number	Duad or dyad, the line
Number correspondences	Yin/Yang, Heaven/Earth
Tree of Life sephira	Chokmah
Traditional meaning	Wisdom
Tree of Life world	Assiah
Color associated with Number and World on the Tree of Life	White flecked red, blue, and yellow
Type of deities associated with number	Father and sky gods
Papus's dialectic	Opposition of Commencement
Number significations	Electrical charge, balance, mirror, equilibrium, opposition, the Other, the "gaze," self-consciousness Choice, crossroads

3 of Pentacles	
Hermetic title (Thoth/*Golden Dawn*)	Work/*Material Works*
Planet ruling decan	Mars
Zodiac	10°–19° Capricorn
Planetary glyph	♂
Zodiacal glyph	♑
Associated planetary major	The Tower
Associated zodiacal major	The Devil
Dates	December 31–January 9
Decan image from the Picatrix	A man with a common ape in front of him.
Decan signification from the Picatrix	Seeking to do what cannot be done and to attain what cannot be known
Decan image from Agrippa	Two women, and a man looking towards a bird flying in the Air.
Decan signification from Agrippa	Requiring those things which cannot be done, searching after those things which cannot be known
Number	3
Geometric forms of number	Triad, triangle, plane
Number correspondences	Father/Son/Holy Spirit; Mother/Maiden/Crone, Trinities
Tree of Life sephira	Binah
Traditional meaning	Understanding
Tree of Life world	Assiah
Color associated with Number and World on the Tree of Life	Grey flecked pink
Type of deities associated with number	Mother and chthonic goddesses; time
Papus's dialectic	Equilibrium of Commencement
Number significations	Collaboration, community Manifestation, action, movement

4 of Pentacles	
Hermetic title (Thoth/*Golden Dawn*)	Power / *Earthly Power*
Planet ruling decan	Sun
Zodiac	20°–29° Capricorn
Planetary glyph	☉
Zodiacal glyph	♑
Associated planetary major	The Sun
Associated zodiacal major	The Devil
Dates	January 10–January 19
Decan image from the Picatrix	A man holding a book which he opens and closes, and before him is the tail of a fish.
Decan signification from the Picatrix	Wealth and the accumulation of money and increase and embarking on trade and pressing on to a good end
Decan image from Agrippa	A woman chaste in body, and wise in her work, and a banker gathering his money together on the table.
Decan signification from Agrippa	To govern in prudence, in covetousness of money, and in avarice
Number	4
Geometric forms of number	Tetrad, square, triangular pyramid, solid
Number correspondences	Elements, seasons, directions, the world of matter, Apostles, Archangels, Humors, Tetragrammaton, Tetramorph
Tree of Life sephira	Chesed
Traditional meaning	Mercy
Tree of Life world	Assiah
Color associated with Number and World on the Tree of Life	Deep azure flecked yellow
Type of deities associated with number	Ruler gods
Papus's dialectic	Commencement of Opposition
Number significations	Order, solidity, stability, the family, accomplishment, stillness

5 of Pentacles	
Hermetic title (Thoth/*Golden Dawn*)	Worry/*Material Trouble*
Planet ruling decan	Mercury
Zodiac	0°–9° Taurus
Planetary glyph	☿
Zodiacal glyph	♉
Associated planetary major	The Magician
Associated zodiacal major	The Hierophant
Dates	April 21–April 30
Decan image from the Picatrix	A woman with curly hair, who has one son wearing clothing looking like flame, and she is wearing garments of the same sort.
Decan signification from the Picatrix	Plowing, working on the land, sciences, geometry, sowing, building
Decan image from Agrippa	A naked man, an Archer, Harvester or Husbandman.
Decan signification from Agrippa	To sow, plough, build, people, and divide the earth, according to the rules of Geometry
Number	5
Geometric forms of number	Pentad, pentagram, square pyramid
Number correspondences	Spirit + Matter, tattwas, Chinese elements
Tree of Life sephira	Geburah
Traditional meaning	Severity
Tree of Life world	Assiah
Color associated with Number and World on the Tree of Life	Red flecked black
Type of deities associated with number	War gods
Papus's dialectic	Opposition of Opposition
Number significations	Disruption—freedom from cycle of matter, creativity, risk

6 of Pentacles	
Hermetic title (Thoth/*Golden Dawn*)	Success/*Material Success*
Planet ruling decan	Moon
Zodiac	10°–19° Taurus
Planetary glyph	☽
Zodiacal glyph	♉
Associated planetary major	The High Priestess
Associated zodiacal major	The Hierophant
Dates	May 1–May 10
Decan image from the Picatrix	A man with a body like a camel, who has cow's hooves on his fingers, and he is covered by a linen cloth. He desires to work the land, sow, and build.
Decan signification from the Picatrix	Nobility, power, rewarding the people
Decan image from Agrippa	A naked man, holding in his hand a key.
Decan signification from Agrippa	Power, nobility, and dominion over people
Number	6
Geometric forms of number	Hexad, hexagram Octahedron (6 points, 8 faces), cube (6 faces)
Number correspondences	As above, so below, union of male and female
Tree of Life sephira	Tiphereth
Traditional meaning	Beauty
Tree of Life world	Assiah
Color associated with Number and World on the Tree of Life	Gold amber
Type of deities associated with number	Solar and sacrificial gods
Papus's dialectic	Equilibrium of Opposition
Number significations	Harmony, beauty, love, reconciliation of opposites, well-being, responsibility, purpose

7 of Pentacles	
Hermetic title (Thoth/*Golden Dawn*)	Failure/*Success Unfulfilled*
Planet ruling decan	Saturn
Zodiac	20°–29° Taurus
Planetary glyph	♄
Zodiacal glyph	♉
Associated planetary major	The World
Associated zodiacal major	The Hierophant
Dates	May 11–May 20
Decan image from the Picatrix	A man of reddish complexion with large white teeth exposed outside of his mouth, and a boy like an elephant with long legs, and with him one horse, one dog and one calf.
Decan signification from the Picatrix	Sloth, poverty, misery, dread
Decan image from Agrippa	A man in whose hand is a Serpent, and a dart.
Decan signification from Agrippa	Necessity and profit, and also misery and slavery
Number	7
Geometric forms of number	Heptad, heptagram
Number correspondences	Planets, days of the week, chakras, musical whole notes
Tree of Life sephira	Netzach
Traditional meaning	Victory
Tree of Life world	Assiah
Color associated with Number and World on the Tree of Life	Olive flecked gold
Type of deities associated with number	Love and Beauty goddesses
Papus's dialectic	Commencement of Equilibrium
Number significations	Imagination, secrets, quests, enchantment, mystery, ego

8 of Pentacles	
Hermetic title (Thoth/*Golden Dawn*)	Prudence
Planet ruling decan	Sun
Zodiac	0°–9° Virgo
Planetary glyph	☉
Zodiacal glyph	♍
Associated planetary major	The Sun
Associated zodiacal major	The Hermit
Dates	August 23–September 1
Decan image from Agrippa	The figure of a good maid, and a man casting seeds.
Decan signification from Agrippa	Getting of wealth, ordering of diet, plowing, sowing, and peopling
Decan image from the Picatrix	A young girl covered with an old woolen cloth, and in her hand is a pomegranate.
Decan signification from the Picatrix	Sowing, plowing, the germination of plants, gathering grapes, good living
Number	8
Geometric forms of number	Octad, octahedron (8 faces)
Number correspondences	*Ba gua*, 8-spoked wheel of Wicca, 8-channel model of consciousness
Tree of Life sephira	Hod
Traditional meaning	Glory
Tree of Life world	Assiah
Color associated with Number and World on the Tree of Life	Yellow-brown flecked white
Type of deities associated with number	Knowledge gods
Papus's dialectic	Opposition of Equilibrium
Number significations	Order, discipline, accomplishment, leadership, success, mastery

9 of Pentacles	
Hermetic title (Thoth/*Golden Dawn*)	Gain/*Material Gain*
Planet ruling decan	Venus
Zodiac	10°–19° Virgo
Planetary glyph	♀
Zodiacal glyph	♍
Associated planetary major	The Empress
Associated zodiacal major	The Hermit
Dates	September 2–September 11
Decan image from the Picatrix	A man of beautiful color, dressed in leather, and over his garment of leather is another garment of iron.
Decan signification from the Picatrix	Petitions, requests, and again, tribute and denying justice
Decan image from Agrippa	A black man clothed with a skin, and a man having a bush of hair, holding a bag
Decan signification from Agrippa	Gain, scraping together of wealth and covetousness
Number	Oppression, evils, and subtltey
Geometric forms of number	Nonad, enneagram
Number correspondences	3 x 3, number of magic
Tree of Life sephira	Yesod
Traditional meaning	Foundation
Tree of Life world	Assiah
Color associated with Number and World on the Tree of Life	Citrine flecked azure
Type of deities associated with number	Lunar goddesses
Papus's dialectic	Equilibrium of Equilibrium
Number significations	Magic, psychic ability, power, completion, idealism

10 of Pentacles	
Hermetic title (Thoth/*Golden Dawn)*	Wealth
Planet ruling decan	Mercury
Zodiac	20°–29° Virgo
Planetary glyph	☿
Zodiacal glyph	♍
Associated planetary major	The Magician
Associated zodiacal major	The Hermit
Dates	September 12–September 22
Decan image from the Picatrix	A white man, with a great body, wrapped in white linen, and with him is a woman holding in her hand black oil.
Decan signification from the Picatrix	Debility, age, infirmity, sloth, injury to limbs and the destruction of people
Decan image from Agrippa	A white woman and deaf, or an old man leaning on a staff.
Decan signification from Agrippa	Weakness, infirmity, loss of members, destruction of trees, and depopulation of lands
Number	10
Geometric forms of number	Decad, decagram
Number correspondences	Digits, decans, sephiroth
Tree of Life sephira	Malkuth
Traditional meaning	Kingdom
Tree of Life world	Assiah
Color associated with Number and World on the Tree of Life	Black rayed yellow
Type of deities associated with number	Harvest goddesses
Papus's dialectic	Uncertainty
Number significations	Renewal

Page/Princess of Pentacles	
Hermetic title (Thoth/*Golden Dawn*)	Princess of the Echoing Hills Rose of the Palace of Earth Princess and Empress of the Gnomes Throne of the Ace of Pentacles
Elemental glyph	▽▽
Elemental title	Earth of Earth
Zodiacal glyph	♈♉♊
Zodiacal decans	0°–29° Aries 0°–29° Taurus 0°–29° Gemini
Corresponding Majors	The Emperor The Hierophant The Lovers
Dates	March 21–June 20
Corresponding Minors	2 of Wands 3 of Wands 4 of Wands 5 of Disks 6 of Disks 7 of Disks 8 of Swords 9 of Swords 10 of Swords
Corresponding Minors Hermetic Titles	Dominion Virtue/Established Strength Completion/Perfected Work Worry/Material Trouble Success/Material Success Failure/Success Unfulfilled Interference/Shortened Force Cruelty/Despair and Cruelty Ruin
Tree of Life sephira	10: Malkuth
Tree of Life world	Assiah

Knight of Pentacles (Rider Waite Smith) **Prince of Disks (Thoth)**	
Hermetic title (Thoth/*Golden Dawn)*	Prince of the Chariot of Earth Prince and Emperor of the Gnomes
Elemental glyph	△▽
Elemental title	Air of Earth
Zodiacal modality	Fixed
Zodiacal glyph	♉
Zodiacal decans	20°–29° Aries III 0°–19° Taurus I & II
Corresponding Majors	[The Emperor] The Hierophant
Dates	April 11–May 10
Corresponding Minors	4 of Wands 5 of Disks 6 of Disks
Corresponding Minors **Hermetic Titles**	Completion/Perfected Work Worry/Material Trouble Success/Material Success
Tree of Life sephira	6: Tiphereth
Tree of Life world	Assiah

Queen of Pentacles	
Hermetic title (Thoth/*Golden Dawn*)	Queen of the Thrones of Earth Queen of Gnomes
Elemental glyph	▽▽
Elemental title	Water of Earth
Zodiacal modality	Cardinal
Zodiacal glyph	♑
Zodiacal decans	20°–29° Sagittarius III 0°–19° Capricorn I & II
Corresponding Majors	[Temperance/Art] The Devil
Dates	December 13–January 9
Corresponding Minors	10 of Wands 2 of Disks 3 of Disks
Corresponding Minors Hermetic Titles	Oppression Change/Harmonious Change Work/Material Works
Tree of Life sephira	3: Binah
Tree of Life world	Assiah

King of Pentacles (Rider Waite Smith) Knight of Disks (Thoth)	
Hermetic title (Thoth/*Golden Dawn*)	Lord of the Wide and Fertile Land King of the Spirits of Earth King of the Gnomes
Elemental glyph	△▽
Elemental title	Fire of Earth
Zodiacal modality	Mutable
Zodiacal glyph	♍
Zodiacal decans	20°–29° Leo III 0°–19° Virgo I & II
Corresponding Majors	[Strength/Lust] The Hermit
Dates	August 11–September 11
Corresponding Minors	7 of Wands 8 of Disks 9 of Disks
Corresponding Minors Hermetic Titles	Valor Prudence Gain/Material Gain
Tree of Life sephira	2: Chokmah
Tree of Life world	Assiah

THE HERMIT'S EPILOGUE

JUST HOW DEEP INTO THE CORRESPONDENCES CAN ONE PERSON GET?

It was just one of those bright ideas that seem so simple at the time. I'd gotten to be friends with Peter Stuart on one of those tarot Facebook groups, and we'd gotten in the habit of chatting about our Card of the Day. *Cards* of the Day, really, since Peter had persuaded me that two was better than one. Problem was, Peter lives exactly half a world away from me in Perth, Australia—twelve time zones away. Now Peter is more nocturnal than most, but even so he'd often be hitting the sack just as I was puttering about getting ready for the morning draw.

Enter Dropbox, the file-sharing platform. How hard would it be, I reasoned, to keep a simple Dropbox database tracking our card draws—one we could check in on at any time we liked, chat about when we felt like it, and ignore if we wanted to? It could be a little Excel spreadsheet, and it would just sit there in virtual space clocking two mornings a day of card draws.

We figured we'd want to search and manipulate the data, so we came up with some ground rules. We'd use an alphanumeric shorthand (6D for 6 of Disks, because Disks are more universal than Pentacles). We'd number courts 11 through 14, so King of Swords would be 14S. To avoid confusing minor and majors, we'd use Roman numerals for majors, and we'd use VIII for Justice and IX for Strength in accordance with Crowley and the older traditions.

So far, so good, I thought, as two neat columns of data began marching up and down the spreadsheet. But how cool would it be if we could color-code them according to element? We could see at a glance if someone was having an Air Attack!

And then: How cool would it be if we could track the frequency of our draws? We could see if one card kept coming up over and over again! Or if there was one card we never got! If one of us thought we were *constantly* getting the Death card, we could see if that was really true!

369

Never again would we suffer from confirmation bias! By this point I had contracted a case of full-blown Virgo OCD.

Anyway, none of those things turned out to be terribly difficult. But then there was: How cool would it be to have a color-coded pie chart representing our elemental balance? How cool would it be to graph which court card each of us drew the most? Or which 1–10 number? And how about the astrology! Which planet influenced each of us the most? How about which sign? And if we were getting a "ton of majors," did they really exceed the 28.21% statistical likelihood of getting a major in any given draw?

That was in 2015. Since then, the little spreadsheet has grown into a sprawling behemoth, its core data extracted and analyzed six ways from Sunday, bristling with colored charts and numeric breakdowns. But I still only enter the card data once—the rest happens automatically thanks to the magic of conditional formatting and Excel's powerful background algorithms.

We've learned a few things along the way:

- **If you draw two cards a day for an entire year, you will eventually get them all**. But there can be interesting holdouts for months at a stretch. Once we both failed to get the 7 of Pentacles (the Lord of Failure!) for half a year.

- **There will be certain cards you see way more than others**. Right now, I'm getting a lot of Ace of Swords, and I have a historical tendency to disproportionally draw Justice, the Fool, and the Star. Air much?!

- **You'll rarely end up perfectly elementally balanced.** Last year in particular I saw a major influx of Air, when I was learning to podcast and sound-edit for the first time.

- **It's possible courts really do skew by gender.** Anecdotally I can tell you that my women clients are constantly getting Queens. But based on the *actual data* I can tell you I really do draw Queens a few percentage points more than any other card.

BUT WHAT DOES IT ALL ADD UP TO?

Tracking your cards can be like the world's most elaborate horoscope column—it tells you something about yourself, or confirms something you already know. It tempts you to a certain fatalism. But at some point you still have to live your life and act. If nothing else, the abundance of data has allowed me to see that I am living within a massive web of patterns, interwoven with elegant synchronicity through my world. In other words, the correspondences have allowed me both to perceive and to navigate.

It's one thing to say "I drew Mercury-related cards 10.74% of the time this year." But it is entirely another thing when one day you happen to draw the Lovers (corresponding to Gemini, *ruled by Mercury*) and the 6 of Swords (the Lord of Science, corresponding to *Mercury in Aquarius*), and it happens to be Wednesday, the *day of Mercury*, and at roughly 3 pm which happens to be the *hour of Mercury*, some random librarian you have literally never seen before in your life, at a library you've never before entered, asks as you walk in, "Are you any good with Excel?" And, because you are a Mercury-ruled Virgo native and a spreadsheet-lovin' fool, and because you are on the road and Mercury is the god of travelers, computers, communication, interpretation, and data, you gladly help and you solve the problem in under 8 minutes, 8 being the number of Mercury. That literally happened to me this week.

It's times like those that you realize that, yes, you live in a web of your own design. But the patterns are more far-reaching and more splendid than you ever did expect. You are a living poem; you are a walking mystery.

I started the spreadsheet perhaps out of a deficit of faith. I thought the power of statistics might provide a healthy dose of realism, to balance the heady mythos of the correspondences. Instead, tracking the correspondences has only bolstered my faith in the patterns backstage; the unseen workings of reality. What I started in a quest for reason, I now continue in a quest for beauty. I may be the tiniest piece of clockwork in those celestial mechanics, yet the rhythm I keep partakes of the whole.

May you, too, keep time with the music of the spheres, listen well enough to know it—and see it in the cards.

BIBLIOGRAPHY

BOOKS

GENERAL TAROT RESOURCES

Amberstone, Wald, and Ruth Ann Amberstone. *The Secret Language of Tarot*. San Francisco: Red Wheel/Weiser, 2008.

Greer, Mary K. *Tarot for Your Self: A Workbook for Personal Transformation*. Franklin Lakes, NJ: New Page Books, 2002.

Greer, Mary K., and Tom Little. *Understanding the Tarot Court*. Woodbury, MN: Llewellyn Publications, 2008.

Hazel, Elizabeth. *Tarot Decoded: Understanding and Using Dignities and Correspondences*. Boston: Weiser Books, 2004.

Katz, Marcus, and Tali Goodwin. *Secrets of the Waite-Smith Tarot: The True Story of the World's Most Popular Tarot*. Woodbury, MN: Llewellyn Publications, 2015.

Katz, Marcus, and Paul Hardacre. *Tarosophy: Tarot to Engage Life, Not Escape It*. Brisbane, Australia: Salamander and Sons, 2011.

Louis, Anthony. *Tarot Beyond the Basics: Gain a Deeper Understanding of the Meanings Behind the Cards*. Woodbury, MN: Llewellyn Publications, 2014.

Nichols, Sallie. *Jung and Tarot: An Archetypal Journey*. York Beach, ME.: Samuel Weiser, 1988.

Place, Robert Michael. *The Tarot: History, Symbolism, and Divination*. New York: Jeremy P. Tarcher/Penguin, 2005.

Pollack, Rachel. *Seventy-Eight Degrees of Wisdom: A Book of Tarot*. London: Thorsons, 1997.

———. *Rachel Pollack's Tarot Wisdom: Spiritual Teachings and Deeper Meanings*. Woodbury, MN: Llewellyn Publications, 2009.

Rosengarten, Arthur. *Tarot and Psychology: Spectrums of Possibility*. St. Paul, MN: Paragon House, 2000.

GENERAL RESOURCES

Battistini, Matilde. *Astrology, Magic, and Alchemy in Art*. Los Angeles: J. Paul Getty Museum, 2007.

Chevalier, Jean, Alain Gheerbrant, and John Buchanan-Brown. *The Penguin Dictionary of Symbols*. London: Penguin, 2008.

Kynes, Sandra. *Llewellyn's Complete Book of Correspondences: A Comprehensive & Cross-Referenced Resource for Pagans & Wiccans*. Woodbury, MN: Llewellyn Worldwide, 2013.

Steinbrecher, Edwin C. *The Inner Guide Meditation: A Primer for the 21st Century*. Wellingborough, Northamptonshire: Aquarian Press, 1988.

THOTH TAROT RESOURCES

Arrien, Angeles. *The Tarot Handbook: Practical Applications of Ancient Visual Symbols*. New York: Jeremy P. Tarcher/Putnam, 1997.

Crowley, Aleister. *The Book of Thoth: A Short Essay on the Tarot of the Egyptians*. New York: Weiser, 1976.

Crowley, Aleister, and Israel Regardie. *777 and other Qabalistic Writings of Aleister Crowley: Including Gematria & Sepher Sephiroth*. York Beach, ME.: Samuel Weiser, 1996.

DuQuette, Lon Milo. *Understanding Aleister Crowley's Thoth Tarot*. Newburyport, MA: Weiser Books, 2017.

TAROT DE MARSEILLES RESOURCES

Ben-Dov, Yoav. *The Marseille Tarot Revealed: A Complete Guide to Symbolism, Meanings & Methods*. Woodbury, MN: Llewellyn Publications.

David, Jean-Michel. *Reading the Marseille Tarot*. n.p.: Association for Tarot Studies, 2011

Jodorowsky, Alejandro, Marianne Costa, and Jon E. Graham. *The way of tarot: the spiritual teacher in the cards*. Rochester, VT: Destiny Books, 2009.

Kabbalah Resources

Kaplan, Aryeh. *Sefer Yetzirah: The Book of Creation*. York Beach, ME: Weiser, 1990.

Kliegman, Isabel Radow. *Tarot and the Tree of Life: Finding Everyday Wisdom in the Minor Arcana*. Wheaton, IL: Theosophical Pub. House, 1997.

Pollack, Rachel. *The Kabbalah Tree: A Journey of Balance & Growth*. St. Paul, MN: Llewellyn Publications, 2004.

Regardie, Israel. *A Garden of Pomegranates: An Outline of the Qabalah*. St. Paul, MN: Llewellyn Publications, 1994.

Wang, Robert. *The Qabalistic Tarot: A Textbook of Mystical Philosophy*. Columbia, MD: Marcus Aurelius Press, 2004.

Magic Resources

Agrippa Von Nettesheim, Heinrich Cornelius, Donald Tyson, and James Freake. *Three Books of Occult Philosophy*. Woodbury, MN: Llewellyn Publications, 2006.

Coppock, Austin. *36 Faces: The History, Astrology, and Magic of the Decans*. Hercules, CA: Three Hands Press, 2014.

Dunn, Patrick. *Magic, Power, Language, Symbol: A Magician's Exploration of Linguistics*. Woodbury, MN: Llewellyn Publications, 2008.

Greer, John Michael, and Christopher Warnock. *Picatrix: The Classic Medieval Handbook of Astrological Magic*. Iowa City, IA: Adocentyn Press, 2011.

Hulse, David Allen. *The Key of It All, book II: An Encyclopedic Guide to the Sacred Languages & Magickal Systems of the World:*. St. Paul, MN: Llewellyn, Publications 2000.

Kraig, Donald Michael. *Tarot and Magic*. St. Paul, MN: Llewellyn Publications, 2003.

Miller, Richard Alan, and Iona Miller. *The Magical and Ritual Use of Perfumes*. Rochester, VT: Destiny Books, 1990.

Regardie, Israel, and John Michael Greer. *The Golden Dawn: The Original Account of the Teachings, Rites, and Ceremonies of the Hermetic Order*. Woodbury, MN: Llewellyn Publications, 2015.

Skinner, Stephen. *The Complete Magician's Tables*. Woodbury, MN: Llewellyn Publications, 2012.

Tyson, Donald. *Portable Magic: Tarot is the Only Tool You Need*. Woodbury, MN: Llewellyn Publications, 2006.

Warnock, Christopher. *Secrets of planetary magic*. IA City, IA: Renaissance Astrology, 2010.

Whitcomb, Bill. *The Magician's Companion: A Practical & Encyclopedic Guide to Magical & Religious Symbolism*. Woodbury, MN: Llewellyn Publications, 2007.

ART CREDIT LIST

1. This is the tree model, letter and astrological attributions used by the Golden Dawn. This version of the tree was drafted by seventeenth-century Jesuit scholar Athanasius Kircher, who derived it from Moses ben Jacob Cordovero, a sixteenth-century Jewish mystic. (Created by the author and Llewellyn art department) pg. 28

2. Here is the same tree used by the Golden Dawn, but with Aleister Crowley's variation, in which the letters Heh and Tzaddi—and therefore the Emperor and the Star—are switched. For a full explanation of the switch , see Part I, Table 4. (Created by the author and Llewellyn art department)   pg. 29

3. The Tree of Life is a cosmology; a model of the emanation of Creation. Emanating from the "three veils" *Ain* ["nothingness"], *Ain Soph* ["limitless nothingness"], and *Ain Soph Aur* ["limitless light"] the light of Kether spills down the Tree, each sephira containing and creating the next. The Four Worlds are an analogue of the Divine Name, Yod-Heh-Vav-Heh, and another representation of the progressive crystallization of matter from the sublime. (Created by the author and Llewellyn art department)   pg. 30

4. This is the tree model conceived by Isaac Luria, the sixteenth-century Jewish rabbi known as the Ari ("the Lion"). It is more widely used in Jewish Kabbalah than Hermetic Qabalah and has a structural elegance lacking in the Kircher tree. The three horizontal paths hold the three elements and mother letters; the seven horizontal paths hold the seven planets and double letters, and the twelve diagonal paths hold the twelve planets and single letters. (Created by the author and Llewellyn art department)   pg. 31

5. Astro Loop. (Created by the author and Llewellyn art department)   pg. 34

6. Round diagram of decans and minor arcana. (Created by the author and Llewellyn art department)   pg. 143

7. Four Qualities, Four Elements diagram. (Created by the Llewellyn art department)   pg. 148

8. 2 of Pentacles "▽ Earth", 2 of Swords "△ Air" (Pictorial Key Tarot)   pg. 152

9. 8 of Cups "▽ Water", 7 of Wands "△ Fire" (Pictorial Key Tarot)   pg. 152

10. Outer Card-Center Card-Outer Card diagram. (Created by the Llewellyn art department)   pg. 154

11. 3 of Cups, 5 of Pentacles, 4 of Cups (Mystical Tarot) pg. 154

12. Queen of Pentacles, 8 of Cups, King of Swords (Pictorial Key Tarot)   pg. 156

13. 5 of Wands, 4 of Pentacles (Pictorial Key Tarot)   pg. 157

14. 8 of Wands and 2 of Pentacles (Steampunk Tarot)   pg. 158

15. 7 of Cups, 4 of Swords (Pictorial Key Tarot)   pg. 159

16. Natural element cycle graphic. (Created by the Llewellyn art department)   pg. 161

17. Queen of Wands (Steampunk Tarot)   pg. 163

18. Knight of Pentacles (Pictorial Key Tarot)   pg. 163

19. Page of Cups (Animal Totem Tarot)   pg. 164

20. Knight of Wands (Pictorial Key Tarot)   pg. 165

21. Ace of Swords, Emperor, 7 of Cups (Mystical Tarot)   pg. 166

115. IX (9) The Hermit Tree of Life. (Created by the author and Llewellyn art department)   pg. 287

116. X (10) The Wheel of Fortune Tree of Life. (Created by the author and Llewellyn art department)   pg. 289

117. XI (11) Justice (Adjustment) Tree of Life. (Created by the author and Llewellyn art department)   pg. 291

118. XII (12) The Hanged Man Tree of Life. (Created by the author and Llewellyn art department)   pg. 293

119. XIII (13) Death Tree of Life. (Created by the author and Llewellyn art department)   pg. 295

120. XIV (14) Temperance (Art) Tree of Life. (Created by the author and Llewellyn art department)   pg. 297

121. XV (15) The Devil Tree of Life. (Created by the author and Llewellyn art department)   pg. 299

122. XVI (16) The Tower Tree of Life. (Created by the author and Llewellyn art department)   pg. 301

123. XVII (17) The Star Tree of Life. (Created by the author and Llewellyn art department)   pg. 303

124. XVIII (18) The Moon Tree of Life. (Created by the author and Llewellyn art department)   pg. 305

125. XIX (19) The Sun Tree of Life. (Created by the author and Llewellyn art department)   pg. 307

126. XX (20) Judgement (The Aeon) Tree of Life. (Created by the author and Llewellyn art department)   pg. 309

127. XXI (21) The World (The Universe) Tree of Life. (Created by the author and Llewellyn art department)   pg. 311

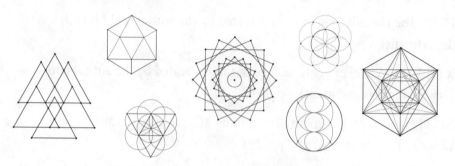

ABOUT THE AUTHOR

T. Susan Chang is a writer and teacher who has for 20 years also been practicing tarot. After moon-lighting as a reader in New York in the 1990s, she took her practice underground for many years, re-surfacing in 2015 and taking up the systematic study of esoteric correspondences in tarot.

Along with deck creator Mel Meleen, Susie hosts the *Fortune's Wheelhouse* esoteric tarot podcast (www.patreon.com/fortuneswheelhouse), which explores imagery and symbolism in the Rider-Waite-Smith and Thoth decks. She is the creator of the Arcana Case® for tarot decks, which can be found at www.etsy.com/shop/tarotista, along with her line of esoteric perfumes. She administers the 78-playlist Tarot Music Project on Spotify, teaches an occasional introduc-tory tarot course, and conducts tarot readings in person at a local shop once a week. She lives in western New England with her husband, two children, and a variable number of chickens.

www.tsusanchang.com